The Good Cook's Guide

more recipes from restaurants
in The Good Food Guide

cooked, written and introduced by
Hilary Fawcett and Jeanne Strang

Consumers' Association

David & Charles
Newton Abbot   London   Vancouver

The Good Cook's Guide
published in Great Britain by
Consumers' Association,
14 Buckingham Street, London WC2N 6DS
and David & Charles (Publishers) Limited,
South Devon House, Newton Abbot, Devon

ISBN 0 7153 6802 8

Illustrations by Mart Kempers
Design by Banks & Miles
Printed by W. S. Cowell Limited

Contents

Foreword

by Christopher Driver
Editor, *The Good Food Guide*

The approach revealed in this book puts back into cookery some of the magic that the technologists have taken out. How far has the Mexican *tomatl* travelled from the Aztecs to this book's recipe for Tetbury Tumkins! To what alchemy has Túróspalacsinta subjected the cheese despised by Shakespeare! In this book Hilary Fawcett and Jeanne Strang begin at the beginning, with food in its raw state, before it has been hewn or pared, marinated or cooked, and in general subjected to all the processes that make it ready to serve to a guest or a customer. Too many cookery writers, and even more restaurants, give the opposite impression: that to create their dishes they have worked backwards from the colour photograph, and have given no thought at all to the fact that there are tomatoes and tomatoes, eggs and eggs; that different strains or seeds, careless or fastidious preservation, can themselves be tasted when the finished recipe comes to table. The restaurants that have kindly furnished recipes for this book (some of them also contributed to its immensely popular companion, *The Good Food Guide Dinner Party Book*) put us all in their debt by finding new and delightful things to do with foodstuffs that have been around, many of them, since Adam dug his first vegetable garden, and Cain killed his first lamb.

Introduction

by Hilary Fawcett and Jeanne Strang

We hope that the introductions to each chapter will provide something new for most cooks. They did for us, even if it were no more than the realisation that almost every foodstuff has been thought by someone to promote both wind and lust. Again and again, too, we were reminded of the need for a larder: so many instructions call for the 'cool, dark place' built into every Victorian dwelling and into every centrally-heated North American home. If British architects knew how to boil an egg, we would surely have alternatives for storage to the refrigerator and the 'custom-designed cupboard unit' in an overheated kitchen.

As in the *Dinner Party Book* (referred to as DPB in the text), we have tested the recipes, in quantities for four unless otherwise stated, using only real stock, homemade mayonnaise, best butter, and so on. They may taste acceptable with substitutes but we do not guarantee it. As before, all spoons are level, all flour plain, and all pepper freshly-ground black. We have used brand names only where they were indicated by the restaurant providing the recipe and where we felt that a different brand might perceptibly alter the flavour of the finished dish.

The editors wish to thank all the people, many of them necessarily anonymous, who contributed information, ideas and criticism to this book. They are particularly grateful for the willing co-operation of busy restaurateurs and trade information bureaux, and for the infinite pains taken by the *Guide*'s own staff.

APPLES

'Coleridge holds that a man cannot have a pure mind who refuses apple dumplings.
I am not certain but he is right.'
CHARLES LAMB, *Essays of Elia*

Origins

Crab apples were probably growing in Britain in neolithic times, but it was the Romans who developed several larger and sweeter varieties, which they stored in the lofts of their villas. One of the earliest named apples was the pearmain, known since the 13th century. Costermongers sold costards in the streets till the 17th century, by which time there were at least eighty named apples.

Even in the 17th century raw fruit was considered to endanger health, and apples were served cooked, often in pies with sugar and spices. They were usually 'greened' by being first stewed in a copper or brass pan, which must have made them almost as lethal as raw apples were thought to be. Once the canal system had been developed, apples became more common in the north of England and Scotland since they could be easily transported from the southern orchards.

Varieties

Of the 1500 different apples supposedly to be found in Britain, depressingly few reach the shopping basket. EEC membership will not necessarily improve this situation, although at least regulations now require grade, name and country of origin to be shown.

The three most popular cooking apples are Bramley's Seedling (available from October to July), Lord Derby (September to November) and Grenadier (August to September). They are all similarly large and green-skinned.

Dessert (eating) apples come in much greater variety. If you like soft apples, you probably choose Beauty of Bath or Jonathan; if medium, Cox's Orange Pippin or Laxton's Superb. Worcester Pearmain, Granny Smith and Newton Pippins rate as crisp, Sturmer Pippins as hard.

In the summer months, when home-grown apples are not in season, Golden Delicious and Granny Smith arrive from Australia, New Zealand and South Africa. French Golden Delicious are with us almost all the year round, and are popular with those who do not echo Morton Shand: 'The French have a poor taste in apples, liking them merely soft and sweet.'

If you had to swear life-time allegiance to only one variety of apple, and if you liked to cook, you might well pick Cox's Orange Pippin, since it is sweet and crisp enough to be a pleasure eaten raw, while still retaining its character cooked. It makes splendid apple sauce and handsome tarts in the French style, with intact, symmetrical slices.

Buying and storing

Apples should look firm and fresh when you buy them. They are now graded (see *Which?*, May 1974), mainly into class I and II, first by the grower and then by the retailer. Unfortunately the only criteria are uniformity of size and freedom from visible blemish, neither of which tells you all you need to know about an apple. Price varies according to supply, so it is worth trying unfamiliar varieties if they look healthy and are cheaper than your usual favourites. Watch out too for the difference in price between, say, French Granny Smiths and English ones, sometimes on the market at the same time.

Dessert apples often become over-sweet and flabby if kept too long after they are fully ripe. Cooking apples can be used unripe without suffering. Ripe apples will keep for a week or two, unripe for longer.

Apples should be kept in a cool place, away from severe temperature fluctuations. Some people find the flavour adversely affected by storage in the refrigerator, but in a centrally-heated house the fridge may be a better bet than a warm room. For long-term storage, home-grown apples will keep for three to four months if wrapped individually in paper, and stored in a single layer in a cool, dark place.

Nutrition

A 4-ounce apple contains a great deal of water, approximately ten carbohydrate grams, 40–45 calories, and traces of vitamins A, B and C. While we would not go as far as a jolly promotional article in calling it 'Nature's toothbrush', we agree that the port shippers' dictum, 'Buy on an apple, sell on cheese', indicates something of the mouth-freshening qualities of an apple. (The saying also provides a useful reminder: if your dessert wine is not first-class, cheese will be kinder to it than fresh fruit.) Apples, as well as being good sources of roughage, have been shown in a recent survey by *Slimming Magazine* to have three times the 'filling power' of the various methylcellulose products sold as slimming aids. Twenty-two overweight people found that eating an apple 15 minutes before each meal affected their appetites to the point where they lost weight without otherwise restricting what they wanted to eat.

Freezing and drying

If you wish to preserve surplus apples, a puree freezes well, either sweetened or not. Apple slices, first blanched in lightly salted water, can also be frozen.

To dry apples, wash them, cut them into slices $\frac{1}{8}$-inch thick, and put them in single layers on racks in an airy place. They will be ready to store in airtight containers when they are leathery but not brittle – this will take 12 hours or more.

Cooking

Use a stainless steel knife to peel apples, or the taste may be affected.

Pour boiling water over cookers before peeling them, and you will find they peel thinly.

Apples have a high pectin content and are therefore useful in helping jams and jellies to set.

Apple sauce needs no water: simmer apples and sugar together very slowly, stir in some butter at the end, and either puree the whole or leave it rough. Some people like lemon or cloves or cinnamon, others do not.

Apples go well with cheese, cream, curry, dried fruit, nuts, pork and chicken. Most of these combinations can be found in the recipes which follow.

Calvados

Apple brandy deserves special mention. It is made in Normandy from the local cider, 'burnt' in a still. For a long time only the Auge district had an *appellation contrôlée* for the production of calvados, and thus many recipes incorporating calvados are called 'vallée d'Auge' (page 9). It is said to recapture the scent of apples uncannily. It appears in many dishes with chicken, fish, tripe and in some pâtés (see Wines and spirits, page 186).

Stuffed apple salad with cheese sablés

Rivermede Country House Hotel,
St Michaels-on-Wyre
chef: Elizabeth Fielding

Sablés are very delicate small biscuits
originating in Normandy.

for the sablés
2 oz flour
¼ teasp salt
a pinch of cayenne pepper
2 oz butter
2 oz grated Cheddar cheese
1 egg

for the salad
4 dessert apples
juice of 2 lemons
1–2 celery hearts
3 tablesp double cream
salt, pepper, sugar

First make the sablés. Sift the flour and the seasonings, rub in the butter and mix in the cheese. Press together to form a ball of dough. Leave it, covered, in a cool place for about an hour. Roll the dough out to ⅛-inch thickness, cut out 2-inch squares and divide these diagonally into triangles. Place the biscuits on a greased baking tray, brush them with beaten egg and bake them in a moderate oven (350°F, mark 4) for 10–12 minutes. Transfer them immediately to a wire rack to cool.

Wash the apples. Cut a lid off the top of each one and remove the cores. Then scoop or cut out the flesh without damaging the 'shell'. (A grapefruit knife helps here.) Chop the flesh and sprinkle it, the lids and the insides of the shells with lemon juice to prevent browning. Chop the celery finely and mix it with the apple, cream and seasoning. Fill the shells with this mixture and replace the lids.

CHEF'S NOTE: these stuffed apples look particularly effective if the apples are from the garden and one or two leaves are left on the stalk.

Céléri bonne femme

L'Aubergade, London
chef/proprietor: M Manciet

6 medium-sized sticks celery
salt, pepper
2 dessert apples, preferably
Golden Delicious

for the dressing
8 fl oz double cream
2 teasp Dijon mustard

Use the best white sticks from the middle of a head of celery. Wash and dry them and remove any strings. Cut the sticks into one-inch lengths, the thickness of a matchstick. Put them into a bowl and season with salt and pepper. Peel and cut the two apples into similar-sized strips and add them to the celery.

Stir the mustard into the cream and pour this over the strips, coating them with the sauce. Check the seasoning and chill in the refrigerator for an hour. Serve on a platter, perhaps decorated with a few lettuce leaves, or in individual dishes.

EDITOR'S NOTE: if you would like the sauce a little thicker, whip the cream lightly before stirring in the mustard.

Loin of pork à la vallée d'Auge

Christopher's, Chichester
chef/proprietor: Christopher A. G. Goff

Calvados du Pays d'Auge is the best apple brandy to be had. It appears often in Norman cooking.

1½–1¾lb piece of boned
middle-cut loin of pork
salt, pepper
2 oz butter
¼ lb mushrooms
2 fl oz calvados
½ pint double cream

If the butcher has not skinned the loin of pork when boning it, do so. Divide the piece into eight slices, approximately ½-inch thick. Season them with salt and pepper and fry them in the butter in a large frying pan. Turn them twice and when they have browned and are almost cooked (after about 20 minutes), add the sliced mushrooms. Cook for a further minute or two. Warm the calvados – then increase the heat under the frying pan, pour in the spirit and set fire to it. Reduce the heat immediately and when the flames have died down, pour in the cream. Stir, check the seasoning and simmer the sauce until it is smooth and creamy.

CHEF'S NOTE: if the sauce gets too hot and separates, add a tablespoonful of cold cream and stir it together again.

Poulet normande

Au Bon Accueil, London
Chefs: Ronald Pearce and José Sanches

1 chicken or 4 chicken joints
2½ oz flour
salt, pepper
3½ oz butter
1 clove garlic
2 large cooking apples
2 bay leaves
7 fl oz dry white wine
3 fl oz calvados
about ½ pint milk
a little grated nutmeg

Cut the chicken into four, or ask the butcher to do this. Toss the pieces in an ounce of seasoned flour. Heat 2 ounces of the butter in a large frying pan or casserole and lightly colour the chicken on both sides, together with the chopped clove of garlic. Peel the apples and cut them into dice. When the chicken is coloured, take it out and quickly colour the apples in the same pan. Take these out and keep them warm. Put back the chicken together with the bay leaves and pour over the wine and the calvados.

Cover and poach for 20–25 minutes until the chicken is nearly cooked. Take it out and keep the juices. Make a roux (DPB, page 169) in a saucepan with the remaining 1½ ounces of butter and flour, and stir in the pan juices, made up to one pint with some milk. Bring this sauce to simmering point and cook it for five minutes, then season it with salt, pepper and a little nutmeg.

Put the chicken and apples back into the pan or casserole and strain the sauce over them. Leave to finish cooking over a low heat for 5–10 minutes.

Pork chops Savoy

Old Crown Inn, Messing
chef/proprietor: Elizabeth Law

4 thick pork chops
2 oz butter
1 large cooking apple
2 oz sultanas
1 teasp grated lemon peel
salt, pepper
¼ pint medium sherry or
　　Madeira

Trim the chops. Heat the butter and brown them in it quickly on both sides. Peel and dice the cooking apple. Add it to the pan with all the other ingredients, cover, and simmer gently on top of the stove for half an hour, or in a warm oven (325°F, mark 3) for 1 hour.

Apple cake (4-6)

Leeming House Hotel, Watermillock
chef: Robert Burton

4 large Granny Smith apples
¼ lb caster sugar
¾ pint water
¼ lemon
2 teasp softened unsalted
   butter

for the topping
¼ lb softened unsalted butter
5 oz caster sugar
3 eggs
2 oz ground almonds
2 teasp lemon juice
pinch of salt

Peel, halve and core the apples (a melon-baller makes a tidy job of the cores); drop them into acidulated water to prevent their going brown. Dissolve the ¼ lb of sugar in the water, add the quarter lemon and the apple halves, and poach them gently until the apples are cooked but still firm. Drain them well. Use the 2 teaspoonsful of butter to grease a baking dish about 10 inches in diameter and 1½ inches deep (just large enough to take the apples in one layer). Place the apples, cut face down, in the dish.

For the topping, cream the butter and sugar until light, blend in the egg yolks one at a time, followed by the almonds, and finally the lemon juice and salt. Fold in the stiffly beaten egg whites and spread the mixture over the apples. Bake the cake in the centre of the oven at 350°F, mark 4, for 25 minutes or until the surface is golden brown.

Serve at room temperature with cream.

EDITOR'S NOTE: it is essential to use apples which do not 'fall' in cooking. You might like to try the cake made with Cox's Orange Pippins.

Apple and walnut pancakes

Pine Trees Hotel, Sway
chef/proprietors: Susan and Gerald Campion

for the pancake batter
¼ lb flour
½ teasp salt
1 egg plus 1 egg yolk
½ pint milk
1 tablesp calvados or kirsch
4 tablesp cooking oil

for the filling
2 lb cooking apples
2 oz butter
¼ lb soft brown sugar
2 oz shelled walnuts
½ teasp cinnamon
grated rind of ½ lemon

Sift the flour and salt into a mixing bowl. Make a well in the centre and break in the egg and the extra yolk. Gradually beat in the milk until the batter is smooth, then stir in the calvados or kirsch. Leave the batter to rest for at least an hour.

Peel, core and slice the apples into a heavy saucepan with the butter and sugar. Stew them very slowly until they are soft and then puree them in the liquidiser. Finely chop the walnuts. Add the cinnamon, grated lemon rind and walnuts to the apple puree and reheat it gently. Taste to check the amounts of sugar and cinnamon.

Add the oil to the batter and, if it has thickened too much, add a little more milk – it should be the consistency of thin cream. Grease a small frying pan, heat it well and make eight pancakes about 6 inches in diameter. Fill each pancake with one or two spoonsful of the filling, roll them up and keep them warm in a buttered, ovenproof dish, covered with foil, in a low oven until all the pancakes have been made. It should not be necessary to grease the pan between cooking each pancake because of the oil in the batter. If they have to be kept warm for a little while, pour some melted butter over them.

Apfel Liechtenstein

Hotel Petit Champ, Sark
chef: Horst Konken

4 medium-sized cooking apples
1½ oz seedless raisins
½ pint red wine
2–3 tablesp brown sugar
juice of half a lemon
good pinch of cinnamon
1 clove
1 tablesp cornflour
whipped cream (optional)

Wash and core the apples. Cut round the skin in a ring half way down each apple with the sharp point of a knife. Fill the centres with the raisins and bake them in a shallow baking tin with a little water in a moderate oven (375°F, mark 5) for about 40 minutes, depending on the quality of the apples.

Heat the red wine in a saucepan, adding the sugar, lemon juice, cinnamon and clove. Simmer for a few seconds, then blend in the cornflour, slaked with a little cold water. When the sauce has thickened, remove the clove, pour the sauce over the apples and serve immediately.

EDITOR'S NOTE: whipped cream goes well with these baked apples.

Crêpes normande

La Bonne Auberge, Heald Green
chef: R G Boutinot

A gateau made up of layers of pancakes and apple, flambéed with calvados.

½ pint pancake batter (DPB, page 172)
1½ lb cooking apples
2 oz butter
2 oz sugar
a pinch of nutmeg
2 tablesp calvados
crème Chantilly

Make a pancake batter and allow it to stand for 1–2 hours. Peel, core and slice the apples. Melt the butter, add the apples, sugar and nutmeg and allow them to cook gently, turning them over from time to time. When the apples are cooked, make eight pancakes, about 6 inches in diameter. As the first one is done, place it on a heatproof serving dish and spread a spoonful of the apples on top. Put it in the oven to keep hot. Build up the pancakes and apple in layers until all eight pancakes are made. Warm the calvados (in a ladle over a flame or in a saucepan), pour it over the crêpes and set fire to it. Serve the gateau immediately while it is still flaming, accompanied by a bowl of crème Chantilly.

EDITOR'S NOTE: crème Chantilly is lightly-whipped cream sweetened with sugar (2 tablespoonsful to ½ pint of chilled cream) and flavoured with vanilla.

Jamaican tart

Old Rectory, Claughton
chef: Mrs P P Martin

6 oz sweet shortcrust pastry (DPB, page 173)
¼ lb white grapes
1 large or two small hard and sweet dessert apples
2 bananas
1 oz glacé cherries
1½ oz shredded almonds
½ oz butter
juice and grated rind of ½ lemon
2 tablesp rum (approx)
sugar to taste

Make the pastry and leave it to rest. Line a buttered 7-inch flan tin with it and lightly bake it blind for 10 minutes in a moderately hot oven (400°F, mark 6). Leave to cool.

Peel and de-seed the grapes, peel and dice the apples and bananas, and thinly slice the glacé cherries. Fry these and the almonds quickly in the butter, turning them over or shaking the pan constantly. Add the lemon juice and rind, rum and sugar to taste, and fry for a few minutes longer.

With a perforated spoon, transfer the drained fruit to the pie shell and arrange it as decoratively as possible. Reduce the remaining pan juices until they have thickened. Pour the syrup over the fruit and return the flan to the oven, reduced to 375°F, mark 5, for 20 minutes. If the pastry is overcooking, cover the pie with foil.

Cool before removing from the flan tin – if your tin has a removable base the job will be much easier. Serve the tart cold.

CHEESE

'Many's the long night I've dreamed of cheese – toasted, mostly.'
R. L. STEVENSON, *Treasure Island*

'If I had a son who was ready to marry, I would tell him: Beware of girls who don't like wine, truffles, cheese or music.' COLETTE

Sound advice, though it is hard to imagine any girl not liking cheese, particularly a French girl who has over 200 varieties to choose from. Even an English girl has a dozen or more. With a choice like that, it is not surprising that cheese has become an important part of our eating and has found its way into recipes for every meal and every course.

Origins

No one knows who first discovered that the addition of rennet (found in the stomachs of some animals) separated milk into solid curds of protein and fat, and whey, but it is thought to have been as early as the first domestication of animals – about 9000 BC.

Primitive cheeses were probably rather yoghourt-like. The wicker basket in which the curds were drained was called a *phormos* in Greek, and from it are derived *formaggio* and *fromage*. From the Latin *caseus* (cheese) we have *käse*, *queso*, *caws* and *cheese*.

After the soft cream cheeses came hard, pressed ones like Emmental and Parmesan, and in the Middle Ages, soft ripened cheeses whose names reveal their monastic origins: Pont-L'Evêque, St Paulin.

Cheese was unfashionable for many years, perhaps because it had connotations, along with other milk products, of being 'food for the poor'. It regained its popularity during the 19th century, and the first cheese factory was opened in Derby in 1870. Until then all cheese had been made on farms. The current picture is a very different one: in 1973 Britain produced almost 179,000 tons of cheese, just over 15,000 tons of it farm-made.

Nutrition

Cheese is a highly concentrated source of protein, two ounces containing the same as four ounces of meat. The harder the cheese, the more protein it contains. The fat content varies considerably, from 65% in a 'double-cream' cheese down to 2% in a rigorously-skimmed-milk cottage cheese. Vitamin A, calcium and some minerals are also present. All cheese is ideal for carbohydrate counters, since it contains none; the calorie picture is less cheerful: an ounce of cream cheese provides 230 calories, an ounce of Cheddar about 120, but an ounce of cottage cheese only 30 (see the cheese and chive soufflé on page 23).

Types

Cheese-making can be as complicated and delicate a process as wine-making, and the differences between one cheese and another can be as subtle, and as unexpected. First of the many variables is the milk: for example, Roquefort, Feta and Pecorino are made from ewe's milk; Chabichou and Chèvrotin are made from goat's milk; true Mozzarella was formerly made from buffalo's milk, but is now made from cow's milk except in some places in southern Italy. Most cheeses are, of course, made from cow's milk, since there is more of it about. Milk also varies greatly according to the time of year (and even day) at which it is produced, and also according to the pasture.

The actual cheese-making produces further differences – the method of obtaining the curds, how they are treated, whether the cheese is ripened or salted, if so for how long, and so on. To oversimplify rather drastically, there are the *hard, pressed and matured cheeses:* Cheddar, Lancashire, Parmesan, Gruyère, for example; *the softer pressed ones:* Caerphilly, Bel Paese, Dunlop, Double Gloucester; *blue-veined cheeses:* Stilton, Gorgonzola, Roquefort; *soft, ripened cheeses:* Brie, Camembert; *soft, fresh cheeses:* cottage cheese, cream cheese, fromage blanc (page 22), Petit Suisse, Boursin, Caboc.

The best known of the English cheeses – Cheddar, Cheshire and Lancashire – are officially separated into farmhouse and creamery cheeses, with the former superior in flavour. Within these two groups, the cheeses are graded into three qualities, the best of each being described as 'superfine' or 'extra selected'. Some Cheddars are matured for up to two years, and have a full flavour. This is not easily captured in foreign Cheddars, although the best of the Canadian ones approach the same quality.

Parmesan is a delicious dessert cheese, if you can find it fresh enough. It has a soft, granular texture and a warm nutty taste. Londoners are lucky in having Italian grocers all over the place who, if they don't stock it, should be encouraged to do so. (The Soho ones already have it.) And even if you want it in grated form, it is cheaper and better bought by the piece, since the ready-grated stuff loses its flavour quickly, and tastes of alien ingredients.

Gruyère and Emmental are closely related, with Gruyère holes the size of a cherry stone, Emmental ones the size of a walnut. Gruyère is the one favoured by the Swiss, although much more Emmental is eaten abroad. Both have a pleasant nutty flavour and cook beautifully. They are always expensive, and if you need something of the flavour, without being able to afford the genuine article, try Jarlsberg, from Norway.

English fresh cheeses are graded according to their fat content: full fat, medium fat, low fat, and skimmed milk soft cheese. Curd cheese, which is made from naturally soured milk, has a more acid flavour.

Buying

Whatever kind of cheese you are looking for, it is best to find a shop which appears to know how to keep and serve it, and which has a good turn-over. Reject hard-pressed cheeses which are dry or sweating. Only cheeses which characteristically have mould should show it. Stilton and Gorgonzola should not have the dark colour of the rind extending too far into the centre. The cheese should smell only of cheese, neither yeasty nor acid – this is particularly important with soft ripened cheeses like Brie. If you are allowed to taste the cheese, check the texture as you handle it. If a pressed cheese feels like soap or putty, it has been incorrectly made. If the taste is bitter this may be the result of using pasteurized milk, which is increasingly common.

Storing

Cheese continues to mature and thus the temperature and humidity of its surroundings are important. If too warm, it will ferment; if too cold, it will rot. The soft ripened cheeses are most sensitive and should not be kept in the refrigerator except in very warm weather. They should, ideally, be stored at 40–50°F. Dampness causes mould, excessive dryness cracking.

A whole soft cheese will keep for several days in a dark, cool place. Pieces of soft or blue-veined cheese should be wrapped in waxed paper, polythene, or foil. If they must be refrigerated, put them in the least cold part, tightly wrapped inside a container. Semi-hard or hard cheese can be covered with a cloth wrung out in salted water and stored in the larder for up to a week.

Fresh cheeses are often date-stamped – useful, since they start to deteriorate within a week, particularly those with a high fat-content. Keep fresh cheeses wrapped, in the fridge. Strong cheese will affect other more delicate foods stored near it, unless securely wrapped, and fresh cream cheeses will take on alien flavours unless similarly stored.

Cheeses which have been refrigerated should be kept at room temperature for at least half an hour before they are served.

Left-over hard cheese can be grated and stored in an airtight jar in the fridge to use in cooking.

Cooking

A well-matured cheese with a high fat content (for example, Cheddar) will blend better with other ingredients than a younger one. It will also grate easily. Lancashire is particularly good for toasting, Gruyère and Emmental melt well (as in Swiss fondue, and in the creamy fritters on page 21), Parmesan is ideal for grating, and its distinctive flavour shows to advantage in the batter for piccata Alfio (page 25). It is the classic topping for a dish which is finished in the oven or under a hot grill (as in the recipe for baked carrots, page 25). Mixed with Emmental or Gruyère, it makes heavenly soufflés, with a good cheesy flavour and a creamy texture.

Cheese should be *melted* rather than cooked, since the twin dangers of 'curdling' (the fat separating from the protein) and toughening into strings are ever-present. Recipes often recommend that the cheese be grated before it is added to a sauce (use a fine grater for hard cheese, a coarse one for soft). You should cook them over a very low heat, stirring constantly, and not allowing them to boil. Generally the cheese is the last ingredient to be added. (Soupe à l'oignon gratinée, page 19, is the honourable exception where the strings are actively encouraged.) Cottage cheese has a firm, curdy texture not always suited to cooking. It can be sieved or put in the liquidiser with some liquid to make it smooth. Cream cheeses, which can be bland, are often made more piquant by the addition of herbs, as in the recipe for fromage blanc (page 22), or of dried apricots, as in the cheesecake recipe on page 26. Ricotta, the famous Italian cream cheese, is particularly well-suited to cooked dishes.

Courgettes and crab au gratin

Wayfarer's Grill, Shaftesbury
chef: Larry Lawrence

8 small or 4 large courgettes
3 tomatoes
1 oz butter
1 small onion
½ lb fresh or frozen white crab
 meat
salt, paprika

for the sauce
1 oz butter
1 oz flour
½ pint milk
1½ oz grated Parmesan
salt, pepper
pinch of nutmeg

½ oz grated Parmesan

Cut the ends off each courgette and simmer them in boiling salted water for 5 minutes. Drain and cool them under running water. Slice them in half lengthways and scoop out the flesh with a teaspoon. Chop it.

Skin, de-seed and chop the tomatoes. Chop the onion finely and soften it in an ounce of butter without letting it brown. Add the chopped courgettes, tomatoes, crab meat and seasoning and cook them gently for 3 or 4 minutes.

Arrange the courgette cases in a buttered gratin dish and fill them with the crab mixture. Make a roux with an ounce of butter and of flour, blend in half a pint of milk and when this sauce has thickened, add the cheese. Season with salt, pepper and nutmeg. Spoon the sauce over the filled courgettes and sprinkle a little Parmesan over the top. Put the dish into a hot oven (425°F, mark 7) for 10 minutes to brown.

Soupe à l'oignon gratinée

Highlander Inn, Ovington
chef/proprietor: Nicole Fayaud

4 medium-sized onions
1½ oz butter
2 tablesp flour
¼ pint dry white wine
1¼ pints boiling water
salt, pepper
5 oz grated cheese (Gruyère or Emmental)
4 thin slices white bread

Peel the onions and slice them thinly into rings. Heat the butter in a heavy saucepan, and cook the onions over a medium heat, turning them from time to time until they have browned – do not let them burn or they will give a bitter taste to the soup. Stir in the flour and allow the mixture to cook a little longer. Heat the wine, blend it in, then add the boiling water. Season. Simmer the soup for a further 15 minutes.

Warm four oven-proof soup bowls, put some cheese in each and ladle the soup into them. Top with the slices of bread and the rest of the cheese. Brown under the grill and serve at once.

CHEF'S NOTE: the cheese at the bottom of the bowls makes the 'strings' which are part of the fun of eating soupe à l'oignon.

Mille-feuilles au fromage

Streets, Hoylake
chef/proprietor: John Street

½ lb puff pastry (page 199)
5 oz Blue Stilton or strong Cheddar cheese
pepper
1 egg yolk
2 fl oz double cream
chopped chives

Roll out the pastry to approximately ⅛-inch thickness and cut out four oblong pieces, 6 inches by 4 inches. Crumble or grate the cheese and sprinkle one ounce of it over one half of each oblong. Season with a little freshly ground pepper. Damp the edges of the pastry and fold the other half over. Seal the edges and brush the tops with beaten egg.

Cook the pastries in a pre-heated oven (425°F, mark 7) until they have risen and browned – in about 12 minutes. While they are baking, whip the cream and stir in some chopped chives. Serve the mille-feuilles very hot, with a sprinkling of the remaining ounce of cheese on top, and a spoonful of cream and chives at the side.

Tetbury tumkins with tomato and tarragon cream

The Close, Tetbury
Peggy Hastings' recipe

for the sauce
2 medium-sized tomatoes
1 tablesp chopped fresh
  tarragon
1 egg yolk
salt, pepper, mustard
1 teasp wine vinegar
½ pint oil
1 teasp tomato puree
juice of ½ lemon

for the tumkins
oil for deep frying
¼ lb dry Double Gloucester
1 tablesp flour
¼ teasp salt
a small pinch cayenne
¼ teasp powdered mustard
chopped parsley and sage
2 egg whites

Prepare the cold sauce first or in advance – it keeps well. Chop the tomatoes and liquidise them. Rub this puree through a sieve into a small pan, add the chopped tarragon and let them cook together for a few minutes. Leave to cool a little. Mix together the egg yolk, salt, pepper, vinegar and mustard as for mayonnaise and start beating in the oil little by little. When half of it has been beaten in, blend in the tomato purée and the liquidised tomato and tarragon. Add the remainder of the oil slowly, and finally the boiled lemon juice – this helps the sauce to keep.

While the oil is heating to just under 400°F, grate the cheese and mix it with the flour, seasoning and just enough parsley and sage to flavour. Beat the egg whites until stiff and fold them into the cheese mixture. Drop round dessertspoonsful into the hot fat where they will puff up and float to the surface. Turn them over after a minute to make them golden and crisp all over and, after another minute, lift them out to drain on absorbent paper. They can be cooked in one or two batches according to the size of the deep fat pan – these quantities make 8 tumkins. Serve them immediately with the tomato and tarragon cream.

CHEF'S NOTE: a little sugar can be added to the sauce, if you like.

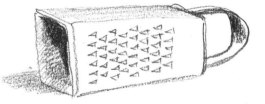

Petits fondus

Cleeveway House, Bishop's Cleeve
chef/proprietor: J G Marfell

A popular dish in Belgium, not to be confused with the Swiss dish of cheese melted with wine and kirsch.

1½ oz Emmental
1½ oz Parmesan
2 oz butter
¼ pint milk
2 oz flour
2 eggs
salt, pepper, nutmeg
1 egg for coating
dried breadcrumbs

oil for deep frying
4 wedges of lemon
watercress or lettuce

Grate the cheese. Heat the butter and milk in a saucepan until the butter has melted, then add all the flour at once and stir the mixture well over the heat until it becomes very thick and smooth, leaving the sides of the pan clean. Add the grated Emmental and Parmesan and continue cooking gently until they have melted. Allow the sauce to cool a little before beating in the eggs, one at a time. Season the sauce generously and put it in the refrigerator to chill and solidify for at least an hour.

Start heating enough oil for deep frying at 375°F. Take a heaped tablespoonful of the cheese mixture and roll it into a ball the size of a walnut. Dip it in beaten egg and roll it in breadcrumbs. Make 12 of these fondu balls and deep fry them, six at a time, in the hot oil for 3 minutes, rolling them over if necessary until they are golden all over. Drain them on kitchen paper and keep the first batch hot while frying the remainder.

Serve immediately on a bed of watercress or lettuce, and with a wedge of lemon.

Gruyère cheese fritters

Old Bridge Hotel, Huntingdon
chef: Alan Scott

6 oz Gruyère
6 whites of egg
1½ tablesp chopped parsley
a pinch of nutmeg
a good pinch of paprika
a pinch of salt
2 oz fresh white breadcrumbs

oil for deep frying

Grate the cheese. Whip the egg whites until they are very stiff, fold in the cheese, parsley and seasonings and leave the mixture to stand for an hour. It may separate by this time but do not worry.

Heat the oil to 'fritter' temperature (375°F). Take small handfuls of the mixture, form them into 12 croquette shapes, about 3 inches long, and roll them in the breadcrumbs. Drop three or four of them into the deep fat. They will rise to the surface quite quickly. Turn them over if necessary and when they are puffed and golden – in two minutes or so – lift them out with a perforated spoon onto absorbent paper to drain. Serve them as quickly as possible.

Cucumber and cheese mousse (6-8)

The Grange, London
proprietor: Geoffrey Sharp

A cool summer lunch dish, or an appetiser for a dinner party.

1 large cucumber
salt
6 oz cream cheese
1 teasp onion juice
salt, white pepper
½ oz gelatine
3 tablesp cold water
¼ pint boiling water
2 tablesp white wine vinegar
1 tablesp caster sugar
a pinch of mace
¼ pint double cream

for garnishing
watercress

Dice the unpeeled cucumber very finely, sprinkle it with salt, and leave it pressed between two plates for half an hour. Beat the cheese with the onion juice and salt and pepper. Soak the gelatine in the cold water for a few minutes, pour on the boiling water and stir until the gelatine is dissolved. Stir in the cream cheese.

Drain the cucumber thoroughly and mix it with the vinegar, sugar and mace. When the cheese mixture is quite cold, fold in the cucumber and lightly whipped cream. Turn it into a lightly oiled 1¼-pint mould and chill until set.

Unmould the mousse, decorate it with watercress and serve it with hot toast.

EDITOR'S NOTES: a small half onion can be squeezed on a lemon squeezer to produce the juice.

If this is served as a lunch dish, garnish it with tomatoes as well as watercress. A ring mould looks pretty, with the watercress in the centre and the tomato slices or wedges round the edge.

Fromage blanc

Wife of Bath, Wye
chef/proprietor: Michael Waterfield

A herby cream cheese, very easy to make, which is served with steaks at the Wife of Bath.

1 pint single cream
juice of ½ lemon
1 tablesp chopped fresh herbs
1 small clove garlic

Curdle the cream with the lemon juice and leave it in a covered bowl overnight in a warm place until it is set. Drain it in a cloth in a colander for a day, then hang it in the cloth in a cool place for another day.

Beat in the chopped herbs and garlic.

EDITOR'S NOTE: this cream cheese is lovely with fruit, in its unherbed state, and on sandwiches or in salads when herbed.

Cheese soufflé with chives

Bowlish House, Shepton Mallet
chef/proprietor: Elaina Gardiner

This is nearer to a soufflé omelette, very light and delicate. Its calorific content is nearly half that of a traditional cheese soufflé. It will serve two as a lunch dish, four as a starter.

4 eggs
salt, pepper
1 8-oz carton cottage cheese
2 tablesp chopped chives
1 tablesp chopped parsley (optional)

Preheat the oven to 425°F, mark 7. Separate the eggs and beat together the yolks and some seasoning. Beat in the cottage cheese, a spoonful at a time.

In a separate bowl whisk the egg whites until they are stiff and fold them lightly into the egg and cheese mixture together with the chopped chives and parsley. Butter generously an omelette pan, about 8 inches in diameter, and one which can go in the oven. Heat it on the top of the stove, and when it is hot, pour in the mixture and leave it to 'set' for a few minutes on the top of the warm cooker or on an asbestos mat over a low flame. Then transfer the soufflé to the hot oven for about 10 minutes by which time it will have risen to double its thickness and turned golden brown on top. Serve immediately.

Spinach tart (6)

Rivermede Country House Hotel,
St Michaels-on-Wyre
chef: Elizabeth Fielding

½ lb rich shortcrust pastry (DPB, page 173)
1½ lb spinach
2 oz butter
salt, pepper
2 oz cottage cheese
2 oz cream cheese
2 oz grated Parmesan
4 fl oz double cream
2 large eggs
a pinch of mace

Make the pastry and leave it to rest for at least an hour.

Line a 7–9 inch buttered flan ring with the pastry and bake it blind for 10–15 minutes in a moderately hot oven (400°F, mark 6).

Wash and drain the spinach and remove the stalks. Cook it gently in the butter with some salt. Drain it very well and chop it finely. Add pepper, and more salt if necessary.

Cream together the three kinds of cheese and blend in the cream, mixed with the lightly beaten eggs, and a pinch of mace. Fold this into the spinach and fill the pastry case with the mixture. Bake it, on a baking tray, in a moderate oven (350°F, mark 4) for 25–30 minutes until the filling has *just* set.

Gebackener Emmentaler

Edelweiss, London
chef/proprietor: Mrs Avenell

Vegetarians like Mrs Avenell's fried Emmental, which she serves with a mixed salad of sauerkraut, potato, tomato, cucumber, beans and red cabbage, all well herbed.

4 3-oz slices Emmental
  3–4 inches square
  and ½ inch thick
2 large or 3 standard eggs
2 oz flour
salt, pepper
¼ lb home-made or baker's
  bread crumbs
cooking oil
1 lemon
a few lettuce leaves

Trim any rind off the slices of cheese. Beat the eggs together in a dish or shallow bowl. Mix the flour, salt and pepper together in a second shallow bowl and put the crumbs into a third dish or bowl.

Pour some cooking oil into a large frying pan to a depth of about 1 inch and heat it over a medium flame or ring. Dip each piece of cheese first into the flour, then into the egg and finally the breadcrumbs. Pat these on well so that the slices are completely covered and shake off any surplus.

When the oil just starts to bubble in the centre of the pan, put the coated slices in. After a couple of minutes, turn them over and reduce the heat slightly. The cheese must not cook too fiercely – the outside must be crisp but the inside should soften without disintegrating. Turn the pieces over again if necessary and as a guide, test each piece with the point of a thin skewer. When they are soft inside, drain them and serve quickly on a leaf of lettuce garnished with a wedge of lemon and accompanied by a mixed salad with a spicy vinaigrette dressing.

Escalopes of veal Dominique

Casa Cominetti, London
chef: Bob Cominetti

4 ¼-lb escalopes of veal
1 egg
salt, pepper
dried breadcrumbs
3 oz clarified butter
4 thin slices ham
¼ lb Bel Paese cheese

Trim the escalopes and beat them out with a meat bat or rolling pin. Dip them in the beaten egg which has been well seasoned with salt and pepper, and coat them with breadcrumbs, pressing them on to give a good coating.

Heat the butter and fry the escalopes for 7–10 minutes, turning them once. When they are cooked and the coating is crisp and golden, transfer them to a flameproof serving dish. Place a slice of ham on top of each one and top that with slices of cheese. Glaze the tops under a hot grill for a few minutes until the cheese browns.

Piccata Alfio

Restaurant Denzler, Edinburgh
chef/proprietor: Samuel Denzler

4 breasts of chicken
seasoned flour
2 eggs
1 tablesp flour
2 oz grated Parmesan
a pinch each of oregano and
**   sage**
1 or 2 tablesp water
oil for shallow frying
¼ lb button mushrooms
1 oz butter
½ pint tomato sauce (page 71)

Skin and bone the chicken and toss the pieces in seasoned flour. Make a coating batter with the beaten eggs, flour, Parmesan, herbs, and just enough water to prevent its being too stiff.

Pour sufficient cooking oil into a large frying-pan to cover the bottom to a depth of ½ inch, and heat it to frying temperature. Dip the chicken breasts into the cheese batter, place them in the hot fat and reduce the heat slightly. Cook them gently for about 8 minutes on each side.

While they are cooking, slice the mushrooms and cook them gently in an ounce of butter until they are just soft. Stir them into the heated tomato sauce.

Arrange the chicken on a serving dish with some boiled rice, risotto or creamed potatoes, and serve the sauce separately.

Baked carrots

Mill House, Milford-on-Sea
chef/proprietor: Colin Cooper English

1 lb carrots
salt
a pinch of sugar
2 oz butter
pepper
3 oz grated cheese (e.g.
**   Cheddar)**
½ oz fresh breadcrumbs

Peel or scrape the carrots and boil them until tender in slightly salted water. Drain and mash them to a puree before blending in the sugar, melted butter and pepper. Stir the mixture over a low heat until very smooth.

Put it in a gratin dish, smooth the top, sprinkle it with the cheese and put the dish under a hot grill. When the cheese begins to bubble, add a thin layer of breadcrumbs and finish browning the top.

CHEF'S NOTE: this is a useful dinner party dish because it keeps hot without spoiling, and can thus be prepared ahead of time.

Apricot cheesecake (6-8)

La Chandelle, Marlow
chef/proprietor: Tom Hearne

½ lb dried apricots
¼ lb pâte sucrée (DPB, page 173)
1¼ lb cream cheese
7 oz caster sugar
1 lemon
3 eggs plus 2 yolks
2 oz double cream
1½ tablesp flour

Soak the apricots overnight. Reserve the liquid. Chop them coarsely, reserving about 8 to decorate the top of the cake.

Line a greased 8-inch loose-bottomed cake tin with pastry, on the bottom only. Bake it blind at 400°F, mark 6 for about 15 minutes. Allow it to cool.

Sieve the cream cheese and combine it with the sugar, the grated rind and juice of the lemon, the eggs and the cream. Sieve in the flour, and fold in the chopped apricots. Turn the mixture into the prepared tin, and bake the cheesecake in a hot oven (425°F, mark 7) for about 15 minutes, until the top starts to brown. Turn down the heat to 350°F, mark 4, and bake the cake for a further 45 minutes to an hour. It should be brown all over and springy to the touch. (Cover the top with foil or greaseproof paper if it browns too fast.)

Allow the cake to cool before removing it from the tin and decorating it with the reserved apricots poached for about 20 minutes in a syrup made with the reserved liquid they were soaked in (about 6 fl oz liquid to 2 oz sugar).

CHEF'S NOTE: we use a St Ivel cream cheese which comes in a 3 lb 'sausage'.

EDITOR'S NOTES: the kind sold by the pound in delicatessens is also suitable, being neither too rich nor too buttery.

If your tin is rather shallow (say, less than 3½ inches deep), you might try using 1 lb cheese, 2 eggs and one extra yolk.

Túróspalacsinta

Gay Hussar, London

Mr Sassie attributes this recipe to Charles Gundel, a famous Hungarian restaurateur who died in Budapest in 1950.

for the pancake batter
5 oz flour
2 eggs
a pinch of salt
a pinch of sugar
¼ pint milk
¼ pint soda water
1 tablesp oil

for the filling
½ lb cream cheese
1 egg
1 oz sultanas soaked in
   1 tablesp brandy
juice and grated rind of
   ½ orange
juice and grated rind of
   ¼ lemon
½ teasp vanilla essence
3 oz sugar

Make the pancake batter in the usual way, using the soda water to dilute it to a thin cream – the thickness of the batter determines the thickness of the pancakes. Leave to stand while preparing the filling, and before stirring in the tablespoonful of oil.

Put the cream cheese into a bowl and stir into it the egg yolk, the brandy-soaked sultanas, the juice and grated rinds of orange and lemon, the vanilla essence and sugar. Whisk the white of the egg separately until it is firm and gently fold it into the mixture. (In warm weather do not beat the mixture or the cream cheese may separate.)

Using a heavy omelette pan only slightly oiled, make eight 6-inch pancakes. Keep each one warm in a low oven while preparing the others. Put a spoonful of the filling in the centre of each pancake, fold in the sides and roll them up. Place the rolled pancakes side by side in a gratin dish, sprinkle a little caster sugar over them and glaze them quickly under a hot grill. Serve very hot.

CHOCOLATE

'Persons who drink chocolate regularly are conspicuous for unfailing health and immunity from the host of minor ailments which mar the enjoyment of life; they are also less inclined to lose weight.'
BRILLAT-SAVARIN, *The Philosopher in the Kitchen*

Since Bournville alone produces more than two million moulded blocks of chocolate a day, Britons apparently take the first observation more to heart than the second.

History

The cacao tree was first cultivated by the Mayas, Incas and Aztecs, who valued the chocolate drink they made from the beans for its nourishing and stimulating properties. Montezuma liked his chocolate flavoured with vanilla, whipped to a froth the consistency of honey, and served in a golden goblet. The cacao tree was introduced to the West Indies by the conquering Spaniards, who preferred their chocolate sweetened with sugar.

The jealously-guarded secret of this exciting new drink reached Europe only in the 17th century, when chocolate, coffee and tea had phenomenal success as non-alcoholic drinks which would 'clear the head and drive away alcoholic vapours'. This is a surprising claim for chocolate as it was first drunk in England, since most of the recipes called for the addition of brandy, wine or sherry. In the chocolate houses, which sprang up as prolifically as did coffee houses, you were likely to be offered a caudle-like brew of claret, egg yolks, chocolate and sugar, milled to a froth. Coffee was supposed to increase men's virility; chocolate was credited with having the same effect on women's fertility. One 18th-century health expert claimed that, by the use of chocolate, his wife was 'brought to bed of twins, three times'. For this, or whatever other reason, the chocolate houses died within fifty years.

Chocolate reappeared in solid form in the 19th century, and since then has been used in all sorts of recipes, as well as being enjoyed as a snack. French children can still be seen clutching a chunk of fresh bread with a bar of chocolate in the middle, and one of the editors sighs nostalgically for a soft Scottish bap sandwiching a Fry's chocolate cream, given up with the other decadent pleasures of childhood.

Nutrition

It is easy to see why chocolate is always found in the packs of Arctic explorers and in emergency rations for fighting forces. The cocoa bean provides vitamins B and D, and is one of the richest sources of iron in an easily assimilated form. Plain chocolate is approximately 31% fat, 4% protein and 55% sugar. An ounce yields 158 calories and 15 grams of carbohydrate. Milk chocolate scores 161 and $15\frac{1}{2}$ respectively.

Types

As far as cooking is concerned, *plain* block chocolate is the most useful, though it appears under a bewildering variety of names, including *bitter* and *dessert*. True *bitter* chocolate is unsweetened and is not normally available retail in this country, though sold as cooking chocolate in the United States. *Couverture* is a smooth high-quality chocolate, used mainly commercially for confectionery, but available for home use in a slightly lower quality. *Milk* chocolate is hardly ever used in cooking, although occasionally you might find it called for in cake decoration.

Buying

When buying chocolate, you usually get what you pay for. Top quality chocolate has been carefully made through all the complex processes of fermenting, roasting, milling, refining, and so on, and is never cheap. Large blocks of 'cooking chocolate' at very low prices taste markedly inferior, and often list several ingredients not found in the best chocolate. It is worth experimenting with various brands of plain chocolate until you find the degree of darkness and sweetness you like. Many restaurateurs specify Chocolat Menier in their recipes, and you can find it in many supermarkets nowadays, as well as in speciality food shops.

Storing

Chocolate is said to have a shelf-life of six months. Remember, of course, that you don't know whether yours is already middle-aged when you buy it. (There are no date-stamping regulations for chocolate as yet.) It normally keeps well for several weeks in a cool place. Once the packet has been opened, the chocolate will quickly absorb alien flavours if it is not carefully rewrapped. Since it does go stale, it is not worth buying larger quantities than you are likely to use, say, within a month.

The bloom which some chocolate develops in hot weather is due only to being stored at too high a temperature, which causes either the butter fat or the sugar to melt and re-form on the surface. It is harmless.

To melt chocolate

Most recipes recommend breaking the chocolate into pieces and melting them in a double boiler or bowl set over a pan of warm (not boiling) water. (You can even grate the chocolate first, if you don't mind the extra washing up.) It *is* possible to melt chocolate without spoiling it, in a heavy pan, especially if you are dissolving it in a liquid. But the heat must be very low (or use an asbestos pad) and the stirring almost constant.

If you are using chocolate as a coating, when it should be glossy, be careful not to let it get too hot, or the shine will vanish. It is probably safer to melt it on a shallow plate over warm water, so that you can judge the heat more accurately. If it does lose its gloss, stir in a small knob of butter or a teaspoonful of cooking oil, beat, and pray. The recipe for Danish chocolate gateau (page 33) incorporates beaten egg to keep the chocolate glossy.

Chocolate in recipes

Chocolate marries well with many other flavours: nuts, coffee, vanilla, rum, orange, brandy – name your own. You might not have thought of some of the earliest experiments, when chocolate-drinkers added pepper, pimento, aniseed and ginger. Hannah Glasse even included in her recipe 'three grains of musk, and as much ambergrease'. Brillat-Savarin considered cinnamon and vanilla the *nec plus ultra*, and Spanish recipes still frequently combine cinnamon with chocolate.

If there is chocolate in a recipe, it is usually the dominant flavour. This is true of all the following recipes for sweets, where it combines variously with brandy, orange liqueurs, coffee, almonds and rum. In the recipe for hare in chocolate sauce, it is barely perceptible, serving to enrich the sauce rather than dominate it. The Mexicans similarly use chocolate in their highly-seasoned molé poblano sauce served with meat, and Italian and Spanish recipes show how well chocolate combines with game.

Dishes such as chocolate mousse seem to improve by being made a day ahead. They ripen and become more mellow, particularly if they also contain spirits. Be sure to cover them so that they do not absorb stray flavours from the refrigerator or develop a skin on top.

Recipes generally specify 'good dessert chocolate' or mention one by name. Flexibility is possible between the various brands of plain chocolate, but you cannot use milk chocolate where plain is called for. The character of the dish would be entirely changed. This is equally true of cocoa, which lacks the butter-fat content of chocolate, and would thus provide the wrong balance of ingredients, ruining the texture as well as the taste.

We feel unqualified to advise on chocolate decorations, disliking commercial 'strands' on taste grounds, and being unable to produce a respectable 'curl'. If confronted by a naked-looking cake or pudding, we have occasionally produced fairly acceptable shavings with a potato peeler, and a fine or coarse dust with a cheese grater.

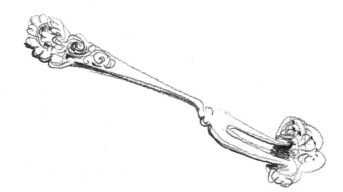

Hare in chocolate sauce (6)

Walnut Tree Inn, Llandewi Skirrid
chef/proprietor: Franco Taruschio

Chocolate is a not uncommon ingredient in savoury dishes in Italy, Spain and Mexico. It does not taste as startling as it sounds, but serves to enrich the sauce and thicken it slightly.

1 hare, jointed
wine vinegar
4 tablesp flour
2–3 oz butter
2–3 oz streaky bacon
1 onion
salt, pepper
½ teasp marjoram
1½–2 pints stock
3 oz sugar
3 fl oz wine vinegar
1 tablesp grated dessert
   chocolate
1 oz pine nuts or shredded
   almonds
1 oz raisins

Wash and trim the pieces of hare, and rinse them in wine vinegar. Pat them dry, toss them in the flour, and sauté them in the butter with the diced bacon and sliced onion. Season the hare with salt, pepper, and marjoram, add enough stock to cover the pieces, cover the pan, and simmer the hare slowly for 1½ hours.

Mix the sugar and vinegar together and add them to the pan, with the grated chocolate, the chopped or shredded nuts, and the raisins. Continue to cook for a further 15–30 minutes, until the hare is tender. If the sauce is very thin, thicken it with a little cornflour.

EDITOR'S NOTE: in some parts of Italy this dish is served with polenta to mop up the sauce. Failing that, some sort of bread and a salad would make appropriate accompaniments.

Chocolate cuisinier (4-6)

¼ lb plain dark chocolate
2 tablesp water
¾ pint double cream
1 tablesp caster sugar
2 egg yolks
grated rind of 1 orange
½–1 tablesp Cointreau

for decoration
double cream

Elbow Room, Totnes
chef/proprietor: Mrs Prunella Kilbane

Break the chocolate into pieces and melt it with the water in a double boiler or heavy saucepan. Bring the cream to just below boiling point, add the melted chocolate to it, and stir the two together well. Beat the sugar and egg yolks thoroughly, and add slowly to the chocolate mixture. Add the finely grated orange rind and the Cointreau. Stir continuously over very low heat until the mixture thickens. Put it in individual glasses or custard cups and chill. Garnish with a blob of cream.

Danish chocolate gateau (8)

Knight's Farm, Burghfield
chef: Meinhard Chibrath

½ lb plain chocolate, e.g.
   Bournville
½ lb butter
1 egg
½ lb digestive biscuits
2 oz flaked almonds
2 oz glacé cherries

Line an 8½-inch cake tin with aluminium foil and, if possible, fit the base from an 8-inch flan ring inside it – this makes the cake easier to turn out and serve. Or use an 8½-inch cake tin which has a removable base and line it with foil in the same way.

Break up the chocolate and put it to melt with the butter over a low heat. When it has melted, whisk in the beaten egg (which gives the chocolate a gloss).

Break the biscuits in half, lightly scoring them across to help make a clean break. Roast the flaked almonds and cut the cherries in half.

Combine the chocolate mixture with the biscuits, nuts and fruit and place it in the mould. Refrigerate the cake until it is cold and has hardened (an hour or two) when it can be removed carefully from its tin and the foil peeled off.

Chocolate mousse (6)

Harvey's Restaurant, Bristol
chef: Raymond Rey

3 oz good plain chocolate
3 medium-sized eggs
¼ teasp instant coffee
1 teasp brandy
1½ oz caster sugar

Put the chocolate pieces into a bowl to melt over a pan of hot water. Separate the yolks from the whites of the eggs and whisk the yolks into the melted chocolate with an electric beater. Then whisk in the instant coffee and the brandy.

In another bowl whisk the egg whites. Add the sugar and continue to whisk until very stiff. Fold these very lightly and swiftly into the chocolate and pour the mixture into a serving bowl or into six glasses or other dishes. Chill the mousse in the refrigerator for a few hours, or even overnight.

CHEF'S NOTE: this sweet can be made only with an electric whisk.

Amaretti Schokoladentorte (10)

Pool Court Restaurant, Pool-in-Wharfedale
chef: David Armstrong

Amaretti biscuits taste of bitter almonds from the apricot kernels which are used to flavour them.

½ lb plain dark chocolate
½ pint double cream
2 tablesp rum
2 tablesp brandy
2 tablesp cider
½ lb Amaretti biscuits

for garnish
whipped cream
angelica

Melt the chocolate in a double saucepan, bring the cream just to boiling point, mix them together and add the rum. Turn the mixture into the bowl of your mixer, and whisk at the speed normally used for cream (slow for a few seconds, high until the cream begins to thicken, and then minimum), scraping down the sides of the bowl frequently during the mixing. When it is ready, the cream will be the colour of milk chocolate and will have reached 'stiff peak' consistency.

Use a round plastic container or straight-sided dish for the torte (about 6 inches in diameter). Spread a thin layer of the chocolate cream over the bottom of the dish. Mix the brandy and cider in a bowl, and quickly immerse about 6–8 of the Amaretti in the liquid, shaking off any surplus as you remove them. Push these into the chocolate layer. Continue with thin layers of cream and moistened biscuits until both are used up. (The final layer, which will be the base of the cake, should be as flat as possible.) Cover the cake, weight it down, and refrigerate it for at least 6 hours, longer if possible.

To serve, warm the container slightly and turn out the torte onto a flat plate. Decorate it with whipped cream, piped if you like, and angelica.

EDITOR'S NOTES: the non-mechanised half of us did the beating by hand, and found it went fairly quickly if the chocolate cream were allowed to cool first. (About 20 minutes should do it, not counting necessary rest periods.)

If you are anti-angelica, decorate the torte with flaked chocolate or a crumbled Amaretti.

Amaretti are cheapest in Italian grocers' shops and in large quantities.

DRIED FRUIT

'What beautiful fruit! I love fruit when it's expensive.'
ARTHUR PINERO, *The Second Mrs Tanqueray*

Many of us have happy childhood memories of stirring the fruit into the Christmas pudding, opening boxes of neatly-ranged sticky dates, or playing snapdragon with raisins flamed in brandy. This orgy of dried fruit at Christmas time is almost the only survivor of the habits of earlier days, when even savoury dishes like meat pottage contained a great deal of dried fruits: currants, raisins and prunes. Mincemeat was once made with meat, the only vestige of which is the beef suet still mixed into the fruit. (The recipe on page 39 has discarded even that.)

Drying

Drying fruit reduces its moisture content and concentrates the sugar, and thus prevents its going mouldy or fermenting. Originally this was always done by leaving the ripe fruit to dry naturally in the sun. The best dried vine fruits are still prepared in this way, although some mechanical processing has been introduced. It takes about four pounds of fresh grapes to make one pound of raisins.

Nutrition

Dried fruits are obviously an excellent source of sugar, in the form of glucose, which is easily assimilated. They also contain vitamin A and some of the B group, as well as salts and minerals. Apricots and peaches are particularly rich in vitamin A, as well as having some vitamin C. The vine fruits have 70–80 calories per ounce, prunes about 38 and apricots 54.

Buying

CURRANTS are made from small, black, seedless grapes, mainly from the Gulf of Corinth which gave them their name. Some, however, are from Australia. The two finest are called Vostizza and Gulf, and they are dried in the traditional way, hanging in bunches in the shade of vine leaves, to give them a delicate blue tint.

SEEDLESS RAISINS are either made from a seedless black grape in California, or seeded before packing, in South Africa and Australia. Look for rich, golden-brown fruit which is firm-skinned and supple. Since raisins contain some moisture, they go 'winey' if kept too long. It is best to buy them in relatively small quantities when you need them.

MUSCATELS are large, juicy dessert raisins from Malaga, dried in bunches. Although they have the best flavour, they are not much used in cooking, because of the tedious business of removing their seeds and stalks.

SULTANAS are made from white seedless grapes, mainly in Australia and Turkey. Their light amber-coloured skin is partly artificially produced. They are also sprayed with a thin layer of oil to keep them separate. For both these reasons, some cooks recommend soaking them in warm water to remove the additives.

PRUNES were first developed by the French, who dried certain varieties of red and purple plums. Their prunes from Agen and Tours are still considered the best, and although most of those sold in Britain come from the Santa Clara valley in California they are grown on Agen plum trees. They are left on the trees as long as possible to acquire as much sweetness as they can from the sun, before being dried out of doors or in wind tunnels. They should be firm and bright in appearance, with a glow to their skins, and they should yield to gentle pressure. They are classified according to size, which seems to bear little relation to flavour. For making purees or pulp, small and medium-sized prunes are most economical.

Some packaged prunes have been pre-treated, or 'tenderized', a process of sterilizing and packing them while they are still hot, thus softening them so that they do not need to be soaked and the cooking time is considerably shortened. Pitted prunes, also from the United States, are particularly convenient if you want to stuff them.

DRIED APRICOTS have a much stronger and truer flavour than tinned, and are some consolation for the short season – and short supply – of fresh ones. They are imported mainly from South Africa and Australia. As with dried peaches and sultanas, a regulated amount of sulphur dioxide is used during processing to preserve the colour of the 'sun eggs', as the Persians called them. It is dispelled by exposure to air, soaking and cooking, so that there should be no danger of the flavour remaining. Apricots should be deep golden in colour and resilient to the touch. Avoid pale, dark-spotted ones which look unattractive and have comparatively little flavour.

Storing

Unopened packets should be kept in a cool dry place, and loose fruit or opened packets in a covered container. Because of their high sugar content they keep well.

Preparing and cooking

Most dried fruit is packaged for sale already washed and ready for use. If you *do* want to wash it at home, rinse it in a sieve in running water and spread it on absorbent paper on a rack to dry. If it is to be used in baking, toss it gently in a spoonful of flour to make sure that it is quite dry and will not sink to the bottom of the cake or loaf.

Most dried fruits need very little soaking before cooking – half an hour in warm water is enough. If prunes seem wizened, blanch them for a couple of minutes first.

Very little sugar need be added during cooking: use the sweetness of the fresh fruit as a guide. For example, apricots need rather more than prunes. Poach the fruit gently with a slice of lemon. Although water is the most usual liquid for soaking and poaching dried fruit, you might enjoy experimenting with tea, red wine, or gin for prunes, for example, or orange juice and water for apricots. The cooking time for prunes varies: follow the packet instructions. Apricots should take 20–30 minutes.

The concentrated, tangy flavour of dried apricots makes them an ideal partner for rich meats, as Apicius proclaimed in his first-century, BC, cookery book, when he combined them with pork. They make fine stuffings for roast lamb or pork. They also make a good soufflé, and combine well with cream or cream cheese, as in the apricot brandy flan (page 40) and apricot cheese cake (page 26). Prunes also go well with savoury dishes. The French combine them with goose, pork or rabbit, and the kebab recipe below uses pork and prunes.

Muesli, the Swiss breakfast dish (page 80) is full of fresh and dried fruit, while the *Dinner Party Book* has an interesting Armenian sweet, kishmish (DPB, page 27), which is a dried fruit compote similar to those found in Muslim cookery in the Middle East.

Pork and prune kebab with orange rice

Spread Eagle, Greenwich
chef: Hannah Wright

24 pitted prunes
a piece of orange peel
2 lb lean pork, leg or fillet
½ teasp powdered thyme
¼ teasp black pepper
½ teasp ground ginger
1 oz butter

for the rice

¾ lb long-grain rice
¼ teasp turmeric
¼ teasp ground ginger
1 orange
salt, pepper
1¼ pints beef stock or water
1 oz butter

Soak the prunes overnight in water with a piece of orange peel. Next day, trim the pork and cut it into 1-inch cubes. Mix together the thyme, pepper and ginger and toss the pork cubes in the mixture. Leave for an hour or so.

Drain and dry the prunes, then thread eight 8-inch skewers alternately with the prunes and pieces of pork, packing them together tightly. Brush them with melted butter and put them to grill slowly for 15–20 minutes, turning them from time to time and making sure the prunes do not burn.

While they are cooking, prepare the rice: wash it and put it to simmer in the stock with the spices and grated rind of the orange for 12–15 minutes.

When it is just cooked, stir in an ounce of butter and the juice of the orange.

Serve the kebabs on their skewers on the bed of rice.

Port and prune fool

Crispins, London
chef: James Stewart

This fool acquires a rich 'vintage' taste, even with cheap ruby port.

¼ lb Californian prunes
lemon zest
6 fl oz ruby port
¼ pint double cream
1 tablesp caster sugar
biscuits

Soak the prunes in cold water for several hours. Poach them till tender in just sufficient water to cover, with a good piece of lemon zest. Cool, remove the stones, and if there is more than 3–4 tablespoonsful of the cooking syrup, reduce it to that amount.

Put the stoned prunes, the syrup and the port in the liquidiser, and blend till smooth. (There will be small flecks of skin.)

Whip the cream, adding the sugar. When it is stiff, combine it with the puree. Put the fool in stemmed individual glasses and chill it.

Serve with biscuits, such as langues de chat.

EDITOR'S NOTES: count the prune stones as you remove them. As well as predicting your (next) marriage partner, this will protect your liquidiser blades.

If you use a more mature port, or more port than we have suggested, you may need a little more sugar.

Mincemeat

Queen's Armes Hotel, Charmouth
chef/proprietor: Mrs D. P. Besley

1 lb cooking apples
¾ lb black grapes
¼ lb almonds
2 lemons
1 lb raisins
1 lb currants
¾ lb sultanas
2 oz candied peel
1 lb brown sugar
2½ fl oz rum

This suetless mincemeat makes six ¾-lb jars and will keep for several months. At the Queen's Armes they make it into large pies – they 'don't go for those dried up little knobs in tartlet tins' – with a fairly rich shortcrust pastry, and serve it with a good dollop of clotted cream.

Peel the apples, peel and de-seed the grapes, and chop them all roughly. Blanch, skin and chop the almonds.

Grate the lemon rind and squeeze the juice. Put the apples, dried fruits, and candied peel through the mincer (not too fine a disc), then add the chopped grapes and almonds, the lemon rind and juice and the sugar, and mix them together. Pour in the rum and let the mixture stand for a couple of hours before putting it into jars and sealing them with waxed papers and pot covers in the usual way.

Apricot brandy flan (6-8)

River House, Thornton-le-Fylde
proprietor: Jean Scott

More sophisticated than it sounds.

½ lb dried apricots (or 1½-lb
  tin apricots)
¾ lb plain chocolate digestive
  biscuits
3 oz butter
¾ oz plain chocolate
9 fl oz double cream
1 fl oz apricot brandy
¼ lb caster sugar
1 oz flaked almonds

Cover the dried apricots with boiling water and allow them to soak overnight.

Crush the biscuits. Melt the butter and chocolate in a double boiler and stir it into the biscuit crumbs. Press the crumb mixture into a loose-bottomed 8-inch sandwich tin, as firmly and evenly as possible to make a shell. Refrigerate it for about 30 minutes.

Roughly chop the well-drained apricots. Whip the cream, apricot brandy and sugar till thick but not buttery. Fold in the apricots, and fill the flan with this mixture. Garnish it with the almond flakes, roasted in the oven till golden brown.

Westmorland raisin and nut pie (6-8)

White Moss House, Grasmere
chef/proprietor: Jean Butterworth

6 oz shortcrust pastry (DPB,
  page 173) or a digestive
  biscuit crumb mixture
  (6 oz biscuit crumbs, 2 oz
  melted butter)
½ lb seedless raisins
6 fl oz boiling water
3 oz sugar
1½ tablesp cornflour
a pinch of salt
juice of ½ lemon and ½ orange
2 oz chopped walnuts
a little rum-flavoured
  whipped cream

Jean Butterworth's version of a local traditional recipe. Instead of a double crust pie, which Mrs Butterworth thinks is too heavy, she spreads the top when cold with lightly whipped cream flavoured with rum, which makes it 'taste like Christmas'.

Line an 8½-inch tin with the pastry and bake it blind. If you are using the biscuit crumb crust, chill it for half an hour before baking it for 10 minutes at 375°F, mark 5.

Cook the raisins in the boiling water for 5 minutes. Mix together the sugar, cornflour and salt and stir this into the raisins. Cook this mixture until it has thickened and, off the heat, add the lemon and orange juices. Leave to cool before stirring in the chopped walnuts.

Fill the prepared flan case with the cooled mixture. Serve with the rum-flavoured cream.

EGGS

'An egg which has succeeded in being fresh has done all that can reasonably be expected of it.'
HENRY JAMES

Much more is expected of the cook. There are said to be a thousand ways to cook an egg, *not* including the one used by Egyptian shepherds and recorded by Mrs Beeton: the eggs were placed in a sling, which was then turned so rapidly that the friction of the air heated them 'to the exact point required for use'. We would welcome evidence of its efficacy.

Nutrition

An egg contains top-quality protein (12.1%), minerals, carbohydrates and vitamins A, B, D, E and K (11.8%), fat (10.5%), and water. It represents 70–90 calories. Because it is relatively cheap and easily prepared, it is extremely good value.

Buying

Eggs sold in Britain must now conform to certain Common Market regulations. They must be coded by the country in which they are packed, *not* the country in which they are produced. If the first number of the code is 9, the eggs were packed in Britain. The date of packing is also given, by week, with the first week of January as week 1, and so on.

Eggs are graded for quality and weight. The current British grades – large, standard, medium, small – are now gradually being replaced by the EEC grades (below) which we shall have adopted completely by 1978.

QUALITY – A means 'fresh eggs, naturally clean and internally perfect'
B is second quality, downgraded because the eggs have been wet- or dry-cleaned, have enlarged air cells, or are preserved in some way
C is 'only suitable for manufacturing purposes', and is not seen in shops
WEIGHT – There are seven EEC weight grades, from 1 at 70 grams or over, to grade 7 at under 45 grams.

Most recipes are based on a 2-ounce egg, 'standard' in the old grading. In future this will probably be a grade 4 egg, with an average weight of between 57 and 59 grams.

It is worth remembering that 'farm' eggs are not necessarily free range, and that carophyll orange is often added to hens' food to produce a yolk of any desired shade.

Freshness

Once you have your eggs home it is easy to test them for freshness: they should feel relatively heavy; if you put them in cold salted water they should sink; when broken, the yolk should bulge and the white cling to it. None of this is practicable in the shop, however, and it is more helpful to find out your grocer's delivery patterns and check on date-labelling and how the eggs are stored.

Storing	Shells are porous and absorb alien flavours. Most people prefer to keep eggs in a refrigerator or larder, pointed end down, away from strong smells. Whites will keep for several days in a covered container in the fridge. Yolks should be covered with cold water before being similarly stored.

Raw eggs in the shell, or hard-boiled eggs, should not be frozen, although both raw whites and yolks freeze satisfactorily separately. Put them in small containers labelled with the number of whites or yolks each contains. Yolks should be mixed with either a half teaspoonful of salt or a teaspoonful of sugar for every two yolks, to prevent coagulation, and labelled accordingly.

Cooking with eggs

'Boiled' eggs should be cooked as gently as possible to avoid rubbery whites. Hard-boiled eggs smell of sulphur dioxide if cooked for more than 12 minutes, and develop a dark ring round the yolk if not cooled quickly in cold water.

Omelettes

Like soufflés, these have prompted a great deal of inflated prose since their reputed invention by Apicius in AD 25 or so. We like the simplicity of Mère Poulard of Mont St Michel, who wrote to an admirer of her omelettes (in 1922):

'Voici la recette de l'omelette: je casse de bons oeufs dans une terrine, je les bats bien, je mets un bon morceau de beurre dans la poêle, j'y jette les oeufs, et je remue constamment. Je suis heureuse, Monsieur, si cette recette vous fait plaisir. Annette Poulard'

Egg whites

BEATING The ideal utensils are a copper bowl and a balloon whisk – the second at least is cheap and easily obtainable. Both should be dry and free from grease. If the whites are to remain uncooked, a pinch of cream of tartar will help stabilise them. You should beat slowly at first, more quickly later, all the time with large gestures to incorporate as much air as possible. If the recipe calls for sugar, the whites will whip more stiffly than they would without it. Do not beat egg whites long before you need to use them, since they will start to deflate and liquefy.

FOLDING IN First stir a large spoonful of the beaten whites into the basic mixture to lighten it. Then scoop the rest of the whites on top, using a rubber spatula. Finally, with the spatula, cut vertically down through the centre of the mixture to the bottom of the bowl or pan, draw the spatula towards you, up the side of the bowl and out. This will have brought some of the basic mixture up over the egg whites. Rotate the bowl slowly while continuing with this movement until the whites have been folded in. The process should take no more than a minute, and it is a mistake to be too thorough in the mixing and thus risk deflating the whites.

Soufflés

Soufflés are easier to contemplate if you remember that they are basically no more than a béchamel sauce with the addition of egg yolks, flavouring of some sort, and stiffly-beaten egg white (see vegetable soufflés, page 48).

Egg-based sauces

MAYONNAISE is neither mysterious nor difficult to make, but it inspires differing sentiments in the hearts of cookery writers. 'You should be able to make mayonnaise by hand as part of your general mastery of the egg yolk', according to Julia Child. Elizabeth David describes the process in more aesthetic terms:

'the pleasure and satisfaction to be obtained from sitting down quietly with a bowl and spoon, eggs and oil, to the peaceful kitchen task of concocting the beautiful shining golden ointment which is mayonnaise'.

We have reproduced the standard recipe, from the *Dinner Party Book*, on page 200. You should not try to incorporate more than six ounces of oil per yolk. If the sauce curdles, either start in another bowl with one egg yolk, and add to it the curdled mayonnaise, teaspoonful by teaspoonful, beating continuously as before, or put a teaspoonful of Dijon mustard in a warm bowl, add a tablespoonful of the curdled sauce, and beat the sauce for several seconds with a balloon whisk. When it is creamy, beat in the rest by teaspoonsful.

Mayonnaise made in the liquidiser needs whole eggs, not just yolks. The texture is lighter, less ointmentlike than a true mayonnaise.

Custards and cooked egg-based sauces, for example hollandaise (page 201), and béarnaise (DPB, page 174) are best cooked in a bain-marie or double-boiler, since yolks reach their maximum viscosity at 145°F, and harden and coagulate at 155°F. If the mixture is uncomfortably hot to the fingertips, it is too hot.

Délices d'Argenteuil

Normandie Restaurant, Birtle
chef/proprietor: Y. R. L. Champeau

Argenteuil – where the best French asparagus is grown.

1½ lb asparagus (1 lb tips)
½ pint pancake batter (DPB, page 172)
4 very thin slices smoked ham, e.g. Parma
½ pint hollandaise sauce

(page 201)

Wash and trim the bottoms from the asparagus, leaving the tip and about 3 or 4 inches of stalk. Poach the tips in about ¼ pint of salted water until they are just cooked, and drain them.

Make four medium-sized thin pancakes, slightly undercooking them. Prepare the hollandaise sauce.

Divide the asparagus tips into four portions, and roll each of them in a slice of ham, then in a pancake. Put them in a single layer in the bottom of a lightly buttered fire-proof dish, and bake them in a moderate oven (350°F, mark 4) for approximately 5 minutes.

Transfer the délices into a clean, *cold* dish – this is important or the sauce may curdle – and coat them with the hollandaise. Put them under a very hot grill for a few seconds until the sauce starts to brown very slightly, and serve them immediately. This dish cannot be kept hot: the sauce will curdle.

Oeufs Lorraine

Pengethley Hotel, Ross-on-Wye
chef/proprietor: Mrs Harvey

4 rashers streaky bacon
butter
2 tablesp finely chopped onion
4 eggs
4 tablesp double cream
4 dessertsp grated cheese

Dice the bacon finely and sauté it gently till brown with the onion in a trace of butter. Transfer the mixture with a perforated spoon to four cocottes or ramekins. Break an egg into the centre of each. Put the dishes in a bain-marie, and bake uncovered in a moderate oven (350°F, mark 4) until the eggs are lightly set (about 10–15 minutes). Spoon the cream over the eggs, sprinkle the grated cheese on top, and place the cocottes under a hot grill until the cheese melts and browns.

Oeufs en cocotte Pascal

Crane's, Salisbury
chef/proprietors: Sue and Tim Cumming

An easy and sophisticated first course, or a
light 'solitary supper' dish.

8 eggs
butter
salt, pepper
chopped parsley

for the topping
6 tablesp lightly-whipped
 double cream
1 tablesp Moutarde de Meaux

Allow two eggs per person, unless either appetites or your cocottes are very small.

Lightly grease the fireproof cocottes or ramekins with butter. Break 2 eggs into each. Season with salt, pepper, and a pinch of chopped parsley. Put the cocottes into a bain-marie with about half an inch of boiling water. Bake the eggs in the upper half of a hot oven (425°F, mark 7) until the whites are almost set and the yolks runny (about 5–7 minutes).

Fold the mustard into the whipped cream and put two spoonsful of the mixture on top of each cocotte, without removing it from the oven. Allow the topping to melt (about one minute) and serve the eggs immediately.

Swiss eggs

Oak Tree Restaurant, Rimington
chef/proprietor: Mary Doyle

4 oz Cheddar cheese
1 oz butter
4 eggs
salt, pepper
2 tablesp double cream

Grate one ounce of the cheese, and cut the remainder into wafer-thin slices. Grease four cocotte dishes generously with the butter, and line them with the cheese slices. Break the eggs carefully into the centre. Season them with salt and pepper, and cover with the cream. Sprinkle the grated cheese on top, and bake the eggs for 15 minutes in a very hot oven (450°F, mark 8). Flash them for a second or two under a very hot grill to glaze the tops.

EDITOR'S NOTE: the cheese acts as insulation here, so that a bain-marie is unnecessary. However, the eggs continue to cook once removed from the oven, and must be served promptly, or cooked for a shorter time if there is any possibility of delay.

Egg mousse (6-8)

Bowlish House, Shepton Mallet
chef/proprietor: Elaina Gardiner

6 hard-boiled eggs
½ pint mayonnaise (page 200)
½ oz or 1 envelope gelatine
2 tablesp cold water
½ pint chicken stock (DPB, page 171)
½ teasp salt
½ teasp curry powder
⅛ teasp white pepper
a pinch of mace
4 tablesp lightly whipped cream

Sieve the cold egg yolks into the mayonnaise and beat well. Soften the gelatine in the cold water, and then dissolve it in the warmed stock. Cool to blood heat. Stir the gelatine into the mayonnaise.

Chop the egg whites finely and add them to the mixture with the seasonings. Chill the mousse until almost set, stirring it from time to time. Add the cream, pour the mousse into oiled moulds (if you wish to turn it out) or ramekins, and leave it to set.

CHEF'S NOTE: the egg whites may be left fairly chunky to provide contrast in texture, but in that case the mousse is better not turned out, as the surface would be lumpy.

Oeufs andalousienne

Hotel Petit Champ, Sark
chef: Horst Konken

4 fresh eggs
1 teasp vinegar
¼ pint mayonnaise (page 200)
1 tablesp tomato puree
2 tablesp dry white wine
salt, pepper
3 or 4 slices garlic sausage
½ green pepper

Poach the eggs by breaking them into a saucer and slipping them into boiling water to which a teaspoonful of vinegar has been added. Bring the water quickly back to the boil and simmer very gently for 3 minutes or so until the white has enveloped the yolk and has set round it. Do not overcook them – the yolk should be soft. Remove each egg with a perforated spoon and slip it into cold water to cool. Then drain it on a cloth or absorbent paper. Trim the edges if necessary, and put one egg into each cocotte dish.

Stir into the mayonnaise the tomato puree, thinned with the wine, and some salt and pepper. Pour this over the eggs and decorate each with a julienne – fine strips – of garlic sausage and green pepper.

Vegetable soufflé

Symonds Down House, Axminster
chef/proprietor: Anne Coubrough

2 oz mushrooms, chopped
1 oz butter
¼ lb freshly cooked spinach,
    chopped
salt, pepper

for the sauce
½ pint milk
1½ oz butter
2 oz flour
salt, pepper
large pinch of nutmeg
5 large eggs (4 yolks, 5 whites)
3 tablesp grated Cheddar or
    Parmesan

Soften the mushrooms in the butter and when they are nearly cooked, mix in the drained, chopped spinach. Season well.

Melt the butter and stir in the flour, letting it cook gently for a few minutes. Off the heat, pour on the boiling milk, whisking well with a wire whisk until it gets very thick. Add seasonings and put the sauce to one side while preparing the eggs. Preheat the oven to 375°F, mark 5.

Separate the eggs, beating 4 of the yolks one by one into the sauce. Stir in the vegetable mixture and 2 tablespoonsful of the cheese. Whisk the whites until they are very stiff, stir one quarter of them into the sauce, then fold in the rest quickly and gently. Turn into a 7-inch buttered soufflé dish and sprinkle the top with the last spoonful of cheese. Place the dish on a baking tray in the middle of the oven and bake for 25 minutes.

CHEF'S NOTES: if kept out of draughts, the prepared soufflé can be left for half an hour before cooking. Once cooked it can be kept 20 minutes in a gas oven if the oven is gradually turned down to mark 2.

Other vegetable soufflés can be made – with 6 ounces of carrots, cauliflower, broccoli or spinach, all pre-cooked with a little chopped onion.

Cucumber sauce (8)

4 egg yolks
5 oz butter
4 tablesp dry white wine
2 tablesp wine vinegar
salt, pepper
1 cucumber, peeled and
    de-seeded
½ pint single cream
1 teasp lemon juice

Rivermede Country House Hotel,
St Michaels-on-Wyre
chef: Elizabeth Fielding

Place the egg yolks and the butter, cut into small pieces, in a double boiler or a large bowl that will fit into the top of a saucepan. Add the wine, vinegar and seasoning. Half fill the bottom pan with water and bring gently to the boil while stirring the mixture in the bowl

An excellent accompaniment to poached salmon, hot or cold.

continuously. As it begins to thicken, remove from the heat and cool the bowl a little. Stir in the peeled, de-seeded and diced cucumber, the lightly whipped cream and the lemon juice and serve the sauce warm or cold (but never straight from the refrigerator).

La truite du souvenir

Old House Hotel, Wickham
chef: Colin White

An attractive light lunch or supper dish: the delicate soufflé sauce exactly complements the flavour of the trout.

4 trout

for the soufflé sauce

1 oz butter
1 tablesp flour
½ pint milk
2 eggs (separated) plus 4 egg whites
2½ oz grated Gruyère or Emmental
salt, pepper
a pinch of nutmeg
a little milk and a little seasoned flour
2–3 oz butter

Ask your fishmonger to clean and bone the trout.

Prepare the soufflé sauce before cooking the trout. Make a roux with the butter and flour and when it has cooked for a minute or two, add the milk and stir until the sauce thickens. Away from the heat stir in the egg yolks, one at a time, then the cheese, and season the sauce lightly.

Wash the trout, dip them in milk, and then in the seasoned flour. Melt the butter in a large frying pan and when it is sizzling, brown the trout in it, turning them after about 3 minutes per side. Add more butter if necessary to cook the remaining trout. When they are brown, arrange them in individual well-buttered gratin or baking dishes.

Whisk the egg whites until they are stiff and gently fold the egg and cheese sauce into them. Cover the trout with this mixture and bake in a fairly hot oven (400°F, mark 6) for about 20 minutes until the soufflé sauce is a light golden brown. Serve immediately.

Iced coffee soufflé (6-8)

Ynyshir Hall, Eglwysfach
chefs: Elisabeth Escolne and Susan Collins

4 eggs
¼ lb sugar
2 oz dessert chocolate
2 tablesp instant coffee
2 tablesp rum
2 tablesp water
½ pint double cream

for decoration

cream, nuts, glacé cherries or angelica

Separate the eggs. Beat the yolks with the sugar until thick and creamy. In a heavy-bottomed pan or a double boiler, melt the chocolate and coffee in the rum and water, over gentle heat. Pour this into the egg mixture and beat thoroughly.

When it is completely cold, fold in the whipped cream and the stiffly whipped egg whites. Pour the mixture into individual coupe glasses or dishes, and decorate each with a little cream and nuts, glacé cherries or angelica.

EDITOR'S NOTE: toasted, flaked almonds go well with the mocha flavour.

GARLIC

. . . 'scorn not garlic like some that think
it only maketh man winke and drinke and stinke.'
SIR JOHN HARINGTON, 1609

Garlic is a perennial member of the lily family (*liliaceae*). It has a bulb made up of 10–12 cloves and a pretty lacy crown of white flowers. It is said to have been used by Odysseus to engineer his escape from Circe, and was thought to be equally effective later against werewolves, vampires and the plague. Slaves building the Pyramids were strengthened by it, as were the first Olympic athletes. It has always been considered a valuable medicinal herb (one of its country names is 'poor man's treacle'), and for every medieval reference one can find an equally convinced-sounding modern claim as to its blood-purifying or digestive properties. It is even said to improve the complexion of human beings (if anyone comes close enough to notice), cure leaf curl in peach trees if planted beneath them, and enhance the scent of roses if grown near them.

Nutrition

Apart from the properties outlined above, garlic has a sulphur compound in its volatile oils (producing its characteristic smell) and traces of iodine, fruit sugar, and vitamins B, C, and D.

Buying

Garlic is now supposed to be labelled by grade and country of origin in accordance with Common Market regulations. Since it is normally sun-dried after harvesting in July or August, it is at its best and freshest in the autumn, but as it comes to Britain from Portugal and Egypt as well as France, Italy, Hungary and Poland, it is possible to buy good garlic all the year round. Look for large firm bulbs, with no damp, crumbling or shrunken cloves. Many people find the white French garlic superior to the pink Italian variety, but within France itself you will find strong rivalries, typified by our recipe for poulet canaille on page 56, where the chef calls for Breton garlic, since 'southern garlic is soft, pulpy, greeny–white and no good'. Do not let this deter you from bringing some back from a Mediterranean or Breton holiday: you will know it is fresh and the nostalgia can only enhance the flavour.

Garlic powder and salt are not true substitutes for garlic since the preservatives they contain seem to distort the flavour.

Growing

The plant is supposedly easy to grow (one of us disagrees), requiring a light, fairly rich, well-drained soil, a sunny spot, and faithful weeding and watering. Plant large healthy cloves in a trench 2 inches deep, 6–8 inches apart, either as a border or in rows one foot apart. If you plant in February or March, you should be harvesting by the autumn. Lift the bulbs when the leaves have died down, and dry them indoors or in a sheltered sunny spot, either hanging, or lying on netting or bracken so that air can circulate.

Storing

If you are storing garlic in quantity, or have successfully grown your own, hang it by its plaited dried stalks, or suspend it in a string bag, in a dry, frost-proof place, since damp makes the bulbs decay.

Preparing

The central core or 'germ' of a bulb is the most indigestible part, and should be removed if anyone you are cooking for is sensitive. Blanching cloves not only makes the flavour less assertive but helps remove their paper-fine skins. Otherwise, pressing lightly on each clove with the flat of a knife squashes it sufficiently to make the skin detach easily.

We cannot find the truth of the matter of crushing versus chopping. Each faction claims that its method preserves the volatile oils and the rival method expels them. Writers we love and trust sound equally convincing on opposing sides.

Cooking

There is more unanimity on the effect of cooking: the garlic will become milder and be more digestible as the sulphurous oils are driven off.

Garlic burns easily, producing an acrid smell and taste. Thus it is often added after onions in a recipe, and fried for only a short time before liquid or other ingredients are added. A mixture of oil and butter is safer than pure butter as the frying medium.

Recipes

Remember that cloves vary in size and strength. The first time we made the delicate terrine of chicken and walnuts (page 165) it could just as well have been called a garlic terrine, because we used lovely new French stuff brought back from the south. You must consider not only what your family and guests will like but also what will make the best balance in a dish.

Some of the recipes which follow – Basque chiorro, the garlic soups, and poulet canaille – use what may seem to be frightening quantities of garlic, but where the cloves are fresh and simmered for some time the final flavour is subtle rather than overpowering. Basque chiorro (page 59) and bourride (page 57) show the affinity between garlic and fish which the French have unnervingly extended even to fish fingers.

Aïoli, which appears in the recipes for bourride and turbot à la monégasque, is one of the most famous Provencal recipes. It is a superbly garlicky mayonnaise, and if you are lucky enough to have some left over, use it instead of butter with jacket potatoes. And any spare garlic butter (mussels with garlic butter, page 58, or mushrooms in garlic butter, DPB, page 127) can be used to make garlic bread: cut through a French or Vienna loaf in thick slices, almost to the base crust, spread both sides of each slice with garlic butter, press the loaf together again, wrap it in foil and heat it in a fairly hot oven (400°F, mark 6) for 15 minutes or so.

For salads, mix finely chopped or crushed garlic with the dressing, or rub a piece of French bread with garlic, sprinkle it with oil and vinegar and put it at the bottom of the salad bowl. This *chapon à l'ail*, as it is called in south-west France, seasons the salad and makes a tasty last bite for the brave. Young fresh leaves of home-grown or wild garlic can be used chopped like chives in a salad. And if your family loves you and your germs rather more than they love the flavour of garlic, you might imitate Francatelli's method of achieving 'a perfect blend of delicacy and excitement in salads': 'At zee last moment I chew a leetle clove of garlic between my teeth and zen I breathe gently over ze salad.'

Aïoli (6-8)

Crane's, Salisbury
chef/proprietors: Sue and Tim Cumming

3 medium-sized garlic cloves
1 tcasp sca salt
3 egg yolks
1 pint olive oil
juice of ½ lemon

In a large mortar or heavy bowl crush the garlic cloves with the salt. When they have broken down into a mushy paste, beat in the egg yolks with a wooden spoon. Continue as for mayonnaise (page 200), adding the oil drop by drop at first, more quickly later. When half of it has been incorporated, stir in the lemon juice (and a little cold water if the emulsion seems too thick). Continue beating in the rest of the oil.

CHEF'S NOTES: if the aïoli curdles, take a fresh bowl with a teaspoonful of cold water in it, and beat in the curdled mixture, a tiny amount at a time.

In the restaurant this is served as a starter with prawns and a cold savoury rice containing nuts and sultanas. It can replace lemon mayonnaise in most recipes, though not those for delicately-flavoured fish.

EDITOR'S NOTES: if the aïoli is required for coating (as in turbot à la monégasque – page 144) it may be thinned with warm water before using.

Aïoli is death to good wine, so serve a modest one with it.

Green summer pâté (8)

Haldon Thatch, Kennford
chef/proprietor: Elizabeth Ambler

A refreshing pâté which gets its summery flavour from the bold use of fresh herbs and spices.

1 lb lettuce leaves (approx 4 lettuces)
1 lb spinach leaves
salt
2 oz butter
2 oz olive oil
2 large onions
4 fat cloves of garlic
2 bay leaves
thyme
marjoram
salt, freshly ground black pepper
allspice
nutmeg
6 oz sausage meat
2 oz boiled ham
6 slices white bread
4 fl oz milk
4 tablesp finely chopped parsley
2 tablesp finely chopped tarragon or basil
4 eggs

for serving
black olives
lemon slices
hot toast

Blanch the lettuce and spinach leaves in boiling salted water for 10 minutes. Drain them well and chop them finely. Simmer the chopped greens in the butter and olive oil until soft. Add the finely chopped onions and garlic, the crumbled bay leaves, thyme, marjoram, salt, pepper and spices to taste. Continue cooking for 10–15 minutes. Remove from the heat and stir in the sausage meat and the diced or minced ham. Remove the crusts from the bread, soften it in the milk, and add it to the mixture. Stir in the parsley and tarragon or basil. Check the seasoning: the mixture should be very flavourful. Mix in the lightly beaten eggs. Blend the mixture in the liquidiser until it is smooth.

Butter a soufflé dish and pour the mixture into it. Cover it and cook the pâté for 45–60 minutes in a hot oven (425°F, mark 7). Weight it and allow it to cool. Leave the pâté to mature for 2 days in the fridge, and then unmould it and decorate it with black olives and lemon slices.

CHEF'S NOTE: we serve the pâté with green mayonnaise (half a pint of mayonnaise thinned with a little white wine, with lots of finely chopped parsley, some chives and a little mint added) or double cream whipped with fresh herbs and lemon juice.

EDITOR'S NOTE: if you have only dried tarragon or basil, use one tablespoonful instead of two.

Baba ganouge

Armenian Restaurant, London
chefs: Aline Tungerian and V. Kevork

A low-calorie appetiser which tastes as good as any fattening one.

4 medium-sized aubergines
  (about 6 oz each)
4 tomatoes
1 green pepper
1 onion

for the dressing
3 teasp cumin
2 cloves crushed garlic
½ teasp cayenne pepper
1 teasp salt
4–6 tablesp olive oil
2 lemons
4 tablesp chopped parsley

Bake the whole, unpeeled aubergines on a shelf in a moderately hot oven (400°F, mark 6) until they are very soft to the touch. Cool and peel them.

Chop the flesh coarsely into a bowl and add the skinned and sliced tomatoes, and the finely sliced green pepper and onion.

Mix the spices in a bowl with the oil and lemon juice and add the dressing to the aubergines. Stir in most of the parsley and use the rest as a garnish.

Serve baba ganouge with Arab bread (page 91) or savoury biscuits for dipping.

EDITOR'S NOTE: another version of this dish calls for the ingredients to be pureed, and for the addition of ¼ pint of tahina paste. It can be served as a salad or as a dip.

Sopa de ajo

Simple Simon, London
chef: Simon Delgado

Jiminy Cricket

ck (DPB,

ron

, crustless

Warm the stock and dissolve the saffron in it. Heat the oil in a large saucepan and gently sauté the whole cloves of garlic in it. As it starts to colour, add the bread, cut into ¼-inch croûtons. Brown these and the garlic, then pour in the stock. Bring to the boil and simmer steadily for 5 minutes. Check the seasoning. Take off

the heat, and pour the soup onto the lightly beaten eggs, stirring continuously. Serve it immediately.

CHEF'S NOTE: the soup does not reheat successfully – 'a soggy bread pudding with garlic will result'.

Sopa de ajo con huevo (6)

Dulcinea, Sheffield Green
chef: L. Benavides

A more sophisticated garlic soup, augmented deliciously by home-made tomato sauce.

6–8 cloves garlic
5 tablesp olive oil
1½ pints water
salt, pepper
1 teasp paprika
1 tablesp chopped parsley
½ pint veal or chicken stock
   (DPB, page 171)
½ pint tomato sauce (page 71)
4 slices white bread, crustless
2 oz butter
6 egg yolks

Pound the peeled cloves of garlic in a mortar until they are creamy, then blend in the olive oil, a little at a time.

Bring the water to boiling point, add some salt, pepper, the paprika and half the chopped parsley. Stir in the garlic and oil mixture and allow it to boil for five minutes. Add the stock and, when it has come back to the boil, the tomato sauce. Continue boiling the soup for 10 minutes, checking the flavour and adding a little water if it is too strong.

Make some croûtons with the bread and the butter and keep them hot.

Put an egg yolk into each of six soup bowls and when the soup is ready pour a little onto each egg yolk, whisking it all briskly while pouring. Sprinkle some croûtons and parsley on top of each helping and serve immediately.

Poulet canaille

Crane's, Salisbury
chef/proprietors: Sue and Tim Cumming

'This dish is infinitely garlicky, but not pungently so.'

2 small roasting chickens,
   about 1¾ lb dressed weight
salt, pepper
2 oz butter
2 tablesp olive oil
20 large cloves of garlic
   (approx 2 heads), preferably
   from Brittany

Joint the chickens and salt and pepper them on both sides. In a heavy-bottomed casserole heat the butter and olive oil until they are very hot and fry the chicken quickly on both sides until it colours.

Throw in the peeled garlic, cover the pan and reduce the heat to the merest flicker.

Cook gently but steadily for 25 minutes, turning the pieces at half time and shaking the garlic down to the bottom of the pan. Serve the chicken with all its buttery, garlicky juices (matching up dark and light meat for each helping), accompanied by potatoes baked in their jackets and a green salad.

La bourride

Dormy House, Broadway
chef/proprietor: Hugh R. Corbett

La bourride, a close relative of bouillabaisse, is also found on the coast of Provence. This recipe was improvised from the various French versions as a starter.

1 lb fish, either a firm white
   fish, eg halibut, haddock *or*
   a selection of white fish,
   scampi, scallops, prawns
½ pint well-seasoned fish
   stock (page 201)
2 fl oz dry white wine
1 clove garlic
½ pint aïoli (page 53)
a little chopped parsley
a few prawns (optional)

Wash the fish and, if using prawns in their shells, shell them. (The shells can be used for preparing the stock.) Bring the stock, wine and garlic to simmering point in a large frying-pan and put in the firm white fish. If scallops and other shell-fish are also being used, add these halfway through so that they are not overcooked.

While the fish is poaching, put one tablespoonful of the fish stock into a double boiler over simmering water. Stir in the aïoli and heat the sauce over the hot water, whisking it continuously. Do not overheat or it will curdle, but try to get it fairly hot.

Drain the fish and divide it into four individual dishes or large cocottes. Spoon the hot aïoli over the top and sprinkle with parsley and one or two prawns if wished. Serve immediately – hot brown toast goes well with it.

Filetti di tacchino alla nerone

Old Bridge Hotel, Huntingdon
chef: Alan Scott

4 fillets of raw breast of
   turkey, 3–4 oz each
1½ oz fresh breadcrumbs
3 tablesp chopped parsley
2 cloves garlic
salt, pepper
2 oz flour
1 egg
2 oz butter
2 tablesp cooking oil
1 lemon

Beat out each turkey fillet under waxed paper or polythene with a meat bat or rolling pin until it is very thin. Prepare the breadcrumbs and mix them with the parsley, chopped garlic and seasoning. Coat each fillet with seasoned flour, dip it in the beaten egg and then in the breadcrumb mixture.

Heat the butter and oil in a frying pan and fry the fillets for about 7 minutes on each side until they are nicely browned and crisp. Serve immediately with wedges of lemon.

Mussels grilled in garlic butter

Priory Hotel, Bath
chef/proprietor: Thea Dupays

*For those who cannot or will not eat snails,
this dish uses mussels instead; the garlic butter
belongs to either.*

for the garlic butter
6 oz salted butter
1–2 cloves garlic
2 tablesp chopped parsley

2 quarts mussels
½ pint dry white wine

Soften the butter in a small bowl and mix into it the crushed garlic – the amount of garlic depending on the size of the cloves and one's fondness for garlic – and the chopped parsley. Cover the butter and put it in the refrigerator to chill for an hour or so.

Put the mussels into cold water and scrub each one thoroughly, chipping off any barnacles and pulling out the beard. Put the cleaned mussels into salted water for at least an hour.

Half an hour before the meal, transfer the drained mussels to a large saucepan and pour in the white wine. Cover the pan and put it over a high heat. After about five minutes, when the mussels start to open, take them out one by one, pulling off the empty half shell and arranging the full halves in four individual fireproof dishes. Sprinkle a teaspoonful of the cooking liquor over each dish. Place a knob of garlic butter on top of each mussel and slip the dishes quickly under a hot grill. As soon as the butter begins to sizzle they are ready to be served, piping hot, with some brown bread and butter.

EDITOR'S NOTES: mussels vary in size and weight. When buying them for this dish, calculate 10–12 mussels per helping. The cooking liquor will make the basis of a good fish soup or stock.

French bread soaks up the garlic butter well.

Basque chiorro

Travellers Rest, Durham
chef: Angela Martin

4 cod or hake cutlets
1¼ lb onions
1 head of garlic
3 tablesp oil
1 tablesp tomato puree
½ pint red wine
½ teasp paprika
salt, cayenne, ground mace
½ lemon
shallot, peppercorns, bay leaf
2½ fl oz dry white wine
4 slices white bread, crustless
2 oz butter
2 tablesp cooking oil

Sprinkle the fish with salt on both sides and leave it to stand for half an hour.

Peel and thinly slice the onions and crush the garlic. Heat the oil in a heavy-bottomed pan and soften the onions and garlic in it with the lid on. When they are transparent, remove the lid and increase the heat to colour them slightly. Off the heat, stir in the tomato puree, red wine and seasoning and simmer the sauce for 10 minutes or so with the lid half on until it thickens. Set it aside to mellow.

Drain off any liquid from the cutlets and sprinkle them with lemon juice. Place them in a large ovenproof dish surrounded by sliced shallot (or a few slices of onion), some peppercorns and a bay leaf, and pour over the white wine. Poach the fish in a warm oven (325°F, mark 3) for 12–15 minutes.

While the fish is cooking, fry the pieces of bread in the butter and oil until they are golden, and place them in four heated individual dishes. Put a cutlet on top of each croûte and top with a good spoonful of the onion and garlic sauce, reheated if necessary. Sprinkle with parsley and serve immediately.

CHEF'S NOTE: although one head of garlic may seem a great deal, it is in fact a conservative amount since when the crushed garlic and onions are simmered together – and this first cooking can be (and should be) done slowly for 15–20 minutes – its flavour mellows and changes into something very hard to describe but very tasty.

GRAINS, PULSES AND PASTA

'A wise man acts always with reason, and prepares his own lentils.'
STOIC MAXIM

'Oats: a grain, which in England is generally given to horses, but in Scotland supports the people.'
DR SAMUEL JOHNSON, *Dictionary of the English Language*

'Full o' beans and benevolence.'
SURTEES, *Handley Cross*

This chapter, which could virtually be subtitled 'staples and starches', deals with the varieties used in the recipes which follow.

GRAIN

Origins

Cereals were planted and harvested in neolithic times, and the first grains were used with nuts and seeds to make pottage. Oats and rye reached Britain in the Iron Age, barley came with the Romans, who also – mercifully – brought the rotary quern and pestle and mortar with them. Pottage then became relatively sophisticated, in Graeco-Roman fashion, and might contain chick peas, lentils, peas, green vegetables, various herbs and spices, with a garnish of chopped cabbage leaves. Cereal pottage remained the chief diet of Anglo-Saxons and other Germanic invaders.

Oats thrived in Britain, particularly in the North, where they could withstand the cold, wet upland weather. Dr Johnson was being less cynical than you might think, since oatmeal pottage did feed man and beast alike in the North. In the South, oatmeal was used mainly to thicken herb and meat stews.

Buttered cereals appeared in Tudor times and even in mid-18th-century London, street vendors sold buttered wheat or barley by the dish. But by the end of the century oatmeal and barley broths were despised in the South because of their workhouse overtones, and hasty pudding and oatmeal porridge were eaten only in the North. (Hasty pudding, 'suitable for labourers', had either milk or beer poured over it.)

Rice, which originated in India and China, came to Britain on medieval spice ships, and was locked up in the spice cupboard by careful housewives. The simplest rice pottage consisted of rice cooked in broth, flavoured with almond milk and saffron. The first ready-to-eat cereal appeared in 1893, followed a year later by Dr John Harvey Kellogg's flakes and Charles Post's ground cereal.

Nutrition

Cereals contain protein, carbohydrate, vitamins B and E, and various trace elements, some of which are lost if the cereals are highly refined. Oats have the greatest food value of any cereal. An ounce of oats or rice (dry weight) contains over 100 calories, and over 20 carbohydrate grams. Oats provide necessary roughage, as does brown rice.

Buying and storing	Cereals (except rice) go stale fairly quickly and should be bought only in quantities which you expect to use within a month. They are now frequently sold cleaned and packaged, but if bought loose should be put in a container before storing in a cool, airy place. Because of its fat content, oatmeal goes stale more quickly than the others.
Buckwheat	This is a seed, not of the grass family like the others in the group, but of a herbaceous plant. However, as it contains a glutenous substance and is made into flour, it is generally associated with them. The flour has very little of the coarse fibre coating included, and is almost as fine as refined white flour, but it has a very distinctive taste. It is used most commonly in variations of the pancake: American griddle cakes, Breton galettes de sarrasin, and Russian blinis (page 69). Whole buckwheat is used in the Russian kasha and as an accompaniment to roast goose, sucking pig, and many other dishes.
Cracked wheat	Known as burghul in the Middle East, this makes a refreshing salad (page 70) and appears in various forms of kibbeh (rissoles) and pilaffs in Middle-Eastern cookery. It can be bought in health food shops, and makes a good crunchy topping for home-made bread.
Oatmeal	Oatmeal and rolled oats contain almost the whole oat kernel, and are thus more nutritious than highly-refined cereals. Because of their high cellulose content they are digested most easily when well-cooked, although many of us take muesli (page 80) in our breakfast stride. (Rolled oats go through a preliminary crushing and partial cooking process.) Oatmeal comes in three grades: *coarse* and *medium*, suitable for porridge, haggis and white puddings, and *fine*, generally used in scones and oatcakes.
Semolina	As well as being the basis of pasta (page 65), the endosperm of durum wheat, when coarsely milled, becomes semolina, used for puddings in Britain (page 78), gnocchi in Italy (page 71).
Rice	India alone has more than a thousand different kinds of rice, of which we probably know only *Patna* (a long-grain rice suitable for boiling and some pilaffs) and *Basmati*, similarly long-grained and used in the same way. It has a particularly fine, nutty flavour. *Carolina* is a fairly long-grained rice, best suited to puddings. *Java*, or *Spanish*, rice has shorter oval grains and does well in risottos and milk puddings. But the best risotto rice, not unexpectedly, is *Italian* (preferably from Piedmont), with a large thick white or reddish grain. *Brown*, or unrefined, rice, still has its resistant bran layer.
Cooking	You are on your own with rice pudding, except for the Armenian gatnaboor on page 78, which almost overcomes our nursery prejudices. We could offer conflicting advice on boiling rice, but it seems less confusing to outline the basic variations and say which we have found successful.

Allow 2–3 ounces of rice per person. Either you wash rice, or you don't. We do (unless specifically advised not to in packet instructions), to remove any foreign particles and some of the starchy surface. Let it dry before proceeding. Next either you turn it in a spoonful of oil over a low flame until the grains are translucent, or you don't. We do sometimes, especially if the rice is rather poor quality and we think the grains may stick together. You then take boiling water – either twice the volume of the rice (for example, one cup of rice, two cups of water) or vast amounts, say, six pints of water to six ounces of rice.

If you are using the first method, you can then add the salted water to the rice, or vice versa, and you can cook the rice in a covered saucepan on top of the stove, or in a covered casserole in a moderate oven. In either case it will take 15–30 minutes to cook, and all the water should have been absorbed. Italian rice absorbs the most and cooks the slowest. Stir a lump of butter into it with a fork before serving.

For the second method, have plenty of water boiling vigorously in a large saucepan, sprinkle in the rice, and boil for 10–15 minutes. Test a grain or two for firmness and stop when they are tender but still firm. Drain the rice in a sieve, put it in a heatproof serving dish, stir in a lump of butter with a fork, and let it warm through, uncovered, in a slow oven for a few minutes. If you are not serving it immediately, put a folded tea towel under the lid to absorb the steam, and put the dish in a slow oven for up to half an hour. Add the butter and fluff it up with a fork just before serving.

Additional flavour can be provided by cooking the rice in stock instead of water, by infusing saffron in the liquid, by adding chopped parsley or other herbs just before serving, or by incorporating onion and coconut, as in the recipe on page 134.

Converted rice, which has already been parboiled, should be cooked by the first method, using $2\frac{1}{2}$ cups of water to one cup of rice. Brown rice takes almost twice as long to cook as milled rice, but the same methods are used.

Risotto

1 oz butter
1 small onion
$\frac{3}{4}$ lb Italian rice
4 fl oz white wine
2 pints chicken stock or water
1 oz butter
1 oz grated Parmesan

Melt the butter in a large heavy pan, and in it fry the chopped onion till pale golden. Add the rice and turn it until all the grains are glistening. Pour in the wine and let the rice cook over a moderate flame until the wine has been almost completely absorbed. Start adding the stock, a cupful at a time, and let the rice simmer uncovered, stirring it occasionally with a fork. When almost all the first cupful has been absorbed, add another and continue in this way until almost all the stock has been incorporated. Test for tenderness – you may not need the last half cupful of stock. The whole process should take no more than half an hour. Stir in the remaining ounce of butter and the cheese and serve at once.

Risotto milanese incorporates an ounce of beef marrow with the butter and onions, and $\frac{1}{8}$ teaspoonful of saffron with the last cupful of stock.

Pilaff

The method is illustrated in paella (page 77), shasliks of lemon chicken tandoori (page 130) and chicken with turmeric (page 121). There is also a recipe on page 174 of the *Dinner Party Book*.

PULSES

PULSE includes the edible seeds of leguminous plants, in effect, peas, beans and lentils. They are grown all over the world, in about 13,000 varieties.

Origins

Pulses have not always been considered the humble fillers we now take for granted. The priests of Egypt judged it a crime even to look at a bean, the very sight of which was unclean. Pythagoras agreed, forbidding his disciples to eat beans, since they were formed out of the rotten ooze from which man was created. The Romans ate them at funerals, thinking they contained the souls of the departed. Somehow they were also thought to cause defective vision. Lentils too were looked on with some ambivalence. Pliny said they produced mildness and moderation of temper, but this was later assessed as indolence and condemned accordingly. In fact, *lentil* is derived from *lentus*, slow.

The Celtic bean was the first pulse known in Britain. Pulses were grown as field crops, in rotation with wheat, and their bines were ploughed back to enrich the soil. Their usefulness in being so easy to dry and store was soon appreciated and they became part of pottage, as well as being ground and added to bread.

Mrs Beeton theorizes that beans and lentils fell into relative disuse in Britain in a fit of post-Reformation fervour, 'for fear the use of them might be considered a sign of popery'. She recommends lentils as ideal pigeon food.

Nutrition

Pulses have a high starch and sugar content, and thus provide energy. Lentils are highest in protein, with dried peas close behind. They contain the B vitamins, calcium, phosphorus and iron. Since they are deficient in fat, they are best served with fatty protein foods like pork and bacon. (How lucky that those combinations taste so good.) A 4-ounce serving of plainly boiled beans or lentils will provide about 100 calories, 20 carbohydrate grams.

Varieties

HARICOT BEANS come in several varieties. The best is thought to be the Soissons bean, which is the one the French would use in cassoulets (page 74) and other bean dishes. (The name is derived from the *haricot* or stew in which they were first used.) The Michigan bean which appears in tinned baked beans is a close relative.

KIDNEY BEANS These are another relative, native to Peru and popular in Mexican cookery, which may have influenced the recipe for spicy red bean salad on page 79.

FUL Egyptian brown beans are related to our broad beans and are virtually an Arabian national dish. They have very tough skins which require long slow cooking.

LENTILS Orange Egyptian lentils, which tend to turn to mush as they are cooked, are ideal for soups. German (or continental) lentils are brown, and hold their shape during cooking, as do the grey-green lentilles du Puy (which, confusingly, are also called lentilles vertes, and turn brown in the cooking.)

Buying and storing

Old beans in particular are tough and relatively tasteless, so it is worth buying the new season's crop which appears in the shops in late autumn. Loose pulses should be stored in tins or jars, and both these and packeted ones should be kept in a cool dry place.

Cooking

Beans require preliminary soaking, but not as long as was once thought. (In fact, if soaked overnight they may start to germinate, which partially remedies their vitamin C deficiency but doesn't do much for your innards.) If you first boil the beans in plenty of water (having washed them of course), and allow them to soak in the cooking liquid for about an hour, they will absorb as much water as if they were soaked in cold water overnight. Most beans absorb two-and-a-half times their weight in liquid during soaking and cooking. A rough guide is to take four cups of liquid for one cup of beans. Broad beans, whether white or brown, require rather longer soaking than other varieties.

It is generally thought that we have also been cooking our beans for far too long. Black-eyed beans need as little as 30 minutes, haricots from $1\frac{1}{2}$ to 3 hours. Beans should be salted at the end of cooking; otherwise they remain tough. Modern processing has made the addition of bicarbonate of soda unnecessary, even with the unyielding chick pea. Since it removed some of the B vitamins and made the texture of the cooked bean unpleasantly soft, this is all to the good.

Beans reheat very well. They may become very much thicker in the process, so have some stock handy for topping up.

Lentils are little helped by soaking, and become tender with about $1-1\frac{1}{2}$ hours cooking. Use the orange ones in soups, the others when you want a starchy vegetable as an accompaniment to meat, as in petit salé aux lentilles vertes (page 75), collar of bacon and lentils, and smoked chicken and lentils (page 76).

PASTA

Pasta, defined as any kind of alimentary paste, is made from the endosperm or heart of a particularly hard variety of wheat (durum wheat), finely milled. The same 'cream of wheat', more coarsely milled, becomes semolina. (Some cheap brands are made from soft flour and become soggy when cooked. Check the packet.)

65

Origins	Pasta comes in hundreds of varieties and stretches far back in history. One legend suggests that it was introduced to Italy by Marco Polo, and yet Roman equipment for making *laganum* (rather like tagliatelle) was found at Pompeii. It was first eaten with tomatoes in the 16th century, and has remained a major part of the diet of Southern Italians ever since. (It is largely replaced by polenta or rice in the North.) Noodles, of course, are popular in many countries, from France to China, and are eaten in soups and sauces, cakes and puddings.

Nutrition	Durum wheat is high in protein and, like other wheats, provides carbohydrates, B vitamins, minerals and calcium. Many pastas are made with eggs, and some with spinach, which provide additional food value. Over the years various dieticians have denounced pasta as fattening, and the Futurist Marinetti blamed *pasta asciutta* for Italy's failure to be a great power. But the fact that it is cheap, satisfying, and easy to cook has kept its devotees wedded to it. They claim that pasta at lunch time, with no more than a salad, cheese and fruit to follow, is not fattening. There are 115 calories and 26 carbohydrate grams in four ounces of pasta, plainly cooked. Butter or sauces count extra.

Varieties	The most important distinction is between home-made and mass-produced pasta. The home-made is used while it is still fresh and soft, and produces a very delicate dish. Since spaghetti and its many tubular relations require special equipment, they are less commonly made at home. Cannelloni and the more ribbonlike noodles, such as tagliatelle, can be made with no special equipment, and many Italian housewives and chefs make their own, although there are often shops round the corner where fresh pasta can be bought. (The same is happily now also true of Soho.)

The names of the various types are charming, and show the familiar affection Italians have for their pasta: *spaghetti* means little strings, *amorini* little cupids, *agnolotti* little fat lambs, *cannelloni* big pipes, *stivaletti* little boots, *vermicelli* little worms, *lingue di passero* sparrows' tongues, and so on.

Pastas can be classified according to their function. There are those for *soup*, for example, semini, pastina, conchigliette. Then there is pasta which is *boiled* and served with oil or a sauce: tagliatelle, fettuccine, capellini, ziti, spaghetti, trenette, and so on. Pasta for *baking al forno* includes lasagne, penne, grosso rigato, spiedini, and many others. And, finally, pasta for *stuffing:* cannelloni, ravioli, manicotti, lumache, etc.

Cooking	A pound of pasta is enough for four people as a main course, six as a first course. Cook it uncovered in plenty of boiling salted water, with a spoonful of oil added to prevent the pan boiling over so readily. Spaghetti should not be broken but should be held with one end of the strands in the boiling water. As they soften, coil the remaining length round,

and keep up the pressure until it is fully covered. Stir fairly frequently with a wooden fork or spoon, to prevent the pasta sticking.

The ideal is to have pasta *al dente*, tender and yet with some 'bite' still in it. Test frequently, since there are many variations in cooking times, depending on the age, composition and size of the pasta. Fresh pasta takes no more than five minutes, factory-made 11–15 minutes. Once cooked, drain it immediately in a colander, and serve at once.

Good fresh pasta tastes delicious when it is dressed very simply, with oil and butter, perhaps a little garlic and parsley. It is also good with cream or cheese, or cream and cheese. And, of course, pesto (page 105). You will notice we have not yet mentioned a meat or tomato sauce, although from Italian restaurants in Britain you might think one or other compulsory. If you do serve a thick sauce, allow about a pint to a pound of pasta. You should have enough to coat and flavour each strand, not enough to leave a puddle at the end.

The recipes which follow are all different to the 'spaghetti bolognese' you may know so well, and the cannelloni recipe (page 73) encourages you to make your own pasta.

Lentil soup (6)

Craigdarroch Hotel, Contin
chef/proprietor: Mrs R. E. Hendry

2 large onions
2 carrots
3 sticks celery
4 tablesp bacon drippings
½ lb orange lentils
3 pints ham stock
salt, pepper
croûtons

Peel and roughly chop the onions and carrots, and chop the celery finely. Heat the bacon fat in a large heavy-bottomed saucepan and fry the vegetables in it for 5 minutes. Add the washed and drained lentils and turn them over in the fat until they are well coated. Pour in the cold ham stock, stir well to remove any fried vegetables sticking to the bottom of the pan, and bring the stock slowly to the boil. Cover the pan and simmer the soup gently for 1–1½ hours.

Put the soup through a vegetable mill or rub it through a sieve. If necessary thin it with a little more stock or water. Reheat and add pepper (and salt if needed). Serve with croûtons.

Ful medames

Armenian Restaurant, Manchester
chef: S. Srabonian

An Egyptian dish, said to be as old as the Pharaohs.

½ lb dried brown broad beans
1 teasp salt
1 clove garlic, crushed
½ teasp cumin
5 tablesp chopped parsley
2 tablesp lemon juice
2 tablesp olive oil
¼ teasp chilli powder
   (optional)

Wash the beans carefully and soak them overnight in 2 pints of cold water. Drain them, and put them in a deep pan with 3 pints of water and the salt, bring the water to the boil, and allow the beans to simmer slowly for 2 hours, or until they are tender. Drain the beans, add the seasonings, the lemon juice and the oil, and mix thoroughly.

Serve hot in bowls with additional oil, lemon wedges or eggs simmered in their shells with onion skins for at least 6 hours *(beid hamine)*.

Italian runner beans

Mill House Restaurant, Milford-on-Sea
chef/proprietor: Colin Cooper English

The Italian rice fields are in Piedmont in the north. This method of serving runner beans, which is common in Piedmont, is simplicity itself.

2 oz long-grain rice
½ lb runner beans
3 rashers streaky bacon
1½ oz butter
salt, pepper
a little chopped parsley

Cook the rice as on page 63. Top and tail the beans and cook them in slightly salted water. Cut the bacon into strips and fry it in a little of the butter or in bacon fat.

When all are cooked, add the rice and bacon to the drained beans, stir in the butter and seasoning and sprinkle a little chopped parsley on top.

Blinis with sour cream and caviar

Leith's, London
proprietor: Prudence Leith

'The first pancake is always a lump': old
Russian proverb to justify the failure of any
first attempt.

for the blinis
$\frac{1}{4}$ lb buckwheat flour
$\frac{3}{4}$ oz fresh yeast (or half
   quantity dried)
1 teasp sugar
$\frac{1}{2}$ pint milk
$\frac{1}{4}$ lb plain flour
pinch of salt
2 eggs
$\frac{1}{2}$ tablesp melted butter
lard for frying

sour cream
caviar, lumpfish roe, smoked
   salmon or herring fillets

Put the buckwheat flour into a large, warm mixing bowl. Cream the yeast with the sugar, add to it half the milk, and mix well. Pour the yeasty milk into the buckwheat flour and mix them to a paste. Cover the bowl with a damp cloth, and leave it in a warm place to rise for about 15 minutes.

Sift the plain flour with the salt into another basin. Make a well in the centre and drop in one whole egg and the other egg yolk, reserving the white. Mix to a batter, bringing in the flour gradually, and adding the melted butter and the rest of the milk. Beat well. Then beat this batter into the yeasty one, cover with a damp cloth again, and leave it in a warm place for 2 hours.

Just before cooking, whip the remaining egg white and fold it into the mixture. Grease a griddle iron or pancake pan with lard, and heat it gently over a steady heat. When it is hot, pour in enough batter to make a saucer-sized blini (about half a ladleful). Turn the blinis when bubbles rise and cook the other side to a gentle brown. Keep the cooked blinis in a warm oven (between two soup plates or in a folded cloth) while you cook the others.

Serve the blinis hot, buttered, with sour cream and caviar. The caviar is spread on the blini, which is then topped with a dollop of sour cream. Danish lump-fish roe tastes good too, or a rolled slice of smoked salmon, or thin fillets of herring.

EDITOR'S NOTE: you may make the blinis before dinner and keep them hot for a little while, as directed in the recipe. Or you can let the batter rise once again at the end, and cook them as you are ready to eat them.

Tabbouleh

Byblos, London
chef/proprietor: Rafic Kreidi

A Lebanese salad using burghul (cracked wheat, obtainable from Middle-Eastern delicatessens and some health shops).

2 oz burghul
1 or 2 spring onions
2 bunches parsley
1 bunch mint
½ lb tomatoes
salt, pepper
juice of 2–3 lemons
2 fl oz olive oil
lettuce leaves, tender vine
   leaves or cabbage leaves

Wash the burghul well and soak it in cold water for an hour. Drain it thoroughly and squeeze it to remove as much water as possible. Chop the onion, the parsley, the mint and the tomatoes very finely, and add them to the burghul. Add the salt, pepper, lemon juice and olive oil and mix together well.

Serve the tabbouleh in a large dish lined with lettuce, vine or cabbage leaves, with additional leaves for people to use to scoop up the salad.

EDITOR'S NOTE: this is a homely dish with infinite variations. Some families serve it in individual bowls; others add cucumber or black olives. You might have to experiment to find the balance of lemon juice to olive oil which you like.

Fettucine imperiale

Don Pasquale, Gloucester
chef: Francesco Laccin

Fettucine is the Roman name for tagliatelle.

1 lb green fettucine

for the sauce
8 large button mushrooms
1 oz butter
4 tablesp béchamel sauce
   (DPB, page 174)
2 fl oz dry white wine
2 oz cooked ham
8 tablesp single cream
salt, pepper

Cook the fettucine in plenty of rapidly boiling salted water until it is *al dente* – tender but still firm.

While it is cooking, prepare the sauce. Slice the mushrooms and fry them in the butter for a few minutes. Stir in the béchamel, mixing it well in before adding the wine, the ham cut into strips, and the cream. Add plenty of seasoning and let the sauce simmer until it is thick and creamy.

Drain the pasta well and put it back into its saucepan over a low heat. Add the sauce and turn the fettucine very gently in it until it is all very hot. Serve the dish immediately.

Gnocchi Pool Court

Pool Court Restaurant, Pool-in-Wharfedale
chef: David Armstrong

A useful dish for an informal supper, since it
can be prepared ahead and baked while the
aperitifs are being drunk.

for the gnocchi
1 pint milk
2 oz butter
nutmeg
¼ teasp salt
pepper
¼ lb semolina
2 egg yolks
1 oz grated Parmesan

for the tomato sauce
14-oz tin plum tomatoes
1 medium-sized onion
2 cloves garlic
pinch of basil
6 fl oz chicken stock or water
salt, pepper
sugar (optional)

for the topping
1 oz grated Parmesan

Bring to the boil the milk, the butter, a little grated nutmeg, the salt and pepper. Rain in the semolina while stirring constantly, and cook the mixture for about 15 minutes, stirring occasionally. (Use a double boiler if your saucepan tends to scorch easily.) The mixture will now be thick enough for a spoon to stand up in it. Remove it from the heat and stir in the egg yolks and the Parmesan. Turn it onto a buttered baking tin or tray and spread it evenly to a depth of about ¾ inch (an area of about 11 inches by 7 inches will achieve this). Leave the paste to cool, preferably overnight.

For the sauce, cook together very slowly in a heavy, open pan the tomatoes, the finely chopped onion, the crushed garlic, the basil, and the stock. You can use the sauce after it has simmered for an hour, but it is even better after 2–3 hours.

Check the seasoning. You may need to add a teaspoonful of sugar if the tomatoes are very acid.

Cut the gnocchi paste into circles and crescents with a biscuit-cutter or tumbler. Put them in a buttered fireproof dish, moisten with a couple of spoonsful of chicken stock, and cover with the tomato sauce. Sprinkle the remaining ounce of grated Parmesan on top, and bake in a moderate oven (350°F, mark 4) for 30 minutes.

EDITOR'S NOTES: if you prefer thinner gnocchi, spread the paste thinner in a larger tray, and arrange them overlapping in the baking dish.

Leftover gnocchi can be reheated with a little cream, and a sprinkling of additional cheese.

Taglierini verde Alfredo

Luigi's, London
chef: Giuntini Fulvio

¾ lb taglierini verde
2 oz butter
2 oz grated Parmesan
½ teasp grated nutmeg
½ pint double cream

Cook the pasta in plenty of salted boiling water until it is *al dente*. This will take about 8 minutes, but check the instructions on the packet, since they vary. Drain the pasta well, return it to the pan, mix in all the other ingredients, and serve immediately.

EDITOR'S NOTES: a little oil added to the boiling water prevents the pasta boiling over quite so readily.

This simple treatment is suitable for all tender noodles and spaghetti. It does not work so well with more solid varieties, such as macaroni. It is particularly delicious made with fresh noodles.

Spaghetti Montparnasse

Bay Tree Hotel, Burford
chef: Fay Shann

A simple first course or light supper dish.

½ lb spaghetti
1 oz butter
1 tablesp cooking oil
1 medium-sized onion,
    sliced
1 medium-sized (about 14 oz)
    tin tomatoes
1 clove garlic, crushed
salt, pepper
4 tablesp grated Parmesan

Put the spaghetti to cook in boiling salted water until just tender.

Meanwhile, heat the butter and oil in a large frying-pan and sauté the onion gently until it is soft and transparent. Add the chopped tomatoes, garlic and seasoning and heat through. Drain the cooked spaghetti and add it to the sauce, mixing them together thoroughly. Serve immediately with the grated cheese either sprinkled on top or handed separately.

CHEF'S NOTE: this dish is equally good if macaroni is used instead of spaghetti.

Cannelloni

Casa Cominetti, London
chef: Bob Cominetti

This recipe for the well-known Italian dish involves making home-made pasta, which, with practice, is not too difficult.

for the pasta
6 oz strong flour
½ teasp salt
1 egg
a little water

for the filling
2 oz butter
1 small onion or 2 shallots
1 clove garlic
½ teasp rosemary
6 oz minced cooked chicken
6 oz minced cooked veal
5 oz chopped cooked spinach
1 tablesp chopped parsley
salt, pepper, nutmeg

for the sauce
½ pint tomato sauce (page 71)
¼ pint double cream
2 oz grated Parmesan

Sieve the flour and salt into a basin. Make a well in the centre and tip into it the beaten egg. Fold in the flour, then stir in sufficient cold water to make a fairly firm dough. Transfer the dough to a floured board and with the heel of the palm, knead it for about 10 minutes until it is very smooth and elastic. Keep the board and your hands well floured. Now roll out the dough with a well-floured rolling pin, stretching it until it is *very* thin. Cut it into eight 4 inch squares and drop these into boiling salted water for one minute. Lift each one out and run cold water over it, then dry it in a cloth.

Prepare the filling by cooking gently together the butter, the chopped onion and garlic, and crushed rosemary for 5 minutes. Mix together the chicken, veal and spinach and strain the flavoured butter into this mixture. Add the chopped parsley and plenty of seasoning, including nutmeg. On each square place some filling in a sausage shape and roll the pasta round it. Put two into each individual buttered ovenproof dish and pour the tomato sauce over them. Heat in a moderate oven (350°F, mark 4) for 10–15 minutes.

Remove from the oven, pour the cream over and sprinkle with grated Parmesan. Glaze the cannelloni under the grill until they are sizzling and golden. Serve very hot.

Cassoulet de Carcassonne (6-10)

Chanterelle, London
chef: Peter du Toit

A hearty family dish from the Languedoc,
where it is eaten at lunchtime on a day when no
great exertions are called for afterwards.

2 lb dried white haricot beans
stock
1 duck
½ small shoulder of lamb,
    boned
1 lb belly of pork or bacon
olive oil
2 onions
2 lb tomatoes
1 dessertsp dried thyme
3 large cloves garlic
1 tablesp chopped parsley
½ teasp pepper
1½ lb Toulouse sausage (or
    pure pork sausage)
salt

Soak the cleaned beans overnight in plenty of cold water. Drain them and cook them slowly, barely covered with stock, for about 1½ hours. Drain them, reserving the liquid.

Roast the duck (DPB, page 162) until it is three-quarters cooked (about 45 minutes at 375°F, mark 5), joint it and cut the breast into large pieces. Leave aside to cool.

Trim the lamb of all fat, skin, and sinew and cut it into large pieces. Remove any bones from the bacon or pork and cut it into ¼-inch cubes. In a large pan, fry the lamb and bacon together in a little oil until they are browned. Add the chopped onions, the skinned and quartered tomatoes, the thyme, crushed garlic, parsley and pepper. Pour in enough of the reserved bean liquid to reach the top of the meat, and simmer very slowly for an hour.

In an ovenware casserole, put layers of beans and the various meats, with the sausage cut into 1½-inch lengths. Add the liquid and, if necessary, enough of the reserved bean liquid to come just below the surface of the mixture. Cover the casserole and cook the cassoulet in a slow oven for at least two hours. Check the seasoning and add salt if necessary.

EDITOR'S NOTES: since this fills more than a gallon casserole, you may wish to experiment with smaller quantities. Like all peasant cookery, the recipe is not fixed, but is varied according to the whim of the cook. The ratio of beans to meat is high, and you may wish to try using only a pound of beans.

This version of the cassoulet is rather liquid, unlike many. A layer of breadcrumbs can be put on top to form a thick crust and absorb some of the liquid and fat. Traditionally, the crumbs are stirred into the cassoulet when they are golden, and a fresh layer is added. This can be repeated yet again, and the cassoulet served when the third crust has formed.

A salad is probably all that is necessary as an accompaniment, with fruit for dessert.

Petit salé aux lentilles vertes (4-6)

Le Français, London
chef/proprietor: Jean-Jacques Figeac

Serve this rich winter dish with a green salad (perhaps lettuce and chicory in a walnut oil dressing).

4 lb hand of pork, pickled
1 lb lentilles vertes (lentilles du Puy) (page 65)
1 onion
3–4 cloves
2 cloves garlic
bouquet garni
½ oz butter
parsley for garnishing

(Check with your butcher as to the saltiness of his brine. If very salty, cover the pork with cold water, bring it to the boil, discard the water and start from there.) Scrub the pork thoroughly with a stiff brush.

In a large saucepan, bring the washed and drained lentils to the boil in about a quart of water. Add the onion stuck with the cloves, the chopped garlic, the bouquet garni and, finally, the pork. Bring the water back slowly to the boil, and simmer for about 2 hours, partially covered. Check that both meat and lentils are tender. Remove the petit salé, the onion and the bouquet garni. Strain the lentils (keeping the liquid), and reheat them in a separate pan with a couple of spoonsful of the cooking liquid and the butter. Check the seasoning.

To serve, remove the skin from the petit salé, cut the meat into thick slices and arrange them on a bed of lentils, on a flattish dish. Garnish with parsley and serve with French mustard.

EDITOR'S NOTES: the cooking liquid is a superb, highly flavoured stock for future soups (try more lentils, or spinach, or mixed vegetables). The colour is a rather menacing brown, so be prepared to adjust it, possibly with finely chopped chives, parsley or grated carrot.

If your family likes fatty meat, this dish can be made with pickled belly of pork.

Smoked chicken and lentils

Crispins, London
chef: James Stewart

¾ lb brown continental lentils
1 medium-sized onion
1 stick celery
2 carrots
1 oz butter
pinch or sprig of thyme
2 bay leaves
pepper
chicken stock or water
1 smoked chicken, 2–2½ lb
parsley or watercress
1 lemon

Soak the lentils for an hour.

Sauté the chopped onion, celery and sliced carrots in the butter in a heavy-bottomed pan until they are soft. Drain the lentils and add them to the vegetables with the seasonings. Cover with plenty of stock or water and simmer for about 1½ hours.

Divide the chicken into four pieces and place them in the bottom of a large pot, then smother them with the cooked lentils and their liquor. Simmer gently for 15–20 minutes so that the chicken is heated through.

Serve in bowls or deep plates with a generous amount of lentils and their juice, garnished with parsley or watercress and a lemon quarter.

EDITOR'S NOTE: smoked chicken, often French, can be found in some delicatessens and large food stores.

Collar of bacon and lentils (6)

Glenwood Room, Rathdrum
chef/proprietor: Mr Cussen

1½ lb collar of bacon
2 oz dripping
12 small onions
1 stick celery
1 lb brown continental lentils
2 small carrots
2 or 3 cloves garlic
salt, pepper
bouquet garni
1 oz butter
a little chopped parsley

Soak the bacon in cold water for at least an hour. Bring it gently to the boil in fresh water and allow it to simmer for 5 minutes. Drain and rinse it in cold water.

In a heavy pan, heat the dripping and brown the onions and chopped celery in it. Put in the lentils, sliced carrot, crushed cloves of garlic, some pepper and a bouquet garni. Place the bacon in the middle and cover with water, put on the lid and simmer very gently until the lentils and bacon are cooked – after about 1½ hours. Towards the end of this time check whether any salt will be needed for the lentils: the bacon may be salty enough to season them.

Remove the bacon, skin and slice it. Arrange the slices in the centre of a warmed serving dish. Strain off the cooking liquor, and remove the bouquet garni. Stir in a little butter and spoon the lentils round the bacon, sprinkling them with chopped parsley.

Paella valenciana (6)

Andalucia, Rugby
chef: Carlos Garcia Gamblor

*A Levantine dish, named after the large
shallow sauté pan with two handles in which it
is cooked and served.*

1 young chicken
2 medium-sized onions
1 clove garlic
6 tablesp olive oil
2 green peppers
¼ pint tomato sauce (page 71)
¾ lb Spanish or Italian rice
½ teasp saffron
salt, pepper
2 pints fish stock (page 201)
1¼–1½ lb mixed shellfish,
    including mussels, shelled
    and unshelled prawns
about 2 oz cooked French
    beans, broad beans or peas
1 red pepper

Cut the chicken into 8 or 10 pieces. Chop the onions and garlic and sauté them in the oil in a paella pan or large, wide casserole. Add the chicken and, when it has coloured, the chopped green peppers. Continue cooking, turning the chicken, for about 5 minutes before stirring in the tomato sauce and the rice. Sprinkle in the saffron and some salt and pepper, and pour in the hot fish stock. Bring it to simmering point and leave, uncovered, over a medium heat for about 15 minutes while the rice cooks. Turn the rice over as the stock is absorbed and towards the end add the shellfish, but not the mussels. Heat these in a little water or fish stock separately until they open.

When the rice is cooked, arrange the mussels round the edge of the dish together with the cooked green vegetables and rings or strips of the red pepper. Put the dish into a warm oven for 5–10 minutes to dry out any moisture in the rice. (Do not stir it again.)

EDITOR'S NOTE: this dish was originally 'poor man's food', made with the ingredients handiest and cheapest. Try variations of your own, with chorizo sausage, rabbit, cubed pork or beef, snails, clams, squid or artichokes.

Gatnaboor

Armenian Restaurant, Manchester
chef: S. Srabonian

¼ lb short-grain rice
1 pint milk
½ pint water
peel of ½ lemon
2 oz washed sultanas
2 oz almonds
5 oz granulated sugar
½ teasp vanilla essence

Put the washed rice in a pan with the milk, water and lemon peel. Bring to the boil and simmer slowly for 15–20 minutes, stirring occasionally. Add the sultanas only 5 minutes before the rice is cooked.

Meanwhile blanch and roast the almonds until they are brown. Stir them into the cooked rice with the sugar and the vanilla flavouring. Leave to cool, remove the lemon peel and chill the pudding before serving. If the gatnaboor thickens too much on cooling, stir in a little more milk or a little liqueur.

Milk pudding de luxe

River House, Thornton-le-Fylde
proprietor: Jean Scott

This is more like a lightly baked sponge than its name suggests, and might convert even dedicated milk-pudding haters.

1 pint milk
¼ lb semolina
5 oz butter
2 oz sugar
2 eggs
strawberry jam
cream

Bring the milk to the boil and sprinkle in the semolina, stirring continuously. Simmer for a minute or two, still stirring, before adding the butter. Off the heat, stir in the sugar and when it has cooled a little, whip in the well-beaten egg yolks.

Whisk the whites until they are stiff and fold them into the mixture. Turn it into a buttered casserole and bake it uncovered in a bain-marie (DPB, page 168) in a moderately hot oven (375°F, mark 5) for 1 hour. Serve at once with strawberry jam and lashings of cream.

Red bean salad (6-8)

Count House Restaurant, St Just-in-Penwith
chef/proprietors: Mr and Mrs Howard

2 15¼-oz tins red kidney beans
5 sticks celery
1 green pepper
1 dill pickle

for the dressing
4 fl oz olive oil
4 fl oz red wine vinegar
4 tablesp chopped parsley
4 tablesp chopped spring
  onions
1–2 cloves garlic, chopped
2 tablesp capers, chopped
1 tablesp fresh basil
1 tablesp fresh tarragon
½ teasp chilli powder
1 teasp sugar
a few drops Tabasco
½ teasp sea salt
pepper

Rinse and drain the beans. Finely chop
the celery and the deseeded pepper, and
dice the dill pickle. Mix all these
together and put them in the bottom of
the refrigerator to chill.

Just before serving, combine all the
ingredients for the dressing, pour it over
the bean salad and toss.

Serve it with fresh pitta bread (page 91)
and plenty of dressing, to be mopped up
with the bread.

CHEF'S NOTE: if you have no fresh herbs,
use a teaspoonful of dried basil and one
of tarragon.

79

Wheatmeal biscuits

Miller Howe, Windermere
chef/proprietor: John Tovey

At Miller Howe, these biscuits are served
with cheese.

½ lb wheatmeal flour
4 teasp caster sugar
1 teasp baking powder
½ teasp salt
large pinch curry powder
2 oz lard
¼ lb butter
2 fl oz milk (approx)

Mix the dry ingredients together, rub in the fats, add enough milk to bind the mixture, and leave it to rest in the refrigerator for about an hour, or even several days, if you wish.

Roll out the dough on a floured board to about ¼-inch thickness, cut into rounds or other shapes, prick them with a fork, and bake them for 10–15 minutes in a moderately hot oven (400°F, mark 6).

EDITOR'S NOTE: the dough is very short and crumbly – you may like to try it with rather less fat.

Birchermuesli

Henderson's Salad Table, Edinburgh
chef/proprietor: Mrs Henderson

A raw-fruit porridge invented by Dr Bircher-
Benner of Zurich – a noted food reform
pioneer.

¼ lb rolled oats, preferably
    compost-grown
1½ oz mixed dried fruit
1½ oz mixed nuts
½ pint fresh fruit juice
1 large cooking apple
2 tablesp molasses
1 tablesp sour cream or
    yoghourt
fresh fruit in season, e.g.
    grapes, oranges, bananas

Soak the oats with the dried fruit and nuts overnight in freshly-squeezed fruit juice.

Next day peel, core and finely grate the apple and add it to the soaked mixture. Stir in the molasses and the sour cream or yoghourt. Spoon the muesli into a large glass bowl or into four individual dishes and decorate the top with slices of fresh fruit – be as generous as possible with the fruit.

CHEF'S NOTE: yoghourt seems more popular than sour cream (it is also less calorific). Use honey rather than molasses for those with a sweeter tooth.

EDITOR'S NOTE: you should be able to find molasses in health food shops, but if not, try black treacle or honey.

BREAD

'... *bread to strengthen a man's heart*'.
THE BOOK OF COMMON PRAYER

'*It is surely a singular fact that the one article of our daily food on which health depends more than any other, is precisely that which is obtained in England with the most difficulty – good, light and pure bread ...*'
ELIZA ACTON, *Modern Cookery*, 1859

It is also a singular fact that over a hundred years after Mrs Acton's protest, and over 700 years after the first laws were passed to regulate the quality of British bread, sales of sliced, steamed cottonwool are higher than they have ever been.

Origins

Bread itself has been with us since pre-historic times: calcined remains of small unleavened barley cakes have been found in Stone Age cave dwellings, and carbonised ones at Pompeii. The Egyptians, generally credited with making the first leavened bread, trod the dough like grapes. Even in the Middle Ages 'bread of wheat' was rare and served only at high table. It was 'fine white bread', and having once become a status symbol, it has remained in demand with all but health food addicts until very recently. Dorothy Hartley suggests that it was the white wafer of the mass in pre-Reformation days which gained white bread its almost magical properties.

Present-day national bread-eating patterns vary greatly. Germany has 200 named varieties of bread, France 40 and Britain twenty. On average, Italians eat $4\frac{1}{2}$ pounds of bread a week, the French and Dutch over three pounds, and the British about two pounds. Almost everyone admires French bread, but it is doubtful whether the British housewife is going to change her shopping patterns to include twice-daily trips to the baker's, necessary because most French bread goes stale in a few hours. However, the chaplain to the Anglican community in Luxembourg feels that there is hope for us: 'I see two good Christian reasons for Britain entering the Common Market – the bread and the wine.'

Nutrition

Bread is rich in carbohydrates, protein, B vitamins, minerals and calcium. A recent government survey found that bread and flour provide 21% of the protein, 22% of the iron, 25% of thiamine and 18% of niacin in our national diet. White flour is, by law, enriched to replace the substances extracted in making it white. Health food addicts would argue that two dozen natural nutrients are removed and half a dozen put back later in synthetic form. However, dieticians are generally agreed that white bread is no less nutritious than brown. A slice of bread yields about 70 calories and 15 carbohydrate grams.

One thing we *are* sure of is that home-made bread tastes much better than any factory product. And baking it is such a joy that it seems almost unbelievable that it can be doing the family good, pleasing them, and saving money, all at the same time.

FLOUR Flours are defined according to their rate of extraction: wholemeal contains all (100%) of the cleaned wheat grain, wheatmeal 80–90%, white 70–72%, and 'patent' flours 40–50%.

Flour is also defined according to its protein content. High protein, or *strong*, flour (with a protein content of 10–15%) comes from hard spring wheats grown in extreme climates like those of Canada and the USSR. *Soft* flour comes from softer winter wheats grown in milder climates found, for example, in England and France. The miller makes his own blends of different wheats.

Strong flour is best suited to bread-making, because it is the protein in it which forms the *gluten*, an elastic substance blown up by steam and air into 'bubbles' which set and become light and crisp on further baking. This dry gluten is the framework for a loaf or cake. Bread baked with strong flour should have a large volume and a light, open texture.

Flour is often not labelled soft or strong, except in health food shops. Strong flour is easier to find in the North. Names to look for are Be-Ro plain, McDougalls Country Life, Prewetts, Allinsons, Marriage and Sons, and Whitworth's Champion. There are also all sorts of other flours to experiment with: granary, bran, oatmeal and rye, which can be added in varying proportions.

Flour keeps best on a cool airy shelf. If your kitchen is damp or steamy, put the bag into a lidded tin or jar. Plain flour keeps for 4–6 months, self-raising for 2–3 months, wholemeal for up to two months.

YEAST should be baker's compressed or dried yeast, not brewer's yeast. It should be creamy and moist in appearance, compact yet crumbly in texture. Fresh yeast is not easy to find, though a baker who bakes his own bread will have it, and many health food shops also stock it. Since it keeps well, it is worth buying relatively large quantities For example, a pound is very much cheaper than 16 separate ounces would be. It can be stored, wrapped in foil or polythene, for up to six weeks in the refrigerator, six months in the freezer. Wrap half- or one-ounce portions individually.

Dried yeast is supposed to give similar results to fresh unless it is stale. (We must confess to being unlucky when we have tried it.) Since there is no date-stamping regulation for dried yeast, you have to trust your grocer. It will keep for six months, but is affected by air, and should therefore be transferred to progressively smaller tins as you use it.

$\frac{1}{2}$ ounce dried yeast = 1 ounce fresh yeast.

The quantity of yeast required varies according to the type of dough, and the rising method used. For 3 pounds of white flour, one ounce of fresh yeast ($\frac{1}{2}$ ounce of dried) is average. With wholemeal flour, double these quantities would be required. An enriched dough, with extra fat, sugar or eggs, requires more than a plain dough. Proportionately more yeast is needed for smaller quantities of flour. A high proportion of yeast to flour gives an open, spongy texture, and sometimes a sour yeasty taste.

Yeast is added to the flour in three possible ways:
(A) the yeast is first blended with the liquid required in the recipe (dried yeast is first reconstituted in the warm liquid with a teaspoonful of sugar, and left to froth for ten minutes.)
(B) a batter is made with one-third of the flour from the recipe, all the yeast, all the liquid and a teaspoonful of sugar. Once the mixture has frothed up like a sponge (after about 20 minutes), the remaining ingredients are added.
(C) the yeast is rubbed into the flour before the other ingredients are added. This method is suitable for quick breads, soft doughs and sweet breads.

Remember that yeast is a living plant, inactive when chilled, at its best just over blood heat, and killed by high temperatures.

SALT gives flavour to the bread, strengthens the gluten and prevents the yeast fermenting too quickly. Rock salt tastes nicest, but should be finely ground or crushed. Using too much will kill the yeast; too little will result in insipid bread. Between a teaspoonful and a tablespoonful to one pound of flour is about right, with the smaller quantity for white bread. It should be mixed with the dry ingredients to avoid killing the yeast.

SUGAR feeds the yeast and starts its action. Modern thinking does not recommend creaming the yeast with sugar, since the high concentration of sugar kills some of the yeast cells. It should also be mixed with the dry ingredients. It helps the crust to brown.

FAT enriches the dough and has a softening effect on it, making it more tender. It also helps delay staling. Lard is more effective than butter or margarine.

EGGS add flavour, help incorporate air, and make the structure firmer. They slow down the rising action, although beaten egg whites produce a greater volume and increased tenderness.

LIQUIDS Different batches of even the same flour vary greatly in their absorption properties. Water, milk, potato cooking water, or whey are all used. Potato water aids fermentation and improves the keeping quality and flavour. Milk and whey slightly increase the nutritive value. Plain water tends to give a better texture to a plain, non-enriched loaf. Too dry a dough will have a close texture; a slack dough will give a very open texture with holes in it. Liquids should be warm when added to the flour and yeast. Blood heat is easy to check, or you can mix equal quantities of boiling and cold water to get a suitable temperature. The liquid mixes in very easily if you use a wooden fork rather than a spoon.

You can put mashed potato or herbs, or almost anything else, into your dough.

Kneading

Kneading, essential to strengthen the gluten and thus give your bread its 'framework', seems to be the most pleasurable part of bread-making, according to cookery writers, even if it does no more than sublimate aggressive instincts. If you remember the Flour Advisory Bureau's thought that 'all kinds of handling, kneading and mixing' will help the necessary toughening of the gluten, you need not be timid in your approach. We cannot improve on Eliza Acton's Joycean description:

'Turn the whole ball out onto the table and press the middle with your folded fist and work it round and round, sides to middle, folding it in and kneading it down till all is one spongy elastic lump of resilience—no dry lumps of flour, no damp spots of yeast, but an even texture   with a lovely alive elasticity which seems to spring back against your fists.'

Other descriptions sound rather like foxtrot lessons, with quarter-turns, gentle rocking, and regular rhythm. If you get the chance to watch a professional, seize it – it is an aesthetic experience as well as educational. However, the hot and heavy-handed half of our partnership was encouraged to find that those very qualities, inimical to pastry-making, are well-suited to kneading. Wholemeal bread is often kneaded only once, sometimes not at all. If you have a dough-hook for your mixer, follow the maker's instructions, though it might be wise to make bread by hand once or twice first to get the feel of it.

Rising

Dough can be set to rise in a warm or cool place – the slower the rising the stronger the dough and the better the bread. To double in size, dough will need about 30 minutes in a warm place, 1–1½ hours at room temperature, and up to 12 hours in a cold larder. If you fancy fresh rolls for breakfast without getting up with the dawn, let them rise overnight in the refrigerator. Warm places are not hard to find: an airing cupboard, the back of the stove, a careful distance from the fire, near a radiator, and so on. In summer, you can make a compact 'warm place' with a hot-water bottle and a thick towel. Cover the dough while it is rising with a damp cloth, or put it in an oiled polythene bag.

Shaping loaves or rolls	Once the dough has doubled in bulk, 'knock it back' (pound the air out of it) and knead it for a further five minutes before shaping it. One of the pleasures of working with a white dough is finding that it is as amenable as plasticine, and that loaves and rolls can be made in virtually any shape.
	For a tin loaf, stretch the dough out into an oblong the same width as the length of the tin. Roll it like a Swiss roll, or fold it in three, and put it in the tin seam side down, with the ends tucked neatly in. A plaited loaf is described on page 90, and rolls on page 89. The crusty bread on page 88 requires no tin, nor does the soda bread (page 92), which is more scone-like than the yeast breads described above. Wholemeal bread looks nice baked in greased, seasoned clay flowerpots.
	Warm and grease your tins, put the dough in them, and slip them back in the oiled plastic bag to *prove* until the dough has doubled in bulk once again, about 30 minutes or so.
Finishes	Brushing the top of a loaf or rolls with salted water makes the crust crisp, butter makes it brown, egg-wash shiny, oil smoothly professional. Sprinkle on poppyseeds, bran, flour, crushed cornflakes, or what you will. Cutting a cross on top either protects you and the bread against evil, or helps it to rise well.
Baking	Bread is almost always started at a high heat (often 450°F, mark 8) which stops the action of the yeast. It is sometimes finished in a more moderate oven. When the bread is cooked, the tin or loaf sounds hollow when tapped on the bottom. For a crisp crust all over, return the loaves to the oven without their tins for five minutes or so. Cool the bread on a wire rack, wrapped in a cloth if you like a soft crust.
Short-time doughs	A modern method of bread-making has been evolved which allows you to finish the entire operation in under two hours. It involves dissolving a crushed 25 mg tablet of ascorbic acid (vitamin C) in the yeast liquid, increasing the yeast to one ounce for $1\frac{1}{2}$ pounds of white flour, adding a teaspoonful of sugar, and using liquid at about 80–90°F in a warm kitchen. The first rising is then reduced to five minutes and the second will take about 45 minutes. Baking temperatures are the same as usual.
Freezing	Bread freezes well and can be put straight into a hot oven (400°F, mark 6) to reheat for 45 minutes. It will smell and taste like fresh bread.
References	We are particularly fond of Elizabeth David's little booklet *The Baking of an English Loaf*, and the home economists at the Flour Advisory Bureau (21 Arlington Street, London SW1), who show patience and humour in the face of even the most inane questions.

Granary bread

Churche's Mansion, Nantwich
chef: Mr Beardsley

½ lb strong bread flour
½ lb granary bread meal
1½ teasp salt
1 oz butter
1 oz fresh yeast
1 teasp sugar
4 fl oz milk
¼ pt water (approx)

In a warm bowl, mix the flours and salt and rub in the butter. Cream the yeast and sugar in a small bowl. Heat the milk and water to blood heat, stir the liquid into the yeast/sugar mixture and finally into the flour. Mix well and add enough warm water (no more than 2 fl oz) to make a dough which is evenly sticky without being sloppy. Cover the bowl with a damp cloth and leave the dough to rise in a warm place for 40 minutes or so, until it has almost doubled in bulk.

Punch the dough down on a floured board and either put it in a greased bread tin or knead it and form it into rolls. Cover, and allow to rise once again in a warm place for about 20 minutes. Bake the bread in a fairly hot oven (400°F, mark 6) for about 40 minutes. The loaf should be nicely browned and should sound hollow when tapped on the bottom. Turn it out on to a rack and cool away from draughts.

Rolls should be baked for approximately 15–20 minutes.

Mr Moffat's soft crusty loaf

La Potinière, Gullane
proprietor: Christiane Moodie

Mrs Moodie has persuaded Gullane's master baker to part with one of his recipes. She serves this bread in her restaurant. Scots may find it sweeter and more brioche-like than the 'crusty' they are used to.

1 teasp salt
2 oz sugar
2 oz white shortening (e.g. lard)
1½ oz fresh yeast
½ pint water at 110°F
1¼ lb strong bread flour
1 egg

Cream the salt, sugar and fat together. Dissolve the yeast in the water and add it to the mixture. Immediately add the flour. Knead the mixture until a smooth, resilient dough is formed (about 10 minutes). Cover it with a damp cloth and leave it to rise in a warm place for 15 minutes.

Turn the dough out onto a board and knead it again for about 5 minutes. Leave it, covered, for a further 10 minutes.

Divide the dough in two, shape each half into a round loaf, put them on warmed baking trays, and leave them to rise, covered, in a warm place, until they have doubled in size.

Glaze them with beaten egg, cut a cross on top with a sharp knife, and bake them at mark 8, 450°F for 25–30 minutes. Cool on wire trays.

EDITOR'S NOTE: in a domestic oven, you may have to bake the bread on two racks. The higher one will almost certainly be ready in 25 minutes, while the lower one may need the extra 5 minutes. This bread can be reheated in the oven, and also makes good toast.

Brown bread rolls (12)

Pine Trees, Sway
chef/proprietors: Susan and Gerald Campion

This recipe calls for an electric mixer with a dough hook.

6 oz Prewetts wholemeal flour
6 oz Prewetts plain (millstone)
   flour
½ oz fresh yeast
2 teasp soft brown sugar
1 oz margarine
1½ teasp coarse salt
¼ pt boiling water
2½ fl oz tepid water
egg-wash or milk

Put both kinds of flour into the mixing bowl of the mixer and blend them roughly together with the dough hook. Break the yeast up into a small bowl and cream it with the sugar. Leave to stand for 10 minutes. Into another bowl or jug, put the margarine, cut into small pieces, the salt and boiling water, and leave it to stand for 10 minutes. Stir both mixtures.

Pour the water and margarine into the centre of the flour and turn on the mixer at slowest speed for half a minute or so until it is roughly mixed in. Stir the tepid water into the yeast syrup, mix them thoroughly and add to the dough. Turn the mixer on again at the slowest speed for roughly 5 minutes or until the dough leaves the sides of the bowl clean. Cover it with a damp cloth and put it in a warm place to rise to double its size, which should take approximately one hour.

Preheat the oven to 450°F, mark 8. Replace the bowl on the machine and again turn it on at the slowest speed for 5 minutes. Transfer the ball of dough to a floured board and cut it in half. Divide each into about 6 small handfuls and roll them into balls. Place them on an oiled baking sheet, slightly warmed, and cut a slit in the top of each roll. Cover the tray with a cloth and leave on the top of the cooker or in any other warm place to prove for 20–25 minutes, when the rolls will be bigger and puffy to the touch – but do not overprove them, thinking they should be huge.

Place the baking sheet in the middle of the oven for 10 minutes, then brush the tops of the rolls with beaten egg or milk. Reduce the heat to 375°F, mark 5 and continue the cooking for about another 5 minutes. Check whether the rolls are done by tapping the bottoms – they should sound hollow. Place them on a wire tray to cool.

CHEF'S NOTE: the rolls can be deep-frozen when lukewarm. To reheat them, put them straight into a moderate oven (350°F, mark 4) for 10–15 minutes.

Plaited cheese loaf

La Potinière, Gullane
chef/proprietor: Christiane Moodie

These quantities make two loaves of bread.
Mrs Moodie serves them with onion soup or
cheese, and tears them into pieces rather than
slicing them.

¼ pint milk
2 oz lard
1½ teasp salt
1 oz fresh yeast
1 teasp sugar
¼ pint water
1½ lb strong flour
black pepper, freshly ground
¼ lb cheese
1 egg
small piece of butter
coarse salt

Warm the milk with 1 oz of the lard and the salt to blood heat. Cream the yeast with the sugar and add to it the tepid water and the milk mixture.

Sieve the flour and pepper together in a large bowl, rub in the remaining ounce of lard, add the finely grated cheese, the egg, and the yeast mixture. Turn the dough out onto a board and knead it until it is smooth. (If it is very dry, you may have to add another drop or two of water.) Leave it to prove in a covered bowl in a warm place for about an hour, by which time it should have doubled in bulk.

Knead the dough again and divide it in two. With each half make four strips and roll them into 'sausage shapes' about 12 inches long. Plait them together to form a loaf, pushing the ends together tidily. Place the two loaves on a floured baking tray and leave them to rise again for half an hour in a warm place.

Brush the loaves with melted butter, sprinkle them with a little coarse salt and bake them in the centre of a very hot oven (450°F, mark 8) for 15 minutes. Lower the heat to 375°F, mark 5, and bake for another 30 minutes. The loaves should sound hollow when tapped, and smell 'ready'.

CHEF'S NOTE: any strong cheese will do. Even Roquefort crumbs and a pinch of parsley make a good loaf.

Pitta bread (6)

Count House, St Just in Penwith
chef/proprietors: Mr and Mrs Howard

A kind of partly-leavened bread, found all over the Middle East, which is delicious eaten hot with soups, hors d'œuvre or salads (e.g. baba ganouge, p. 55), or as a sandwich with a kebab filling.

½ oz fresh yeast
about ½ pint tepid water
1 lb strong flour
½ teasp salt
1 tablesp olive oil

Dissolve the yeast in 3 or 4 tablespoonsful of the tepid water and stir in enough of the flour to thicken it a little – this should start the yeast fermenting.

Sift the flour and salt into a warm mixing bowl and pour the yeast mixture into a well in the centre, adding enough of the tepid water to make a firm dough, though not a hard one. Knead it for about 15 minutes until it is very smooth and elastic. At this stage, if a tablespoonful of oil is kneaded into the dough, it will make a softer bread. Then oil the mixing bowl and roll the ball of dough around it to grease it all over which will prevent its cracking while rising. Cover the bowl with a damp cloth and leave it in a warm place for 1½–2 hours, when the dough should have almost doubled in size.

Punch it down and knead it again for a few minutes. Then divide the dough into 6 pieces and roll these in the hands until they are round and smooth. Roll out each one with a rolling pin on a floured board until it is barely ¼-inch thick, as even and as circular as possible. Dust them with flour and cover with a floured cloth. Leave them to rise in a warm place for 20–30 minutes.

Preheat the oven to maximum heat (450° or 475°F, mark 8 or 9), putting in two large oiled baking sheets half way through the heating period. When the oven is hot, slide the thin rounds of dough on to the hot sheets, dampen the tops to prevent their burning, and bake them for 10 minutes. Do not open the oven door during this time, but, after that, open it cautiously to see if the pitta have puffed up. They may need a little longer but should not be overcooked. They should be soft, with a hollow pocket in the centre.

CHEF'S NOTE: if the bread is not eaten hot straight away, it can be stored in the refrigerator in plastic bags and quickly heated up under a very hot grill after brushing the top with olive oil or paprika butter.

Irish soda bread

Purple Heather, Kenmare
chef: Maura O'Connell

¾ lb wholemeal flour
¼ lb white flour
1 teasp bicarbonate of soda
1 teasp salt
1 oz margarine
1 egg
1 teasp golden syrup
½ pint sour milk

In a large bowl, sieve together all the dry ingredients. Rub in the margarine. Make a well in the centre and add the beaten egg, the golden syrup and most of the sour milk. Mix the dough quickly and lightly with a wooden spoon. The mixture should be slack but not wet (rather like a scone dough); if it is too stiff, add a little more milk.

Put the dough on a floured board, and with floured hands pat it into a circle about 1½ inches thick. Put it on a baking sheet and make a large cross on the top with a floured knife. Bake it in a moderately hot oven (375°F, mark 5) for 30–35 minutes. Test the centre with a skewer before removing the bread from the oven.

If you like a soft crust, wrap the bread in a tea towel. It should not be cut for at least four hours, and keeps for a day or two, though it is at its best the day it is made.

EDITOR'S NOTES: dip the spoon in boiling water before measuring the syrup, and it will slide off cleanly.

If you have no sour milk, either sour some with a little lemon juice, or add ¾ teaspoonful cream of tartar to the dry ingredients.

Lahma-bi-ajeen (8-10)

Armenian Restaurant, Manchester
chef: S. Srabonian

An Arabian pizza, which can be rolled or folded and eaten in the hand at a 'stand up' party, or served more conventionally as a first course at a dinner, or as a tasty supper dish.

for the dough
¾ lb flour
½ oz fresh yeast
1 teasp sugar
1 teasp salt
½ teasp allspice
7–8 fl oz water

for the topping
1 lb minced lamb (shoulder)
1 onion
1 small bunch parsley
1 medium-sized green pepper
½ clove garlic
1 lb ripe tomatoes
½ tablesp tomato puree
1 teasp salt
1 pinch cayenne pepper
⅛ teasp black pepper
1–2 lemons

Sift the flour into a large bowl. Cream the yeast with the sugar and leave for a few moments to liquefy. Add to the flour the sugar, salt and allspice, the yeast mixture, and, finally, enough lukewarm water to make a soft dough. Knead it vigorously for 12–15 minutes, by which time it should be resilient and leave the sides of the bowl clean. Cover the bowl with a damp cloth and leave the dough to double in bulk in a warm place, for 2–3 hours.

Meantime make the topping. Mix the lamb, the finely chopped onion, the chopped parsley, green pepper and garlic. Add the skinned and chopped tomatoes, the tomato puree and the seasonings.

After the dough has risen, divide it into golf-ball-sized pieces, and allow them to rest for 10 minutes to make them easier to handle. Either pull them in your hand into circles about 6 inches in diameter, or roll them out on a floured board to the same size.

Spread a generous layer of the topping over the entire surface of each circle, and place them on greased trays as they are being made, leaving adequate space between. Bake them in a hot oven (450°F, mark 8) for 15 minutes. The dough should be cooked through, but still pale and soft enough to fold.

Serve the lahma-bi-ajeen with a wedge of lemon and a salad. If they are thin enough, they can be rolled like a pancake.

CHEF'S NOTE: these reheat well. Stack them in a covered container, in a cool place, till needed. Reheat them on baking sheets in a warm oven for about 10 minutes.

English summer pudding (6)

La Chandelle, Marlow
chef/proprietor: Tom Hearne

1½ lb mixed raspberries, redcurrants and blackcurrants
½–¾ lb sugar
¼ pint water
8–10 thin slices white bread

Clean the fruit, topping and tailing as necessary. Add the sugar and water to the currants and simmer them for a minute or two to draw the juices. Add the raspberries for the last minute only.

Remove the crusts from the bread and carefully line a 1½-pint pudding basin with it, trimming and filling so that there are no gaps. Fill the mould with the fruit (use a perforated spoon), save any excess juice, and cover the top with more bread slices. Place on top a plate slightly smaller than the inside of the bowl, so that it can be pressed down on the pudding with a 3–4 lb weight. Leave the pudding for 24 hours in the refrigerator, turn it out, cover any bare patches of bread with the reserved juice, and serve it with thick cream.

CHEF'S NOTE: blackberries or gooseberries may be substituted for one of the fruits listed above.

EDITOR'S NOTE: if your fruit is rather sweet, cut down on the sugar and have a sugar sifter on the table.

Bread and butter pudding

Craigdarroch Hotel, Contin
chef/proprietor: Mrs Hendry

An interesting variation on the old nursery favourite, with crunchy sides and top, and a custard-like middle.

5 slices white bread
2 oz butter
3 oz mixed dried fruit
1 oz chopped mixed peel
½ pint milk
2 large eggs
1 teasp cinnamon
1 tablesp sugar

Trim the crusts from the bread and cut the slices in half. Melt the butter in a shallow pan or heatproof plate. Dip one side of each slice of bread in it. Use approximately two pieces to line the base of a 1¼-pint pie dish or soufflé dish, and four pieces to line the sides, all buttered side out. Sprinkle with half the fruit and peel, put another two pieces of bread on top, buttered side down, add the remaining fruit and peel, and, finally, the last two pieces of bread, buttered side up. Heat the milk a little, mix it with the lightly beaten eggs, and strain the mixture carefully over the bread. Sprinkle the mixed cinnamon and sugar on top, and bake the pudding at 350°F, mark 4 for about 45 minutes.

GREEN PEPPERS & TOMATOES

Peppers and tomatoes, in common with potatoes, are part of the nightshade family (*solanaceae*), and this may account for the suspicion with which they have all been regarded at some time or other. They came from South America, and the tomato spent years as an ornamental greenhouse plant before anyone thought of eating it. It was suspected of causing cancer at one time, lust at another, and according to one of Mrs Beeton's medical friends, was a sovereign cure for dyspepsia. The first variety was yellow, hence the name golden apple (*pomodoro* in Italian). Its aphrodisiac properties (or its Moorish source, depending on whom you read) led to the name *pomme d'amour*, which became love apple in English (a name used until relatively recently). *Tomatl*, the Mexican name for a tomato, gives the modern name.

The pepper, being little known in Britain until about twenty years ago, is short on picturesque legends, but compensates with a confusing variety of names: *capsicum* in the West Indies, *poivron* or *piment doux* (France), *pimiento* (Spain), *bell pepper* (North America), *peperoni* (Italy) and *paprika* (Hungary). There are many varieties, some hotter than others, but we deal here only with the mild 'sweet' pepper, green when unripe, red when fully mature. (Chillies are discussed in the curry section, page 125.)

Nutrition

Both peppers and tomatoes are rich in vitamin C: two medium-sized tomatoes will provide the day's requirements. Tomatoes contain vitamins A and B also. Both vegetables are low in carbohydrates. Green peppers contain about eight calories per ounce, tomatoes five. Vitamins are lost during cooking and canning, and over-ripe peppers or tomatoes have fewer than ripe ones in good condition.

Growing

Green peppers are now featured in several 'exotic seeds' offers, but we have never tried growing them. Tomatoes are a different story, and not only do they have more vitamins when ripened on the vine and eaten promptly after picking, but they also taste better. The variety to avoid is the one most commonly on sale, Moneymaker, which produces a high yield of symmetrical, medium-sized, tasteless tomatoes. Find a good nurseryman, or consult a wise friend, and choose an outdoor variety with some character.

Buying

Green peppers should be dark green and shiny, relatively heavy for their size, with firm, unwrinkled flesh. Look out for any soft patches or discolouring (other than the natural tendency to turn red). Although they are available all the year round (from Israel, Kenya, Ethiopia, Holland, Rumania and the Canaries) they are at their best in late summer.

Tomatoes should be firm, shiny and red – light red if you are a 'rock hard' fan, as they say in the markets, rich red – but still unwrinkled – if you prefer a more mature flavour. When they are over-ripe the skin becomes dark and wrinkled and the tomatoes are best used for cooking. Asking for 'cooking tomatoes' sometimes produces some relatively healthy specimens at half the price of 'salad' tomatoes. Greenish, under-ripe ones will ripen at room temperature, best away from direct sunlight.

Tomatoes are most plentiful and cheap in August, when home supplies are at their peak. In winter they come from Spain, North Africa and the Canaries; Guernseys start appearing in June, along with Dutch tomatoes. The large, green-flecked, excellently flavoured though misshapen Marmande tomatoes (originally French but now mostly from Morocco) are stocked sporadically by enlightened greengrocers.

Green peppers will keep for a week, wrapped in plastic or foil, in the salad drawer of the refrigerator. A cut pepper will also keep well if carefully wrapped. Green ones will ripen to red if wrapped in tissue and kept in a cool place. They can be blanched and frozen.

Tomatoes will keep for a week in a cool larder if they are stored not touching each other. In the refrigerator they will keep one to two weeks in a polythene bag or other container. Check them frequently for bad spots. For freezing, they are best as a puree. If you are lucky enough to have a glut, they can be simmered slowly until they reduce almost to a paste, and stored for some weeks in the fridge with a layer of oil on top.

Cut round the hard stalk of the pepper and pull it out with as many of the seeds as possible. If you wish to stuff the pepper, rinse it in cold water to flush out the last of the seeds, and, if necessary, level the bottom so that it will not overbalance while baking.

Some people who find raw peppers indigestible are happier if they first blanch them in boiling water and refresh them in cold. If you wish to remove the skins, hold them on a long fork over a flame or put them under a hot grill until the skin chars, when it will rub off easily. Tomatoes can also be peeled by charring the skin, but it is more usual to drop them into boiling water for a minute, and then into cold.

With many of the tomatoes we are forced to buy, the watery pulp is no asset to a dish, and should be discarded, along with the seeds if your sauce is a smooth one as in the Tetbury tumkins recipe (page 20). For a spaghetti sauce or stew, it is not worth the extra trouble.

Stuffed peppers and tomatoes are known all round the Mediterranean, and recipes for these are to be found in many cookery books. The two vegetables combine well together, as in a ratatouille (DPB, page 54) or pisto (page 100). Green peppers also go well with orange, as in the refreshing salad and the pork with an orange and green pepper sauce (page 146). The green pepper soup (page 99) is unusual and delicious, made even more so by the last-minute addition of finely chopped raw peppers. As a vegetable, peppers can be soaked in oil and grilled, or blanched and sautéed in butter. They are perhaps at their best in salads when the brilliant colour and firm crunchiness are unimpaired.

Tomatoes are also splendid in salad, with their flavour helped along by good salt and pepper and an oily vinaigrette. Onion, garlic, parsley and sugar are optional extras, as are various herbs: basil or tarragon if fresh ones are to hand, oregano if you have to use a dried one. Those same herbs are classic for cooked tomato dishes.

Tomato sauce – even in Italy – is often made with tinned tomatoes, the best of which are Italian plums (see page 71). If you have plenty of ripe tomatoes (luckily they taste best when they are most plentiful and, therefore, cheaper) try making the same sauce with them. At other times, you may find that you need to add a little tomato puree to help both flavour and colour, but don't overdo it, or your sauce or soup will develop the distinctive 'tinned' taste you are working to avoid. Tomato sauce seems to thrive on extremes of cooking times: very brief cooking produces a fresh-tasting sauce, prolonged cooking a mellow one. Choose accordingly. Dishes with tomatoes in them – whether fresh or tinned or puree – almost always need a little sugar as well as the salt.

Peppers à la toulonnaise

1 tablesp finely chopped onion
½ tablesp butter
½ tablesp olive oil
3 sweet red peppers
1 small can tomatoes
1 teasp tomato puree
½ teasp chopped fresh basil
1 clove garlic
3 fl oz dry white wine
1 tablesp chopped ham
1 tablesp chopped black
 olives
1 tablesp walnuts
6 fl oz double cream
½ teasp Dijon mustard
1 tablesp chicken stock
1 egg yolk
1 tablesp grated Parmesan

Penny Farthing, Shrewsbury
chef: Chris Greenhow

Sauté the onion till it is transparent in the butter and oil. Add the sliced peppers and cook them over low heat for about 15 minutes, until they are tender. Add the tomatoes, the tomato puree, the basil, the garlic and the white wine. Simmer the mixture for a further 5 minutes. Add the chopped ham and olives.

To make the sauce, grind the chopped walnuts in a mortar (or coffee grinder) and simmer them gently with the cream, mustard, stock and egg yolk for a few minutes, until the sauce has thickened. Blend it in the liquidiser for a second or two.

Place the ragout of peppers in individual gratin dishes or ramekins. Cover with the walnut sauce and a sprinkling of Parmesan, and brown the tops under a hot grill.

Green pepper soup

Rothay Manor, Ambleside
chef/proprietor: Bronwen Nixon

2 large green peppers
1 large onion, chopped
1 oz butter
1 pint white stock, chicken,
    pork or veal (DPB, page 171)

for the white sauce
1 pint milk
1 oz beurre manié (DPB, page
    169)
salt, pepper, nutmeg

juice of ½ lemon

Quarter the peppers and remove the core and pips. Reserve one piece. Chop the rest roughly and sauté gently in the butter with the onion in a covered pan until they have softened without browning. Blend them in the liquidiser with a little of the stock until you have a smooth puree. Return it to the soup pan with the rest of the stock, bring it gently to the boil and simmer for 10 minutes.

Meanwhile make the white sauce: heat the milk to boiling point and whisk in the beurre manié. Season well and leave to simmer very gently till thickened. When both preparations are ready, whisk the sauce into the pepper puree. Just before serving, chop the remaining quarter of pepper roughly and liquidise it with a little of the soup (or chop it finely). Stir it into the soup and add the lemon juice. This gives a sharper flavour, texture and colour to the soup.

Tomatoes en cocotte

Cherwell Boathouse, Oxford
proprietor: Mrs A. Verdun

This is an ideal dish when tomatoes are in high season.

16–20 tomatoes (approx 2 lb)
thyme, sage, parsley, chives
salt, pepper
6 fl oz double cream
4–6 oz grated Cheddar

Choose fairly deep individual ovenproof bowls. In each one put 4–5 quartered tomatoes. Sprinkle them with herbs to taste, and salt and pepper, and cook them for 10 minutes at 350°F, mark 4. Put about 3 tablespoonsful of cream on top of each one, sprinkle them with the grated cheese, and brown the tops under the grill.

EDITOR'S NOTE: skin the tomatoes first if you find skins objectionable. However, doing so will change the colour and texture of the dish.

Pisto

1 large Spanish onion
4 cloves garlic
4 tablesp olive oil
1 or 2 bay leaves
3 green peppers
½ lb courgettes
1 carrot
2 rashers streaky bacon
salt, pepper
1 lb tomatoes
1 aubergine
a little chopped parsley
paprika, basil, thyme,
   Tabasco
3 fl oz dry white wine
a few rings of red pepper

Dulcinea, Sheffield Green
chef: L. Benavides

The Spanish version of the Mediterranean ragout of vegetables of which ratatouille and peperonata are other variations.

Slice the onion into rings and chop the garlic. Heat the olive oil in a large frying pan or casserole and soften the onion and garlic in it, together with the bay leaves. Deseed the peppers and slice them into rings, along with the courgettes and carrot. Cut the bacon rashers into thin strips. When the onion is soft, add all these to the pan with a teaspoonful of salt and some black pepper and let them cook gently. After 10 minutes put in the peeled and chopped tomatoes, adding the aubergine, cut into 1½-inch cubes, 7–10 minutes later. Season with a little chopped parsley, paprika, basil, thyme and a few drops of Tabasco. Pour in the wine, cover the pan and simmer slowly for 15 minutes or so – the vegetables should be stewed rather than fried to bring out their flavours. Uncover the pan for a final 5 minutes to reduce the sauce a little. Decorate with a few thin slices of red pepper on top and serve hot.

Onion, tomato and basil flan (4-6)

The Grange, London
proprietor: Geoffrey Sharp

6 oz shortcrust pastry (DPB,
   page 173)
1 lb onions
3 oz butter
1 lb tomatoes
1 teasp chopped fresh basil
salt, pepper
3 eggs
¼ pint double cream

Make the pastry and leave it to rest in a cool place while preparing the filling.

Chop the onions finely and soften them slowly in the butter for 10 minutes. Peel, deseed and coarsely chop the tomatoes. Add them to the onions, cover the pan, and let them cook together for another 10 minutes. Stir in the chopped basil and plenty of salt and pepper. Lightly beat the eggs, add the cream and mix into the onion and tomato.

Roll out the pastry and line a buttered 8-inch flan ring. Pour the filling into the case and bake it in a moderately hot oven (400°F, mark 6) for about half an hour.

Poulet provençale

Highlander Inn, Ovington
chef/proprietor: Mlle Fayaud

1 chicken or 4 chicken joints
2 tablesp olive oil
1 large onion
½ green or red pepper
3 cloves garlic
4–5 tomatoes
½ lb button mushrooms
2 tablesp tomato puree
½ bottle dry white wine
¼ pint water
a few black olives
salt, pepper, thyme, rosemary,
  basil, parsley

Cut the chicken into four (or get the butcher to do this). In a large casserole, brown the pieces in the olive oil. Remove them and put in the finely chopped onion to brown.

Deseed the pepper and slice it, chop two of the garlic cloves and peel the tomatoes. Trim the mushrooms. When the onions have browned, stir in the tomato puree, then the wine and water. Put the chicken back in the casserole together with the prepared vegetables, the olives, seasoning and a good pinch of each of the herbs. Cover and put into the centre of a warm oven (325°F, mark 3) for 1½ hours.

Transfer the chicken pieces to a serving dish and surround them with the vegetables and some of the stock, reduced a little if necessary. Chop the third garlic clove finely, mix it with some chopped parsley and sprinkle this over the top.

Salade niçoise

French Partridge, Horton
chef/proprietor: D. C. Partridge

4 eggs
½ lb tinned tuna fish
vinaigrette (DPB, page 172)
1 lettuce
2 tomatoes
12 black olives (approx)
8 anchovy fillets

There is really no exact recipe for this salad. Cooked French beans and onion rings are other traditional ingredients.

Hard boil the eggs, cool them under running water and shell them. Drain and flake the tuna fish.

Put some vinaigrette dressing in a salad bowl and in it toss enough lettuce leaves for four. On top arrange as decoratively as possible the eggs and tomatoes, cut into wedges, interspersed with the black olives and strips of anchovy. In the centre pile the flaked tuna fish.

As an alternative, the salads can be prepared in individual bowls and, as a finishing touch, the piece of tuna fish decorated with a piped star of mayonnaise (page 200).

Escalopes biscayenne

Cardinal Restaurant, Wetherby
chef: Jacques Castel

2½ oz butter
5 tablesp oil
1 large onion
½ lb green peppers, seeded and
    sliced
3 cloves garlic
1 lb tomatoes, skinned,
    seeded and chopped
salt, pepper
4 veal escalopes
4 tablesp flour
2 fl oz dry white wine
3 fl oz double cream
chopped parsley

Heat 1½ ounces of the butter and 3 tablespoonsful of the oil in a frying pan, and cook the sliced onion, peppers and chopped garlic for 5 minutes over a low heat, stirring them from time to time. Add the tomatoes and some salt and continue the cooking, turning the mixture occasionally, for 30–35 minutes. Be sure the peppers are properly cooked and quite soft or they will be indigestible. If the mixture becomes too dry at the end, add 2 or 3 tablespoonsful of water.

While the vegetables are cooking, beat out the escalopes with a meat bat or rolling pin. Dust them with seasoned flour and sauté them gently for 20 minutes in the remaining butter and oil. Transfer them to a heated serving dish and keep them hot. Drain off any excess fat from the pan before deglazing it with the white wine. Put in the vegetable mixture and the cream. Check the seasoning – it will probably need more, particularly freshly-ground black pepper.

Allow the sauce to reduce a little until it becomes thick and creamy. Cover the escalopes with it and sprinkle with chopped parsley.

Pilau rice goes well with this dish.

HERBS AND SPICES

*'O! mickle is the powerful grace that lies
In herbs, plants, stones, and their true qualities.'*
SHAKESPEARE, *Romeo and Juliet*

*'Nose, nose, jolly red nose,
and who gave thee this jolly red nose?
Nutmegs and ginger, cinnamon and cloves
and they gave me this jolly red nose.'*
BEAUMONT AND FLETCHER, *Knight of the Burning Pestle*

We all like to think that what we eat, apart from tasting good, is doing us good. That is how herbs and spices entered cookery. Nowadays we look on them collectively as flavourings, but they were originally used for curing people or curing food.

Origins

HERBS – grow best in temperate climates. Originally wild, they were cultivated even in Babylonian gardens for medicinal purposes. The Romans believed that tarragon would cure bites and stings and named it after the dragon. Rosemary, 'for remembrance', was worn as a crown by Greek students during their exams.

In medieval England, herbs were cultivated mainly in monastery gardens for use in treating diseases. Their enlivening of a diet of salted and dried food was of secondary importance. Today we regard that as their primary function, although recently there has been a revival of interest in the medicinal and cosmetic use of herbs.

SPICES, on the other hand, were first valued for their preservative properties – an essential in the hot climates where they originate. Their pungent flavours also helped to disguise or improve poorer foodstuffs. The Arabs first perfected their art of monopoly on the lucrative spice trade, which brought most spices overland to Europe from the Middle and Far East.

The Greeks loved the perfume of spices, the Romans their implications of affluence. The Crusaders brought the vogue to western Europe, and even after the early explorers had found new spice routes, spices were so expensive that when first introduced to England they were kept in locked cupboards by the wealthy, whose spicy winter dishes became part of traditional English cooking. One or two Puritans condemned spices as exciters of passion, but they survived despite – or because of – that verdict, and the taste for them has been reinforced by our historic links with the East, by our contemporary holidaying abroad, and by the multiplication of continental restaurants in this country.

Sales have more than doubled in the last six years, and we spend nearly £5 million a year on prepacked herbs and spices, distributed under a dozen brand names, the market leader of which sells over seventy different items. Herbs apparently sell well all over Britain, but Northerners are suspicious of spices.

The information below concerns only those herbs and spices which we find particularly useful in the kitchen, or which feature in the recipes which follow. Other, more exotic spices are dealt with in the curry section on page 125.

HERBS

Buying and storing

FRESH HERBS are, happily, appearing with increasing frequency. Parsley, mint and chives can be found in most greengrocers' and many supermarkets, which are also beginning to stock fresh thyme, bay leaves and sage. Health food shops are another likely source. Stored in their polythene bags or covered packs, these cut herbs will last for a day or two in the refrigerator, though they gradually wilt. They can also be kept for a short time in a cool place with their stems in fresh water.

DRIED HERBS are easy to come by. Do not be tempted by the all-too-pretty containers in which they are often packed, since you will be paying a high price for them, and they might tempt you to keep them out on display, which does the herbs nothing but harm. They go stale and lose their fragrance fairly quickly, so buy small quantities, and pitch out old ones ruthlessly every so often. Keep them in the larder, or other cool, dark place, in airtight jars.

PLANTS can be bought from some nurseries and greengrocers, and they are often cheaper than cut herbs, besides keeping considerably longer, even if you have a northern exposure and a black thumb. It is rewarding to grow your own herbs, either from these potted plants or from seed, and they require only indoor pots, window boxes, or a small area of garden – preferably near the kitchen door for easy forays in mid-omelette. If success overwhelms you, you can dry the herbs surplus to your immediate needs. For sensible help, consult *Herb Gardening* by Claire Loewenfeld (Faber) or *Herbs for Health and Cookery* by Loewenfeld and Back (Pan).

Basil

Sweet basil is worth growing (indoors), since it does not dry well and is seldom found in shops. It is at its best with tomatoes in a salad, or in pesto – the Italian sauce of pounded basil, pine kernels, Parmesan and olive oil – which transforms spaghetti.

Bay leaf

The sweet bay produces leaves containing a strong volatile oil, released when crushed or heated. One leaf is often added to stews or marinades, and, along with a sprig of parsley and thyme, makes up a *bouquet garni*. The bay is a hardy and ornamental evergreen, but it reveals a certain amount of temperament in choosing where it will grow successfully. It dislikes exposed spots. The leaves dry well. If you are buying them, choose dark green ones rather than brown.

Chervil

Chervil is a useful alternative to parsley, with ferny leaves and a slight aniseed flavour. It is nice raw in salads or as a garnish, and delicious in soups. An easy-to-grow annual, it withers quickly when cut.

Chives

A perennial, easily grown, even in indoor pots, which thrives on being cut from March to October. Its mild onion flavour makes it useful in salads. The freeze-dried version is fairly successful. With parsley, chervil and tarragon, chives make up the *fines herbes* for the omelette of that name.

Dill

This Scandinavian favourite which goes well with fish (see gravlax on page 114), has silky green fronds with a slight caraway flavour. The seeds, rather sharper in flavour, are used in pickling, and as a condiment by those on salt-free diets.

Mint

Mint, another easily grown perennial, is wedded in English cookery to 'mint-sauce-with-lamb'. It is worth experimenting with the lemon and mint sauce with duckling (page 148). A Turkish salad, jeryik (DPB, page 75) combines mint, cucumber and yoghourt. There are several varieties (e.g. applemint, spearmint).

Oregano

Wild marjoram with a spicy, astringent taste, characteristic of Italian pasta dishes.

Parsley

There are several kinds, with the curly-leafed variety the most common. It is fairly easy to grow (although slow to germinate), easy to buy, and keeps fresh for some days if rinsed in cold water, shaken gently, and stored in a sealed plastic bag in the crisper drawer of the refrigerator. It is a rich source of vitamin C as well as being an attractive garnish for salads and soups. To chop it quickly, use a sharp knife with a triangular blade, hold the point steady on the chopping board with one hand, and move the blade round in a wide arc with the other, chopping as you go.

Maître d'hôtel butter (butter, parsley, lemon juice and seasonings, pounded together and chilled) is often served with steaks, or try the fromage blanc on page 22 as an interesting alternative. Deep-fried sprigs of parsley (a minute or two at 375°F) make an attractive crunchy garnish, and go especially well with fish. Parsley stalks are full of flavour and are useful in soups and in a bouquet garni. Use parsley as a substitute for fresh coriander in Indian and Middle-Eastern recipes.

Rosemary

This spiky herb has a strong flavour – too strong for some of us. It goes well with lamb or, according to Italian chefs, with sauté potatoes and with buttered pasta. Along with juniper berries, it flavours pickled belly of pork most delicately (page 117). It is decorative and dries well, though the spikes then become somewhat lethal, unless pounded.

Sage

Another strongly flavoured herb, but an appetising one, particularly when used fresh in certain Italian veal dishes. It also goes well with pork chops. It is a perennial shrub, with silvery green leaves.

Sorrel

Sorrel has been a pot-herb for centuries. It grows freely wild, but can also be easily cultivated. It is broad-leaved, rather like spinach in flavour, but sharper because of its oxalic acid content. It makes a good soup and interesting sauces, where the rather bitter flavour adds piquancy, as in the green puree served with pickled pork (page 117) and the sauce vert-pré served with fish (page 118).

Tarragon

This is one of the best-tasting herbs, slightly aniseedy, with a strong affinity with chicken (see chicken Mère Michel, page 190). It is easier to grow from a cutting, since seeds are hard to find. Be sure you have the French variety, not the Russian. The dried variety has much less flavour, although the French have greater success, and a jar brought back from any French supermarket will keep you happy all winter.

Thyme

Garden thyme, an easily grown small shrubby plant, is the variety to cook with. It is very aromatic and a sprig is usually enough, even for a bouquet garni. It retains its character in dried form.

SPICES

Spices may be the dried fruit of a plant (paprika), or berries and seeds (coriander, juniper, mustard, nutmeg). Cloves and saffron are parts of flowers; cinnamon is a dried bark; turmeric and ginger are root spices.

Spices keep rather longer than herbs, but also lose their flavour over the months, and should be bought in small quantities and stored in airtight containers. Whole spices, such as cinnamon sticks, cloves and nutmegs, will last for years, but fade quickly in their ground form.

Cinnamon

The dried bark of a laurel found in Ceylon. Buy it in sticks for pickling, preserving or mulling. Use it in its powdered form for baking, and grind your own for an authentic curry. Cinnamon is one of the traditional flavourings in drinking-chocolate. It is used for cinnamon toast at cosy winter teas, and when mixed with sugar and butter makes an interesting crumbly topping for streusel cake.

Clove

The nail-shaped dried flower bud of a type of myrtle grown only in Zanzibar. Cloves are pungent and are associated particularly with apples and with bread sauce, where they are studded in an onion, as in the recipe for petit salé aux lentilles vertes (page 75). Use the powdered form in cakes.

Coriander

The crushed seeds give off a distinctive aroma which adds an unusual flavour to three of our cooked dishes, as well as appearing in a delicious salad with mushrooms and lemon (page 160). Buy the whole seeds and crush them as you need them, with a pestle and mortar or rolling pin (in a polythene bag). Ready-ground powder lacks the exotic fragrance of the freshly crushed seeds.

Juniper

The berries take two or three years to ripen on the tree and are then dried. Since they are the main flavour in gin, they may surprise you with their strong 'gin-like' bitter-sweet flavour. They are usually crushed before use. They go particularly well with game, as in the hare terrine (page 113) and the sauce served with pigeon breasts (page 123).

Mustard

Mustard is the 'British spice' by tradition, although it grows all over the world. It comes in several colours, including black and white, and mustard powder is a mixture of those two with additional colouring matter (often turmeric). English mustard is usually mixed with water (occasionally milk); aromatic French mustards are made with wine vinegar and spices. In powder form mustard keeps well; once made up it develops an impermeable skin with amazing rapidity. Dijon is one of the best and most famous kinds of French mustard, although recently Moutarde de Meaux, with its chunks of crushed mustard seed giving it an interesting texture, has run it a close second. (See œufs en cocotte Pascal, page 46.) As every pub-luncher knows, mustard goes well with cold beef or ham, and sausages. It also combines well with cheese (tarte à la moutarde, page 112) and certain oily fish, such as herring and mackerel.

Nutmeg

Nutmeg is the dried kernel of a fruit whose outer husk is made into the similar but stronger mace. Buy whole nutmegs, which keep for years, and grate them as needed. A little enhances cream and bolognese sauces, egg and cheese dishes, spinach and green beans.

Pepper

Peppercorns are berries of a pepper tree, and come black, white or green. The white are fully ripe berries without their outer husk, the black, immature berries from the same tree, used unhusked. The black are more aromatic, but the white can be useful in seasoning a pale-coloured dish where black flecks would detract from the appearance. A mixture of the two, *mignonette*, can be easily achieved by filling a peppermill with both white and black peppercorns. Ready-ground pepper has the heat but not the flavour of berries milled as required.

While black and white peppercorns are used dried, green ones are soft, fresh unripe berries, available tinned from Madagascar. They are gentler in their pepperiness, but do wonders for a mass-produced chicken or a steak – or even bread and butter.

Saffron

The most expensive spice in the world is made from the dried stigmas of a variety of autumn crocus, with up to 200,000 of them per kilo. It has spread from its native Mediterranean (even as far as Cornwall and Saffron Walden, where it was cultivated in earlier times), and is found in oriental as well as European cookery. It has a distinctive almost bitter flavour and a beautiful golden yellow colour, both seen at their best in bouillabaisse, paella valenciana (page 77) and chicken with lemon and mushrooms (page 147). You can buy it powdered or in whole filaments, and if measuring by spoonsful (or quarter spoonsful!), you will need twice as much of the filaments as the powder. It is often dissolved in liquid before being incorporated in a dish. Beware a golden-yellow impostor which is very much cheaper but has none of the flavour of saffron.

Soupe au pistou (4-6)

Le Sorbonne, Oxford
chef/proprietor: A. P. Chavagnon

A summer soup, originally from Genoa, but also found in Provence. The pistou (or pesto in Italian) is a creamy pommade of pounded garlic, fresh basil leaves and olive oil which is stirred into the vegetable soup just before it is served.

2 oz dried white haricot beans
2 ripe tomatoes
1 medium-sized onion
1 small stick celery
2 medium-sized courgettes
1 medium-sized carrot
1 small leek
¼ lb French beans
2 tablesp olive oil
salt, pepper
2½ pints water (or chicken
    stock)
2 rashers smoked bacon
    (optional)
2 teasp tomato puree
1 medium-sized potato
2 oz spaghetti

for the pistou
1 large clove garlic
2 sprigs parsley
4 sprigs fresh basil
1 tablesp olive oil

4 tablesp grated Parmesan
    (optional)

Soak the dried beans for 24 hours in salted water. Next day drain them, put them into a pan of cold, salted water and simmer them gently for about an hour until they are cooked. Peel, deseed and dice the tomatoes. Cut the onion, celery, courgettes and carrots into small cubes, chop the leek finely and cut the beans into ½-inch lengths.

Heat 2 tablespoonsful of olive oil in a large casserole or pan and soften the diced vegetables in it for 10 minutes; stir them frequently and do not let them brown. Season them lightly. Add the water or stock, the diced bacon, if you are including it, and the tomato puree. Bring the soup to the boil, cover and simmer it for about 30 minutes. Add the potato, cut into small dice, and the spaghetti,

broken into ½-inch lengths, and continue simmering the soup for a further 15 minutes before tipping in the drained haricot beans which have been cooking separately.

While the soup is cooking, make the pistou: finely chop the garlic, parsley and basil leaves and put them with the oil into a mortar, or if you have no pestle and mortar, use a bowl and wooden spoon. Pound them together until they amalgamate to form a smooth cream. Put this into a large serving bowl and slowly pour the soup in, whisking it all together. Taste to check the seasoning before serving – with or without a spoonful of grated Parmesan cheese sprinkled over each helping according to taste.

Lettuce and tarragon soup (4-6)

Leeming House Hotel, Watermillock
chef: Robert Burton

1 **good head of lettuce**
1 **small onion**
1 **oz butter**
½ **teasp dried tarragon**
1 **tablesp flour**
2 **pints chicken stock** (DPB, page 171)
½ **cucumber**
2 **egg yolks**
¼ **pint double cream**
salt, pepper, nutmeg
fried croûtons

Cut the washed and dried lettuce into ribbons and finely chop the onion. Melt the butter over a gentle heat and sweat the onion until it is transparent. Stir in the lettuce and tarragon and continue to cook gently for another 5 minutes until the lettuce is soft. Off the heat, stir in the flour, return the pan to the stove and gradually add half the stock, a little at a time, blending it in. Simmer for 25 minutes. While this is cooking, peel and deseed the half cucumber, then cut it into fine matchsticks.

Allow the soup to cool a little before pureeing it in the liquidiser or rubbing it through a fine sieve. Return it to the pan and add the rest of the stock. Prepare a liaison by beating together the egg yolks and cream, then stir into them some of the warm soup – to prevent any chance of curdling the liaison – and blend this back into the soup. Season well. Add the julienne of cucumber and reheat the soup but do not allow it to boil. Serve with croûtons, fried in butter.

EDITOR'S NOTE: this soup tastes even more delicious with fresh tarragon.

Carrot and coriander soup

Miller Howe, Windermere
chef/proprietor: John Tovey

2 medium-sized onions
1 clove garlic
2 oz butter
1 lb carrots
salt, pepper
½ tablesp coriander seeds
3 fl oz sherry
½ pint chicken stock
   (DPB, page 171)
½ pint milk

for garnishing
double cream
chopped parsley
croûtons

In a soup pan, sauté the finely chopped onions and the crushed garlic in the butter until they are golden brown. Add the thinly-sliced carrots, the seasonings and the sherry. Take a large piece of greaseproof paper and wet it thoroughly on one side. Place the wet side face down on the vegetables, cover the pan, and simmer them slowly for 30 minutes.

Remove the paper, add the stock and simmer the soup for a further 30 minutes. Liquidise it and strain it back into the rinsed saucepan. Add the milk, heat the soup and serve it with a swirl of cream, a sprinkling of parsley, and croûtons handed round separately so that they remain crisp.

CHEF'S NOTE: this method can be applied to parsnip and curry, turnip and dill (1 teaspoonful of seeds), or to smoked bacon and sprouts (garnished with ground hazelnuts).

EDITOR'S NOTE: lacking greaseproof paper, use foil.

Tarte à la moutarde (4-6)

Hotel Portmeirion, Penrhyndeudraeth
chef: Hefin Williams

6 oz shortcrust pastry (DPB,
   page 173)
2 dessertsp strong French
   mustard
¼ lb Gruyère cheese
5 tomatoes
2 egg yolks
2 fl oz double cream
salt, pepper

Bake an 8–9 inch pastry case blind (DPB, page 173) and allow it to cool.

Spread the mustard over the base to a thickness of ⅛-inch and sprinkle over it the grated Gruyère cheese. Blanch and peel the tomatoes, cut them in half and remove the seeds. Arrange the halves, cut side down, on top of the cheese and pour over the egg yolks, lightly whipped with the cream and some salt and pepper.

Bake the flan on a baking sheet in a moderate oven (350°F, mark 4) for 30–35 minutes until it is golden brown.

Terrine de lièvre genièvre (12-14)

Clifton Hotel, Nairn
chef/proprietor: Gordon Macintyre

A gamey pâté which freezes well, so that the large quantity produced by the recipe need not be daunting.

1 fresh hare
2 trotters or 1 calf's foot, split
2 onions
8 cloves
4 cloves of garlic
salt, pepper
6–8 oz belly of pork
½ lb liver pâté
3 tablesp chopped parsley
2 fl oz gin
3 fl oz port (optional)
16 juniper berries
1 clove garlic
½–1 lb streaky bacon

Joint the hare (or ask your butcher to do it) and wash the pieces carefully. Scrub the trotters or calf's foot. Put them with the onions, each stuck with 4 cloves, the chopped garlic and the salt and pepper in a large saucepan. Add enough cold water to cover the meat, bring it to the boil slowly, and simmer gently for 1½–2 hours, until the hare is tender. (Skim off scum as it rises.)

Cut the belly of pork in a few large pieces and fry it for a few minutes to make it easier to chop. (Save the juices for the stock.)

Remove the hare, leaving the pan on the stove. Strip the flesh from the bones and return them to the pan. Continue to simmer the stock, allowing it to reduce. Mix the coarsely minced or finely chopped hare and belly of pork with the pâté, the parsley, the gin, the port, the juniper berries and the crushed clove of garlic.

Line one or more terrines with the streaky bacon, leaving some slices overhanging the sides of the dish to cover the top finally. Pack in the pâté, cover with the bacon, and pour over the reduced and strained stock. Cover the pâté with greaseproof paper or foil

before putting on the lid. Cook it at 350°F, mark 4 for 1½–2 hours (the longer time if you have used only one large terrine). Uncover it, if you wish, for the last 15 minutes, to brown the top a little.

Press the pâté, and tip off some of the fatty juices. Cover it, weight it, and allow it to cool. Top up the dish with some of the stock, which will form a lovely jelly.

The terrine keeps well in the refrigerator for several days, and tastes better after a day or two's maturing. Serve it from the terrine, in slices, with watercress and toast.

CHEF'S NOTE: 'game comes to us very much on a feast-or-famine basis, and we make our terrines in this way, 8 or 10 at a time, from teal, widgeon, chicken, grouse, pheasant, guinea fowl, mallard, pig's head, hare, duckling – what you will.'

EDITOR'S NOTES: if you chop the meat rather than mincing it, you will not find it a difficult job, and the texture is pleasantly coarse.

If you like the flavour of juniper, you might try crushing the berries.

Gravlax with mustard sauce (14-16)

The Grange, London
proprietor: Geoffrey Sharp

2 lb middle-cut fresh salmon
1 large bunch fresh dill
4 tablesp chopped parsley
    and chives, mixed
2 tablesp sugar
2 tablesp coarse salt
1 teasp ground white pepper

for the sauce
6 tablesp dark French or
    German mustard
2 teasp mustard powder
4 tablesp sugar
4 tablesp wine vinegar
8–10 tablesp olive oil
4 tablesp chopped dill,
    parsley and chives, mixed

for garnishing
lemon slices

Split the salmon lengthways and remove all the bones (or ask your fishmonger to do this). Wipe and dry the fish and place one half, skin side down, in a deep dish. Wash the dill and place it on top, then sprinkle over the chopped herbs, the sugar, the salt and pepper. Place the other half of the salmon on top, skin side up. Cover it with foil and then with a heavily weighted dish, and leave it in a cool place for 48 hours. During this time, baste the fish inside and out with the liquid which gathers.

To serve, remove the gravlax from the marinade and herbs, separate the two halves, pat them dry, and place them skin side down on a dish or board and garnish with lemon. Cut the gravlax in thin diagonal slices (as for smoked salmon) and serve it with the mustard sauce.

To make the sauce, mix the two mustards to a paste with the sugar and vinegar. Gradually beat in the oil to make a thick, vinaigrette-type of sauce. Stir in the chopped herbs, and, if you like, a little of the juices from the gravlax.

CHEF'S NOTE: the flavour of the dill is essential to this dish. If yours is not fresh and highly flavoured, chop it finely with the parsley and chives before strewing it over the fish.

EDITOR'S NOTE: if the weather is very warm, marinate the gravlax in the bottom of the refrigerator.

Barbecued spare ribs of pork

Pine Trees Hotel, Sway
chef/proprietor: Susan Campion

An English version of a Chinese dish.

4–6 lb spare ribs

for the marinade
4 tablesp soy sauce
2 tablesp dry sherry
1 teasp fresh grated or ground
  ginger
2 cloves garlic, crushed
freshly ground black pepper
4 star anise

for the roasting sauce
3 tablesp molasses
2 tablesp orange marmalade
2 teasp sea salt
pepper
1 tablesp wine or cider
  vinegar
1 teasp arrowroot or cornflour
2 cloves garlic, crushed

Chinese mustard
2 tablesp dry mustard
1 teasp turmeric
2 tablesp wine vinegar
cold water to mix

Trim the racks of ribs of excess fat and remove the transverse bone if the butcher has not already done so. Combine the ingredients for the marinade and brush it on both sides of the racks. Break the star anise into pieces and sprinkle them on top. Leave the ribs to marinate in a roasting or baking tin for about 1 hour. Cover the tin tightly with aluminium foil and steam the ribs in the oven for 1 hour at 325°F, mark 3.

Take the ribs out of the tin and allow them to cool. Pour the juices from the pan into a saucepan and add the ingredients for the roasting sauce, first mixing the cornflour with a little cold water. Heat the mixture slowly to boiling point, and if you are using cornflour, allow it to cook for a few minutes. Liquidise the sauce and allow it to cool. Remove any fat which has hardened on the surface.

Cut the cold racks into individual ribs and pack them sideways on edge into roasting tins (you will probably need two). Pour the roasting sauce over the ribs, using a pastry brush to ensure that each rib is covered. Roast them for 30 minutes in a very hot oven, as near the top as possible. After 15 minutes, take the tins out of the oven, baste the ribs with the sauce and sprinkle them with ground sea salt, before returning them for the last 15 minutes.

Serve the ribs with rice flavoured with plenty of freshly ground black pepper and a good pinch of nutmeg, and moistened with a little olive oil. Add soy sauce to taste and serve separately the following Chinese mustard, which is very hot, and should be dipped into guardedly.

For the Chinese mustard, mix the mustard powder and the turmeric thoroughly. Add the vinegar and enough water to make a very thin paste. Each diner takes a little mustard and dips a rib in it – it is very hot!

CHEF'S NOTES: the baking tins will be very dirty and should be soaked immediately after the ribs have been removed.

The initial steaming can be done ahead of time, and the roasting sauce can also be prepared beforehand, so that only the final cooking remains to be done before dinner.

Sweet and sour barbecue pork

Crispins, London
chef: James Stewart

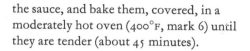

4 large loin pork chops

for the marinade
2 crushed cloves
I teasp ground cinnamon
**I dessertsp crushed coriander
    seeds**
I dessertsp Demerara sugar
**I dessertsp English mustard
    powder**
I large clove garlic, crushed
I tablesp soy sauce
I tablesp olive oil
I tablesp vinegar

for the sauce
I onion
I carrot
I stick celery
I small green pepper
I oz fresh ginger root
6 fl oz wine vinegar
6 fl oz water
3 tablesp sugar (approx)
**2 tablesp tomato purée
    (approx)**
I tablesp cornflour

for frying
2 tablesp oil

Trim the chops of excess fat. Blend the marinade ingredients to a thin paste and rub them into the chops. Leave them for several hours to absorb the flavours.

To make the sauce, chop finely the onion, carrot, celery, green pepper and ginger. Boil the vegetables for 5–10 minutes in the vinegar and water, adding the sugar and tomato puree near the end. Adjust the quantities to give a sweet-sour effect to your liking.

Brown the chops quickly on both sides in the oil, transfer them to a casserole with the sauce, and bake them, covered, in a moderately hot oven (400°F, mark 6) until they are tender (about 45 minutes).

Put the chops on a serving dish and keep them warm while you thicken the sauce with the cornflour, first dissolved in a couple of spoonsful of water. Pour the sauce over the chops and serve them with plain boiled rice.

EDITOR'S NOTE: if you cannot find fresh ginger, use preserved ginger and adjust the quantity of sugar.

Pork and juniper berries (4-6)

Horn of Plenty, Gulworthy
chef/proprietor: Sonia Stevenson

Ask your butcher to put the boned belly of pork in brine for 4–5 days.

2½–3 lb boned pickled belly of
    pork
20–30 juniper berries
8–12 black peppercorns
6–10 sprigs rosemary
½ pint dry white wine
½ pint water (approx)

for the puree
¼ lb split peas
1 lb spinach (or ½ lb frozen)
1 bunch watercress
1 bunch sorrel
1 teasp freshly-ground
    nutmeg
2 oz ice-cold butter

Remove the skin and excess fat from the pork. Crush the juniper berries and peppercorns, using a pestle and mortar, and chop the rosemary. Sprinkle them over the inside of the pork, roll it up tightly, and tie it at intervals with string.

Poach the pork in an enamelled pan in the mixed wine and water for about an hour, or until it is cooked.

To make the puree, cook the split peas in water or stock; lightly cook the spinach, and chop it coarsely; blanch and refresh the watercress and sorrel, removing any coarse stems or roots. Blend all these to a puree in the liquidiser, adding a little stock if necessary. Reheat the puree, add the grated nutmeg, and check the seasoning (remembering that the pork will be fairly salt). Add the ice-cold butter in pieces and beat the puree until the butter has melted.

Serve the sliced pork with the puree as a sauce.

CHEF'S NOTE: if the pork is very salty, wash it before stuffing it. If it is under-salted, rub the interior with salt before stuffing.

EDITOR'S NOTE: Mr Stevenson considers the green puree an integral part of the dish, and does not recommend serving the pork without it. We have to confess to finding the cold, left-over spiced pork delicious on its own with a salad or as a sandwich filling.

Cypriot beef stew

Travellers Rest, Durham
chef: Angela Martin

2 lb topside of beef
2 tablesp cooking oil
a pinch of cinnamon
a pinch of ground cloves
salt, black pepper
2 bay leaves
2 tablesp red wine vinegar
3 tablesp tomato puree
½ pint stock (approx)
1 lb button onions

Trim the meat and cut it in 1½-inch cubes. Brown it quickly in the oil. Add the seasonings, the vinegar, the tomato puree and enough stock barely to cover the meat. Cover. Simmer the stew gently until the meat is almost tender. Brown the onions in a little oil and add them for about 45 minutes' additional cooking time. (2 hours should do in all.)

Serve the stew with rice.

Sauce vert-pré

Wife of Bath, Wye
chef/proprietor: Michael Waterfield

Mr Waterfield serves this sauce over poached fish, or bakes fillets in butter with the sauce for about 10 minutes.

2 oz butter
4 spring onions
1 oz flour
4 fl oz dry white wine
4 fl oz chicken stock (DPB, page 171)
6 green peppercorns (page 108)
1 small bunch sorrel
1 small bunch sweet herbs (eg. basil, tarragon, thyme, marjoram)
salt
4 fl oz double cream

In a saucepan, melt the butter and add the finely chopped spring onions. Cook them slowly until they are soft, stir in the flour, and cook for a few minutes before adding the wine, stock and all the seasonings. Simmer the sauce for 10 minutes, then blend it to a puree in the liquidiser. Add the cream and heat the sauce gently to just below boiling point.

EDITOR'S NOTE: if you cannot find any sorrel, try the sauce with watercress or spinach. The taste will not be quite the same, but you will have a pleasant 'green' sauce.

Emmentaler Schafsvoressen

Restaurant Denzler, Edinburgh
chef/proprietor: Samuel Denzler

A light, fat-free stew, suitable for dieters but tasty enough for anyone.

2 lb shoulder of mutton
   (boned weight)
¾ pint stock or water
¼ pint dry white wine
salt, pepper
1 teasp saffron threads or
   ½ teasp powdered saffron
1 clove garlic, crushed
1 teasp Worcestershire sauce
1 bay leaf
¼ teasp each thyme, sage,
   oregano
½ lb onions
¼ lb celery or celeriac
¼ lb turnips
½ lb carrots
½–1 tablesp cornflour

Trim the meat and cut it into one-inch cubes. Make stock with the bones and trimmings (DPB, page 170). Blanch the meat briefly in boiling water, and then refresh it by pouring cold water over it in a colander.

Put the meat, stock, wine, seasonings, herbs and spices in a stew-pan and simmer slowly for 35–45 minutes. Add the coarsely chopped onions and the diced celery, turnip and carrot and continue to simmer until both meat and vegetables are tender. Thicken the juices with the cornflour blended with a little water and correct the seasoning.

Serve the stew with plain boiled potatoes and the following beetroot salad.

Beetroot salad

4–6 whole fresh beetroot
French dressing
salt and vinegar to taste

for garnishing
4–6 large lettuce leaves
1 hard-boiled egg

Clean the beetroot and boil them in salted water in their skins until soft. Peel the beetroot, slice them and toss the slices carefully in French dressing, adding extra salt and vinegar if necessary.

Line a salad bowl with the lettuce leaves, arrange the slices of beetroot on top, and garnish with the finely chopped egg.

EDITOR'S NOTE: if you dislike lettuce leaves stained with beetroot juice, the salad would look pretty in a white dish garnished with the chopped egg and a little parsley.

Poussin Limpopo

*Pengethley Hotel, Ross-on-Wye
chef/proprietor: Mrs Harvey*

The name is a family joke, suggested by Mr Harvey when the dish was invented, to commemorate Kipling's 'great, grey, green, greasy Limpopo'. Forget Kipling – this is a delicious and elegant dish.

4 poussins, or 2 small
   chickens
2 oz butter
salt, pepper

for the spiced butter
¼ lb butter
1 teasp ground coriander
½ teasp ground cloves
1 teasp ginger
salt, pepper

for the sauce
2 medium-sized onions
1 oz butter
1 tablesp olive oil
1 teasp turmeric
½ teasp ginger
4 fl oz yoghourt
1 tablesp currants
2½ fl oz double cream

Skin and flatten the poussins. To do this, first remove the backbone by cutting along either side of it from neck to tail. Then turn the bird over and press down on the top of the breastbone. If you are using chickens, split each one completely in two, starting at the breastbone. Place the birds or halves in one large or two smaller roasting tins and smear them with a little butter and some salt and pepper. Put them to roast in a moderately hot oven (400°F, mark 6) for 20 minutes, basting them from time to time. While they are cooking, make the spiced butter by creaming together all the ingredients.

Allow the birds to cool before coating them thickly with the spiced butter.

Brown them under the grill or in a hot oven (425°F, mark 7) for 10 minutes, while making the sauce. Finely chop the onions and sauté them till golden in the butter and oil. Add the turmeric and ginger and cook slowly for 3 or 4 minutes before adding the yoghourt, currants and cream. Heat the sauce carefully but do not allow it to boil. Check the seasoning.

Arrange the chickens on a heated serving dish, and either coat them with the sauce or serve it separately. Plain boiled rice goes well with this dish.

Chicken with turmeric

Ballymaloe House, Shanagarry
chef: Mrs M. Allen

a roasting chicken
salt, pepper
2 medium-sized onions
3 medium-sized tomatoes
2 oz butter
a little sugar
3 teasp turmeric
1 large clove garlic
½ lb patna rice
1 pint water or stock
½ oz beurre manié (DPB,
page 169)

Skin the chicken and rub a little salt and pepper over it. Peel the onions and tomatoes and chop them finely. Melt one ounce of the butter in a large casserole and cook three-quarters of the chopped onion in it until it is transparent. Then put in the chicken, breast side down, to brown. Season the chopped tomatoes with salt, pepper and a little sugar and when the chicken has browned, sprinkle them round it, together with 1½ teaspoonsful of turmeric and the chopped clove of garlic. Turn the chicken over onto one side, cover the casserole and put it in a pre-heated moderate oven (350°F, mark 4). After 20 minutes turn the bird over onto its other side and continue cooking for another 20 minutes. During this time, in another casserole, cook the remaining chopped onion in the other ounce of butter until it is soft. Stir in the remaining turmeric and the rice and fry these together for a few minutes, turning the rice over. Pour on 1 pint of stock or water, seasoned with a teaspoonful of salt. Bring to the boil, cover and put into the oven for 15 minutes while the chicken finishes cooking. Transfer the chicken to a warm dish to keep hot.

Strain off any fat from the juices in the casserole, and thicken them with the beurre manié. Allow to cook for a few minutes while carving the chicken into joints. Arrange these in the centre of the dish and coat them with the sauce. Surround the chicken with the savoury rice and serve immediately.

EDITOR'S NOTE: if you do not have two large casseroles, the rice can, of course, be cooked in a saucepan on top of the stove.

Poussins La Potinière au basilic

La Potinière, Gullane
chef/proprietor: Christiane Moodie

At the restaurant, customers are given bibs to protect their clothes and are encouraged to eat the poussins in their fingers.

2 poussins, each 1¼ lb dressed
  weight
2 tablesp olive oil
salt, pepper
1 bunch fresh basil (or 4 teasp
  dried basil)

Wash and dry the birds, then brush them generously all over with olive oil and rub some salt and pepper over them. Sprinkle them with half of the chopped basil, pressing it well on to the skin. Put the poussins into a shallow baking dish or tin, breast side down, and cook them in a fairly hot oven (400°F, mark 6). When the backs become golden, turn them over and baste them with the pan juices, adding a little more oil if necessary. Sprinkle the rest of the basil on their breasts and continue cooking until they are golden. For chickens of this size, allow 25–30 minutes per pound and pierce them with a skewer to test if they are cooked – the juices should run clear with no trace of blood.

Before serving them, take each poussin and, with poultry shears if you have them, cut first along either side of the backbone, discarding it, and then along the breastbone, to give two neat halves. Serve them on a bed of tossed salad.

CHEF'S NOTE: at La Potinière the poussins are accompanied by sautéed carrots and apples: carrots cooked until they are *al dente*, then sautéed in butter with quartered dessert apples and finished with a ladleful of the pan juices from the cooked chickens.

Pigeon breasts
with juniper berry sauce

Snaffles, Dublin
chef/proprietor: Rosie Tinne

4 pigeons
2 oz butter
4 slices brown bread
4 rashers streaky bacon

for the sauce
2 oz butter
1 small onion
1 stick celery
1 oz flour
½ pint red wine
1 dessertsp redcurrant jelly
15 juniper berries
1 chicken stock cube
6 peppercorns
¼ pint port

for decoration
watercress

Using poultry shears, cut the complete breast off each pigeon and skin it. Rub the breasts with some butter, set them on the lightly-buttered slices of bread, and cover each with a bacon rasher. Roast them in a hot oven (425°F, mark 7) until they are cooked but still pink (about 15–25 minutes).

For the sauce, sweat the finely chopped vegetables in the butter until they are soft. Add the flour and cook gently until it is golden brown. Stir in the wine, the redcurrant jelly, the crushed juniper berries, the stock cube and the peppercorns. Bring the sauce to the boil and simmer it very slowly for 20 minutes. Add the port and cook it for 5 more minutes. Strain the sauce, pour some of it over the pigeons, garnish the serving dish with watercress, and hand round the rest of the sauce separately.

CHEF'S NOTE: this sauce is good with any game.

EDITOR'S NOTES: the remainder of the carcases make a good stock.

The sauce may be made ahead of time: add a little more port if it thickens too much.

You may wish to set the cooked birds on croûtes or toast instead of the bread, which becomes rather soggy if the pigeons are cooked for the longer time.

Tarragon cream

Miller Howe, Windermere
chef/proprietor: John Tovey

For serving with poached pears stuffed with Boursin cheese, poached apples stuffed with walnuts and plumped raisins, or poached leeks covered with grated carrots, served very cold.

¼ lb caster sugar
4 eggs
4 fl oz tarragon wine vinegar
a little single cream
fresh mint (optional)

Lightly beat together the sugar and the eggs and then beat in, a little at a time, the tarragon wine vinegar. Pour this sauce into a double boiler and heat it slowly over simmering water, stirring it continuously, until it thickens. Do not overcook it. Leave it to cool.

Before serving, thin the sauce if necessary with a little cream to whatever thickness you like, and spoon it over the pears or apples, perhaps decorating them with a sprig of fresh mint.

CHEF'S NOTE: poach the pears or apples very slowly in a sugar syrup, after peeling them and removing the cores from the bottom, leaving their stalks on. Stand them upright in a roasting tin covered with a piece of tinfoil, allowing the stalks to stick up through the foil.

This tarragon cream will keep for 4 or 5 days in the refrigerator.

CURRY AND
OTHER SPICED DISHES

Curry may bring one of two sensations to mind – the searing heat of an incautiously-ordered Madras in an Indo-Pakistani restaurant, or the deadly re-appearance of the weekend joint in a shroud of khaki, adorned with apples and raisins and served, of course, with Major Grey's mango chutney. It is cheering to think that most Indians, Pakistanis and Bangladeshis are totally unfamiliar with either.

Curry

Curry (from *kari*, a sauce) is used to describe a highly seasoned stew with lots of sauce.

In Britain, until relatively recently, curry meant the use of curry powder (most often bought at the grocer's, but occasionally sent home in bulk by supporters of the Raj). Two of the recipes which follow are, in fact, 'English' curries, using ready-mixed powder as an adjunct to the other flavours – nuts and sour cream in one case (page 139), honey and ginger in the other (page 136). They are both delicious and no one is pretending they have much to do with Indian food.

But for fragrance and complexity of flavours, rather than heat alone, you must mix your own herbs and spices. The liquidiser and coffee-grinder make the task easier, though less picturesque, than it would be when done by pounding on stone slabs. (Spices linger determinedly on plastic, and you might decide to keep a grinder especially for them, rather than risk serving exotic coffee by mistake. You can clean the grinder by whizzing a little bread in it after the spices.) If you try one or two of the recipes which follow, you will realise how varied the flavours are, and how much more sensible it is to choose the seasonings which suit individual dishes, rather than have one all-purpose mixture.

It is worth remembering that India is a continent with almost thirty different states and territories, over 500 million inhabitants, enormously varied climate and geography, and the strong influences of past invasions and present religious customs.

For example, you find people in the north (except for Orthodox Hindus) eating any meat except beef (or in the case of Muslims, pork) dishes that are rather dry, with various breads as accompaniments.

Pakistani dishes show the Middle-Eastern influence in kebabs and the use of coriander, with light spicing typified by tandoori cooking: marinated chicken and puffy nan bread cooked in the clay oven called a *tandoor*.

Bangladesh shares many Pakistani traditions, but the cooking is made distinctive by its use of fish, and the unusual spicing. For example, mustard appears as a dominant flavour, and a great deal of frying is done in mustard oil.

In the mainly vegetarian south, dishes tend to be much more liquid; oil is used rather than ghee; garlic and coconut appear frequently; and rice is served rather than bread.

Goa is famed for its fish and pork dishes, unique in India, and acceptable there because Christianity has had a firm base since Portuguese days. Our vindaloo recipe (page 132) is fairly typical – and the made-up paste would be tolerated by a Goan in this one dish.

The Parsees of Gujarat produce, perhaps, the most westernised food, rather bland and delicate. There is even a dish of scrambled eggs called *ekuri* (or *ackoori*), more interesting than our usual breakfast version. Dhansak recipes, deceptively simple at first mouthful, usually contain three types of lentils, pumpkin, aubergine, tomatoes, onions, spinach and coriander leaf.

Spices

Spices were originally used for flavour, to preserve food, and because they were believed to be good for you, having a 'purifying effect on the intestines', and stimulating the liver. Ginger was cooked with peas and lentils to counteract their flatulent effect.

The selection and quantity of spices is very much a matter of individual taste. Each cook chooses what he wants and grinds them together to make the *masala* for a particular dish. The individuality is partly a matter of pride, partly a result of recipes being passed on orally, with great variations in both ingredients and spelling. We have given exact quantities in the recipes which follow, usually as indicated by the restaurant providing the recipe, so that you have something to start with. From then on, experiment.

The usual spices are turmeric *(haldi)*, coriander *(danya)*, cumin *(zeera)*, fresh ginger root *(adrak)*, fenugreek *(methe)*, saffron *(kesram)*, fennel seed *(soonf)*, as well as cinnamon, cardamom, poppy seeds, mustard seeds, cloves, nutmeg and mace.

GARAM MASALA (which can be bought ready-mixed) is usually a blend of coriander seeds, caraway seeds, cloves, cardamoms and cinnamon. It is seldom used in fish dishes, since its pungency would kill the delicate flavour. Unlike turmeric, which requires long cooking to mellow its rather acrid taste, garam masala is sometimes sprinkled on a dish just before serving.

The spices commonly used in sweet dishes are cardamom, saffron and cinnamon.

An Indian cook would roast or fry the spices before grinding them, and some recipes recommend this. You will find that they are cooked in oil or ghee before the other ingredients are added. It is worth doing this also with commercial curry powder.

Chillies	Chillies, along with peppercorns, provide the 'heat' in Indian recipes. Since chillies were not introduced to India from America till the 16th century, and must have spread only gradually, it is easier to understand why there is a tradition of mildly spiced dishes in parts of India, as well as fiery ones. Chillies require careful handling, since their volatile oils can burn sensitive skin and eyes. Avoid touching your face while preparing chillies, and rinse them in cold water before removing stem and seeds.

Herbs	The most commonly used herbs are coriander leaves, mint, basil, thyme and neem or curry leaves (which look like small bay leaves and can be found fresh or dried in Indian grocers').

Ghee	Ghee or clarified butter can be bought tinned, and keeps for months once opened. Or you can clarify your own (DPB, page 168). It does not burn as readily as butter and is ideal for frying. Vegetable oil is the other frying medium.

Dahi	Dahi or curd is properly made from buffalo milk. The best substitute is plain yoghourt, preferably kept for a day or two before using, so that it increases in acidity. As well as being used in cooking (masala muchlee, page 136), it is the basis for various cooling salads called raitas (page 130).

Dhal	Dhal or lentils come in many varieties, with the red Egyptian and the green moong dhal among the most common. Chana dhal are chick-peas; urd dhal, either white or black, small beans (usually bought shelled and split).

Coconut	Coconut is generally used fresh, grated and steeped in water to yield a milk or cream. Creamed coconut makes an adequate substitute, and can be found in health shops in block form.

Tamarind	Tamarind *(imli)* is used to provide a fresh, lime-like tang to dishes. The fruit comes in dried block form, looking rather like pressed dates, and is infused before use.

Atta	Atta is the wholemeal flour used for Indian breads.

Rice	Rice deserves most of a chapter to itself, and has it on page 62.

Buying and storing	In even the most sedate suburb or backwaterish town you are likely to find at least *some* spices. Do not neglect your chemist or health shop, which may have quite a range.
	All spices go stale quickly, so buy them in small quantities, whether whole or ground, and store them in a cool dry place in air-tight containers. Fresh coriander is popular

with Middle-Eastern and Chinese cooks as well as Indian ones, so you may be lucky with that. If not, parsley at least provides the colour. Fresh ginger, once you have tracked it down, keeps for months, peeled, sliced, and stored in the fridge in a covered jar filled with dry sherry. (The liquid adds a piquancy to clear soups – start with a teaspoonful and work up.)

If all this sounds terribly difficult, please have the courage to try one of the recipes, even without *all* the ingredients. The fresh fragrance will delight you, even if the taste is not absolutely authentic.

Chutneys

Just as an authentic curry does not come from a tin, the most interesting chutneys do not come in bottles, but are freshly made, and often completely raw, created with whatever fruits and vegetables are to hand. Fresh mango, thinly sliced, with coriander, ginger, salt and pepper, is so delicious that you will realise why the Major never became a general.

Salads

Salads are of two main types: the yoghourt-based raitas mentioned above, or simple mixed raw vegetables, seasoned with lemon and chillies.

Planning an Indian meal

With a very wet curry, like the lamb or beef curry on page 137, serve rice. With a drier curry you could try the paratha on page 134, which the Golden Orient serves with curried pigeon. Serve only one meat dish, with a vegetable dish (niramish vegetables or spinach bhaji both on page 135), and possibly a raita (page 130) or a salad, some chutneys or sambals, and poppadums. For large appetites, the onion bhajia on page 133 makes a good extra dish.

Each guest helps himself to some of each of the dishes. If you wish to be absolutely authentic, you must have a deep round metal tray, called a *thali*, for each guest, on which are arranged portions of the various dishes, in small bowls, or, in the case of rice, directly on the tray.

Reading

This section is no more than an introduction to Indian cooking. The 1974 *Good Food Guide* contains a short essay on eating in Indian restaurants. In more detail, you might enjoy *Indian Cookery* by Dharamjit Singh (Penguin), or *The Cooking of India* (Time/Life).

Shasliks of lemon chicken tandoori

Golden Orient Restaurant, Dublin
chef/proprietor: Mike Butt

An East Asian recipe, refreshingly lemony,
and not at all 'hot'.

2 2-lb chickens
4 lemons
1 clove garlic, crushed
½ teasp turmeric
sea salt
1 green pepper
1 red (sweet) pepper
1 Spanish onion
1 teasp grated nutmeg
2 oz butter

for the rice
½ lb Basmati rice
1 pint stock
bouquet garni indienne
   (onion, garlic, cloves,
   cinnamon, cumin seed,
   coriander seed)

for the raita
2 tomatoes
½ cucumber
8 fl oz yoghourt

Joint the chickens, skin and bone them, and cut them into pieces roughly 1½ inches square. Make a stock with the chicken carcase and giblets (DPB, page 171). Remove the skins from the lemons as thinly as possible, and cut them into fine julienne. Blanch them in boiling water for 1 minute, drain them and leave them to dry. Combine the lemon juice, garlic, turmeric and salt and roll the chicken pieces in the mixture. Leave them to marinate for at least an hour.

Cut the peppers in 1½-inch squares. Separate the onion into layers and cut it also into 1½-inch squares.

Thread the skewers, alternating chicken, onion and peppers. Pack them tightly and dust them with the freshly grated nutmeg. Paint them liberally with the melted butter, and cook them under a very hot grill for 10–20 minutes. Baste with the juices from the pan once or twice, and turn the skewers frequently.

Cook the rice in the stock with a 'bouquet garni indienne'.

To make the raita, skin and dice the tomatoes and cucumber and fold them into the yoghourt.

To serve the shasliks, lay the rice pilaff on a flat dish, lay the kebabs diagonally over it, and strew them liberally with the julienne of lemon. Hand round the raita separately. A simple green salad goes well with this dish.

EDITOR'S NOTE: raita is often served spiced, if it is to accompany a less elaborate dish: add a half-teaspoonful of crushed cumin and coriander if you are using it with a plainer curry.

Malayan chicken curry

Plough Inn, Fadmoor

Mrs Kathlyn Brown's version of the curry she prepared in Singapore, adapted to ingredients obtainable here.

1 large roasting chicken or
   4 large joints
4 tablesp ground coriander
1½ tablesp ground aniseed
1 tablesp ground cumin
1½ teasp turmeric
1 teasp cinnamon
1 teasp chilli powder or
   ground chillies
1 pinch nutmeg
1 pinch powdered cloves
½ lb onions
1 oz fresh ginger root
2 cloves garlic
6 tablesp oil
1 star anise
2 cardamoms
¾ pint chicken stock or water
1 tablesp salt
1 lb potatoes
¼ lb desiccated coconut
½ pint milk
1 tablesp lemon juice
1 tablesp brown sugar

Joint the chicken. (Use the carcase to make the stock required later.) Sieve together the 8 powdered spices and rub them into the chicken joints. Mince the onions, ginger and garlic, and fry them gently in the oil with the star anise and cardamoms. Add the chicken joints and any surplus powdered spices and cook them slowly, turning the joints, until the oil and spices separate. Add the chicken stock or water, and the salt. Simmer the curry gently for 15 minutes. Add the peeled and quartered potatoes and continue to simmer until both chicken and potatoes are cooked. Remove from the heat.

While the chicken is cooking, make coconut milk by infusing the desiccated coconut in the warm milk for about half an hour, then squeezing the liquid through muslin. Add this to the curry, along with the lemon juice and brown sugar.

Serve the curry with plain boiled rice, prawn crackers, chutney, raita (page 130) and so on.

CHEF'S NOTES: stem ginger can be used instead of fresh ginger, though you may then wish to cut down on the sugar. The cardamom and star anise can be omitted. If you can find it, use tamarind pulp instead of lemon juice.

Coconut cream (2 oz) can be used instead of the desiccated coconut and milk infusion.

If you are using a boiling fowl the pieces should be skinned and cooked longer.

EDITOR'S NOTE: if Mrs Brown is serving this curry to her family, she also provides a side-dish of pickled pork vindaloo (page 132), described as 'rather fiery' and not generally served in the restaurant.

Pickled pork vindaloo

Plough Inn, Fadmoor

A friend of Mrs Brown's gave her this recipe for the Indian equivalent of a confit, *which keeps for a considerable time and can be dipped into whenever you wish to pep up a curry – or any other dish. It is very fiery.*

3 lb fresh belly of pork
2 large onions
3 cloves garlic
12 fl oz cooking oil
½ jar (3½ oz) vindaloo paste
½ lb tinned tomatoes
8 fl oz vinegar

Cut the pork in two-inch pieces, removing any large bones. Fry the sliced onions and crushed garlic in the oil gently until they are transparent. Add the paste and cook it for a few minutes, stirring constantly, until the paste sticks to the spoon. Add the tomatoes and the meat and stir until the meat is sealed. Add the vinegar and cook for a further minute. Cover the pan with a cloth to absorb condensation and leave it to stand overnight.

Next day cook the mixture very slowly for 2 hours in a covered saucepan. Pour the vindaloo into a stone jar or other suitable container and do not cover it until the vindaloo is quite cold. Keep the jar in a cool place or the refrigerator.

Use the vindaloo as required, as a side dish with a bland curry, or as a 'pepper-up' of dishes, where even a spoonful of the fat can make a difference to the flavour.

Once you have removed some of the vindaloo, reheat the jar so that the fat melts and covers the meat again completely. Do not cover it until it is cold.

Breasts of pigeon or pheasant

Golden Orient Restaurant, Dublin
chef/proprietor: Mike Butt

4 pigeons (not game high)
2 oz clarified butter (DPB, page
   168) or ghee
1 medium-sized onion
½ teasp turmeric
1 tablesp ground coriander
1 pinch ground chilli
1-inch fresh root ginger
1 tablesp raisins or muscatels
24 black and white grapes

This dish has developed from Mr Butt's earliest cooking attempts. At the age of ten or so he would shoot pigeons with a home-made catapult in the woods near his home in Kenya. They were cooked over an open fire with a stolen handful of his mother's herbs and the wild berries growing nearby. If he forgot to take a pan with him, he roasted the birds on the end of a stick.

Wipe the pigeons with a damp cloth, remove their breasts with poultry shears, and wash off any dark blood in the interior.

Melt the butter in a heavy pan, and in it fry the finely chopped onion until it is light brown. Add the spices (the ginger finely chopped) and fry them for five minutes, stirring all the time with a wooden spoon. Toss the pigeon breasts in the mixture until they are coated all over. Cover the pan, and pot roast the breasts until they are tender, either in the oven (300°F, mark 2) for 1½–2 hours, or on top of the stove. Add the cleaned and chopped raisins and cook for a further 5 minutes. Add the halved and seeded grapes only long enough to heat them through.

Serve each pigeon breast on a paratha (page 134) or croûte with the residual gravy and the grapes spooned over it.

Onion bhajia

Anarkali, London
chef: Abdul Aziz

5 medium-sized onions
¼ lb self-raising flour
¼ teasp ground cumin
¼ teasp ground coriander
1 pinch chilli powder
½ teasp salt
1 tablesp ghee
2 fl oz water (approx)
oil for deep frying

Slice the onions finely, add the flour, the spices and the salt. Mix them well, add the ghee and enough water to make the onions hold together when you squeeze them into a ball (about the size of a golf ball). They will look untidy but improve in appearance as they cook.

Fry them, a few at a time, in deep oil at

Crisply shaggy golden balls of onion, soft in the centre.

375°F – 400°F, for about 3 minutes, until they are crisp and golden, turning them half way through. Drain them on absorbent paper and serve very hot along with a 'wet' curry.

EDITOR'S NOTE: if you cannot obtain ghee, use clarified butter (DPB, page 168) instead.

Bhoona paratha

Golden Orient Restaurant, Dublin
chef/proprietor: Mike Butt

½ lb wholemeal flour
8 fl oz water
a pinch of salt
1–2 oz butter

This flat bread – 'fine, thin, speckled brown and appetising' – can be used as a substitute for rice with many Indian dishes. In the Golden Orient it is used as a base for the pot-roasted game described on page 133.

Mix the flour, water and salt together in a bowl, to form a dough. Allow it to rest for 2–3 hours, covered with a damp cloth. Roll the dough out on a heavily floured board, paint the top lightly with melted butter, fold it over and repeat once again. Take pieces of dough about the size of puff-balls and roll each one out as thinly as possible into a circle.

Heat a heavy frying pan or griddle until it is fairly hot, and put the circles on it. Once again paint the tops lightly with butter, turn the parathas as soon as they come free from the pan, and shake the pan to and fro to keep them moving. Paint the top and repeat the turning and shaking for half a minute.

EDITOR'S NOTE: we have not yet conquered this process and plan to practise until we can produce light parathas, rather than the heavy ones which resulted from our earlier attempts.

Coconut rice

Vijay, London
chef: P. G. Ramalingam

½ lb Patna rice
salt
2 tablesp cooking oil
¼ teasp black mustard seeds
½ teasp urd dahl
1½ oz desiccated coconut
fresh curry leaves (optional)

Cook the rice in plenty of salted water until it is three-quarters cooked. Strain it in a colander and pour boiling water over it.

Heat the oil in a heavy-bottomed pan and, when it is hot, add the mustard seeds and allow them to fry a little. When they start to spit, add the urd dahl and coconut. Fry them until they are brown, stirring frequently. Add the rice and reduce the heat. Stir the spices and coconut through the rice, and add a little more salt if necessary. When the mixture is thoroughly heated, serve it with fresh curry leaves (if available).

The whole process should be very quick.

EDITOR'S NOTE: even without the spices, the coconut makes a delicious addition to the rice.

Niramish vegetables

Ganges One, London
chef: Mrs Ahmed

2 lb mixed vegetables
(cauliflower, potatoes, peas,
carrots, beans, okra, etc)
3 oz ghee or 8 tablesp corn oil
½ teasp panch-phoran (five
spices: cumin, fennel,
fenugreek, mustard seed,
onion seed)
1 large onion
½ teasp turmeric
salt
2 tomatoes
1 teasp lemon juice
¼ teasp sugar (optional)
1–3 green chillies (optional)

A sophisticated vegetable dish from the Ganges delta region of Bangladesh and West Bengal. The original version contained no onions or ghee, since it was created for Hindu widows observing their religious restrictions.

Cut the larger vegetables into bite-sized pieces, and boil them all separately until they are three-quarters cooked.

Heat the ghee or oil in a heavy-bottomed pan. Remove it from the heat, add the panch-phoran, cover the pan to protect yourself from popping seeds, and cook it for half a minute over low heat. Add the sliced onion and fry it till it is pale brown. Add the turmeric and salt and cook for a further minute. Put in the pre-cooked vegetables and fry them in the oil and spices for 3–4 minutes, stirring them frequently and gently so that the vegetables are not broken up. Finally add the sliced tomatoes, the lemon juice, the sugar and the chopped chillies, and leave to simmer for a minute or two before serving.

EDITOR'S NOTES: if you cannot find panch-phoran, make up the half-teaspoonful with any of the spices you have. They are used whole, not ground.

We experimented with a ½-lb packet of mixed frozen vegetables as a base, and found they added colour and variety to our mixture.

Spinach bhaji

Vijay, London
chef: P. G. Ramalingam

1½–2 lb spinach, or ¾–1 lb
frozen leaf spinach
1 tablesp cooking oil
½ teasp black mustard seed
1 teasp urd dahl
1 small onion
1 pinch chilli powder, salt
1 tomato

Drain the blanched spinach and chop it roughly. (If you are using frozen spinach, allow it to thaw before draining and chopping it.) Heat the oil in a heavy frying-pan, and when it is hot add the mustard seeds and urd dahl (which will spit). Add the sliced onion and fry them together until the onion is brown, stirring frequently. Add the spinach, chilli powder, salt, and peeled, chopped tomato and turn constantly until the spinach is lightly cooked – about five minutes. Serve very hot.

Masala muchlee

4 ¾ lb soles
1½ tablesp tomato puree
¼ pint yoghourt (at least 3
   days old)
2 large cloves garlic
1 lime
2 tablesp chopped onion
1 red or green chilli pepper
½ teasp ground turmeric
1 teasp sea salt
1 tablesp chopped coriander
   leaf (or parsley)
¼ lb butter

Golden Orient Restaurant, Dublin
chef/proprietor: Mike Butt

Ask the fishmonger to skin the fish.
Score them in a criss-cross pattern on
both sides, and dry them thoroughly.

In the liquidiser, blend the tomato puree,
the yoghourt, the garlic, the lime juice,
the onion, the deseeded chilli pepper, the
turmeric, salt and coriander. Paint the
fish heavily with this paste, filling all the
gashes. Leave it in a cool place to
marinate for 2 hours.

A Kenyan dish made with a coarse fish called
talapia found in Lake Victoria. Dover sole,
plaice, sea bream, bass or hake are
acceptable substitutes.

Fry the fish slowly in the butter until it is
golden brown on both sides. Use the
residue paste, which will have a dark
brown, granular appearance, for topping
the fish to enhance the flavour.

Serve the fish with new potatoes boiled in
their jackets, and lots of watercress 'for
eating, not for garnishing'.

EDITOR'S NOTE: if you are timid, use half a
chilli the first time.

Chicken with ginger, curry
and honey sauce

4 boned chicken breasts
2 onions
2 sticks celery
6 slices root ginger
½ pint dry white wine (approx)

for the sauce
1 oz butter
1 oz flour
¼ pint single cream
1 teasp curry paste
2 teasp honey
salt, pepper

toasted almonds

Miller Howe, Windermere
chef/proprietor: John Tovey

Put the chicken breasts on a wire cooling
tray. In a roasting tin arrange the diced
onions, celery and ginger. Heat the wine
and pour it over the vegetables. Put the
wire tray on top of the roasting tin and
cover the chicken and tin securely with
foil. Bake it in a hot oven (400°F, mark 6)
for about 40 minutes.

Strain off the juices, and keep the chicken
warm while you make the sauce. Reduce
the strained juices to about ¼ pint over

high heat. Make a roux with the butter
and flour. Stir in the reduced juices and
the cream and cook the sauce gently for a
few minutes. Add the curry paste and
honey and allow it to cook for another
few minutes. Taste it and adjust the
honey/curry ratio to suit yourself. Add
salt and pepper if necessary.

To serve the chicken, remove the skin
and cover the supremes with the sauce
and a garnish of toasted almonds.

Lamb or beef curry

Prince of India, London
chef: Abdul Quddus

1½ lb lamb or beef
½ lb onions
½-inch fresh root ginger
4 cloves garlic
3 tablesp ghee or cooking oil
2 bay leaves
1 stick cinnamon
½ teasp chilli powder
1 teasp turmeric
½ teasp ground coriander
pinch of cumin
12 fl oz water
salt

Cut the trimmed meat into large cubes. Mince or finely chop the onions, ginger and garlic. Heat the oil in a heavy pan, and fry the onions for about 5 minutes. Add the ginger, the garlic and the other spices, and fry them for 5 minutes before adding 3 fl oz of water. Add the meat cubes and stir them for 10 minutes. Add salt to taste, and the remaining 9 fl oz water. Cover the pan, and simmer the curry slowly for 30 minutes to an hour, until the meat is tender. Remove the bay leaves and cinnamon stick.

Serve the curry with rice and chapatis to mop up the gravy.

CHEF'S NOTE: you may substitute two teaspoonsful of curry powder for the chilli, turmeric and coriander.

EDITOR'S NOTES: topside or leg of lamb would cook in half an hour; humbler stewing cuts may take the hour.

Bobotie (4-6)

Pinks, Fairford
chefs: Susan Kennaway and Jane Hill

1 large onion
½ oz dripping
1 lb minced beef
2 slices brown bread
6 fl oz rich gravy
1 tablesp curry powder
    (approx)
juice of 1 lemon
1 tablesp chopped almonds
8 drops almond essence
salt, pepper
herbs (e.g. thyme, oregano)
2 eggs
½ pint milk
1 bay leaf

Fry the finely chopped onion in the dripping until golden, add the minced beef and brown it, stirring frequently. Soak the bread in the gravy and mash it thoroughly with a fork. Add this to the beef along with the curry powder, the lemon juice, the chopped almonds, the almond essence and the seasonings. Cook the mixture for a few minutes before turning it into an open pie dish or other baking dish. (It should be quite thick.)

Beat the eggs with the milk and pour the liquid gently on top of the beef. Float the bay leaf on top, and cook the bobotie in a moderate oven (350°F, mark 4) for about 45 minutes, until the top is set, golden brown, and bubbling at the edges. (A knife inserted in the centre of the custard should come out clean.) Serve the bobotie with rice, and possibly a salad.

CHEF'S NOTE: if you have no gravy to hand, use a bouillon cube dissolved in boiling water.

EDITOR'S NOTE: another version of this South African dish uses white bread instead of brown, and 2 teaspoonsful of Angostura bitters instead of the almond essence.

Noisettes of lamb with cream curry and nut sauce

Grape Vine, Cavendish
chef: Mrs S. A. Roberts

2 racks of lamb (best end of neck), each with 6 cutlets

for the sauce
½ pint brown stock (from the lamb bones)
1 medium-sized onion
1 tablesp oil
½ lb salted peanuts
2 dessertsp curry powder
1 clove of garlic
1 cooking apple
2 dessertsp mango chutney
¼ pt sour double cream

for garnishing
watercress or parsley

Ask your butcher to trim the cutlets well and bone and roll them separately.

Make stock from the lamb bones (DPB, page 170).

Chop the onion and fry it gently in the oil. Wash and dry the peanuts, chop them coarsely, and add them to the onions with the curry powder. Stir for a minute before adding the crushed garlic (or its pressed juice) and the peeled and chopped apple. Cook for a few minutes. Add the chutney and the stock and simmer the sauce for half an hour. This can be done ahead of time.

Grill or bake the noisettes to the desired degree, remembering that they are juicier when pink but that the fat will drain off better if they are cooked a little longer.

At the same time, add the sour cream to the sauce and simmer it very gently for a few minutes. This step can also be carried out ahead of time if the sauce is simmered over a *very* low flame. If it is too thin, it can be gradually reduced for an hour.

To serve, put the noisettes on a serving dish and spoon the sauce over them. Garnish with watercress or parsley.

EDITOR'S NOTES: as a contrast to both flavour and texture, serve simple spring vegetables and a grated cucumber and yoghourt salad (page 130) with the lamb.

If you do not wish to cook the noisettes at the last minute, grill or bake them rather less than you want for the final dish, and keep them hot in a very slow oven (275°F, mark 1) for up to half an hour. Do not pour the sauce over them till just before serving, as some fat will drain from them in the oven.

You might like to try the recipe with commercially soured cream.

LEMONS AND ORANGES

'Knowst thou the land where the lemon trees bloom,
Where the gold orange glows, in the deep thicket's gloom?'
GOETHE

Lemons and oranges began to be imported into England from Spain and Portugal in medieval times. From what we know of medieval cookery, they were used in spiced sauces to eat with meat, and to make marmalade, a solid confection (then if not now . . .) borrowed from the Portuguese. The French used the juice of lemons as an alternative to vinegar and also candied both peels.

Varieties

LEMONS The lemon differs from other citrus fruits in blossoming several times a year, so that mature fruit is available on the tree during most months. The main producers are Israel, Cyprus, Spain and South Africa, though we are so insatiable that they are even imported from the United States and Turkey to keep the supply continuous.

ORANGES Sweet oranges come in three main varieties, the Shamouti, the navel and the Valencia. The name Jaffa (from the area in Israel where they were first grown) is often used to describe a kind of orange, although it now covers all three varieties. The Shamouti is oval, with a thick, easily peeled skin. The navel (from Spain, Morocco and South Africa, as well as Israel) is an extra-large, winter variety, with a navel formation at the blossom end and a tiny orange inside the larger one. It is convenient in the kitchen because it peels easily, separates into segments tidily and has no pips. The Valencia is a summer variety, with a few seeds and plenty of juice. One or other of these varieties is available from October to July.

For a month or so on either side of Christmas, one sees clementines and satsumas from Spain and Morocco, and in February mandarins are also available. Their distinctive, oriental taste is inextricably mixed with festivity, and their ease of preparation is typified by the American variety names, *zipper* and *kid-glove*.

Bitter oranges – mainly used for marmalade, though working wonders in a bigarade sauce – arrive in January and February. The finest, Sevilles, have a rough skin and are a deep orange-red. Choose soft, ripened fruit, which will contain plenty of pectin, the setting agent in jams and marmalade.

Buying and storing

Thin-skinned varieties of lemon are usually better than thick-skinned. A greenish skin does not imply an inferior lemon, since many of the shiny bright yellow ones are artificially ripened, and some varieties are naturally less bright than others. Large oranges are not necessarily the juiciest – it is weight in relation to size that counts. Quite often smaller, cheaper oranges hold just as much juice as larger ones. The sheen on the skin, which was once a sign of freshness, can now be artificially achieved. Fresh oranges have dimples on the skin which fade with age. The 'orientals' are best bought at the beginning of their season, since they dry out rapidly if incorrectly stored.

The fruit continues to mature after being picked and will eventually rot. But this process can be slowed up by keeping it cool. Oranges and lemons should be stored in a cool larder, where they will keep for a week. Better still, they will keep for up to a fortnight if they are stored in the bottom of the refrigerator in polythene bags, to prevent their drying out. A cut lemon or orange can also be kept for several days if stored in this way. Lemons tend to go mouldy more quickly than oranges. Both fruits freeze well, either whole, in segments, or as juice.

Nutrition

Lemons and oranges are a valuable source of ascorbic acid, vitamin C, so much so that lemons and limes were part of the diet of sailors for many years, as protection against scurvy. An adequate daily intake, when other sources of vitamin C are less readily available, is one lemon or orange. Tests carried out on Florida fruit showed that smaller oranges have proportionately more vitamin C. This deteriorates if the fruit containing it is stored for some time, and also if cut fruit is exposed to light and air, so the ideal is to have fresh fruit, freshly prepared. A lemon provides about 15 calories, the sweeter orange about 40. In carbohydrate grams, the lemon wins again with only 4 to the orange's 9. Commercially-packed lemon juice is available in various forms. While it may provide the daily ration of vitamin C, no one could pretend that it tastes anything like a fresh lemon.

Preparing

To make peeling oranges easier, drop them into boiling water for a few seconds. Before squeezing either fruit, roll them over a hard surface to 'loosen' the juice. To remove the zest (thin outer skin) in shreds use a zester or grater. For julienne, fine matchsticks of peel with no bitter pith attached, use a potato peeler or sharp stainless knife.

Cooking

The very mention of lemons starts us off on a greedy stream of consciousness touching affectionately on lemon curd, lemon marmalade, lemon meringue pie, home-made lemonade and candied peel. However, more practically, the high acid content of lemon juice inhibits the oxidation which turns cut surfaces brown, so that if you drop peeled apples or pears into water with a dash of lemon juice, they will stay white. A slice of lemon cooked with rice helps keep that white, and lemon juice also whitens your hands or prevents the discoloration of an aluminium pan if it is boiled along with eggs.

Pancakes on Shrove Tuesday and whitebait or smoked salmon on expense-account lunches are blessed with a squeeze of lemon juice. For these, cut the lemon lengthwise into wedges, which squeeze easily, unless you wish to emulate the Greeks and serve a half per person. Italian and Greek restaurateurs are also now teaching us to spread the blessing to an escalope milanese or a lamb kebab. The Italians invented gremolata, made of grated lemon rind, chopped parsley and garlic, to sprinkle over osso buco. The same freshness is apparent in the recipe for shasliks of lemon chicken tandoori (page 130).

Lemon sharpens a soup, a sauce or a casserole in the same way that wine or wine vinegar might, but with its own piquancy. It accentuates flavour better than extra salting (one of us even uses it on melon, while the other sticks to salt). It can be used as an alternative to vinegar in a salad dressing or mayonnaise, and goes especially well in fishy mayonnaise.

The acidity in citrus fruits 'cuts' the richness in a fatty dish. That is why duck and oranges go well together, although the roast duck with lemon and mint (page 148) is an even nicer combination, with a much fresher taste.

Oranges go well with chocolate (DPB, page 124) and orange is often the flavouring called for in chocolate mousse. The only lemon liqueur we know about came from a Dutchman in Canada: take a bottle of old Genever (Dutch gin, tasting alarming *au naturel*, but have faith), remove a teacupful from the bottle and replace it with a teacupful of sugar. Add the thinly peeled rind of a lemon, and prepare to wait four to six weeks, shaking the bottle gently on the first day or two until the sugar is dissolved. It tastes the way freshly-grated lemon rind smells, and can be the spirit of Christmas in our homes any year.

Carrot and orange soup (6)

Toastmaster's Inn, Burham
chefs: Christopher Dimech and Gregory Ward

1 medium-sized onion
1 oz butter
15½-oz tin carrots
1½ pints chicken stock (DPB, page 171)
6½-oz tin frozen orange juice
salt, pepper
8 fl oz cream
chives

Chop the onion and cook it in the butter until it is soft but not coloured. Drain the carrots and liquidise them with the onions and a little of the stock. Return the puree to a saucepan, add the remaining stock, the undiluted orange juice, the seasonings and the cream. Heat the soup slowly to just below boiling point, adjust the seasoning, and decorate it with snipped chives.

'Although it goes against the grain,' says Mr Ward the proprietor, 'the use of tins for this recipe is important. It needs the intense colour of the carrots and the concentrated orange flavour.'

EDITOR'S NOTE: at the Toastmaster's this soup is sometimes served cold, although we preferred it hot. If you plan to try it chilled, we suggest using oil instead of butter so that no hardened flecks spoil its smoothness.

Avgolemono

Ardnagashel House, Bantry
chef: Audrey Kaulback

2 pints strong chicken stock
  (DPB, page 171)
2 oz long-grain rice
3 eggs
4 tablesp fresh lemon juice
salt, pepper

Bring the chicken stock to the boil and add the washed rice. Allow this to cook for 12–15 minutes until it is tender. Then reduce the heat so that the stock is barely simmering. While the rice is cooking, beat the eggs until they are light and frothy, and stir in the lemon juice. When the rice is cooked, slowly add two ladlesful of the hot stock to the egg and lemon mixture, stirring vigorously all the time. Then pour this back into the soup. Check the flavour, adding more lemon if necessary, and salt and pepper. Reheat the soup very carefully: it must not boil, or the eggs will scramble.

Turbot à la monégasque

L' Etoile, London
chef: Jorge Ribeiro

1½ lb turbot
1 onion
small bunch of parsley
10 peppercorns
1 teasp salt
3 oz peeled prawns
½ mild onion or shallot
juice of 1½ lemons
2 fl oz olive oil

for garnishing
lettuce or watercress
¼–½ pint mayonnaise or aïoli
  (page 53)
few prawns (in shell)
black olives

Put the fish, onion, a few stalks of parsley, the peppercorns and salt in just enough cold water to cover them. Bring it slowly to the boil and simmer gently until the fish is cooked but still firm (about 10 minutes or so). Allow it to cool in the water, before removing the skin and bones, and breaking the fish into large pieces.

In a bowl, gently mix the fish, the prawns, the chopped half onion, and the remaining parsley, also chopped, with the lemon juice and olive oil. Leave to marinate for an hour.

To serve, put the drained fish on a bed of lettuce or watercress, cover it with a thin layer of mayonnaise or aïoli, and decorate with the remaining prawns and black olives. Serve the remaining mayonnaise or aïoli separately.

EDITOR'S NOTE: if turbot is prohibitively expensive, use some other firm-fleshed fish, such as halibut or sea-bass.

Fillets of trout marinated in spices, lemon and orange

Chanterelle, London
chef: Peter du Toit

¼ pint peanut oil
4 medium-sized trout
flour
4 tablesp dry white wine
4 tablesp tarragon vinegar
2 cloves garlic, crushed
2 teasp salt
1 teasp peppercorns, crushed
12 cloves
juice and rind of 2 oranges
juice and rind of 2 lemons
bouquet garni

Heat the oil in a large frying pan. Clean the trout and remove their heads, roll them in flour, and fry them on each side until cooked (about 3–4 minutes a side, depending on their size and the heat of the oil). Arrange the trout in a large earthenware dish which will hold them without overlapping, and which will also take the marinade.

Add all the remaining ingredients to the pan, return it to the heat, and boil it for a few minutes over moderate heat to bring out the flavour of the garlic and spices.

Line a sieve with butter muslin, strain the liquid through it over the trout, and then tie the solids in the muslin with string. Put the muslin bag in the liquid and refrigerate the dish overnight. Before serving, fillet the trout, squeeze out the muslin bag and baste the fillets with the liquids.

CHEF'S NOTE: peanut oil is not only cheaper than olive oil, but also does not mask the fresh flavours of the fish and fruit.

Farouk

Vane's, Thatcham
chef: Valerie Vane

4 oz Californian prunes
4 oz fresh prawns (shelled weight)
4 large Jaffa oranges
¼ lb cooked ham
4 fl oz sour cream
salt, pepper
fresh mixed herbs (parsley, oregano, basil and dill)

Soak the prunes overnight in water. Cook them gently for five minutes and put them aside to cool. Shell the prawns (or defrost best quality frozen ones) and put some aside for garnishing. Remove the top of the oranges and scoop out the flesh. Remove any pith or pips. Chop the flesh and mix it with the chopped ham and prunes. Fold the mixture into the sour cream and season to taste. Spoon it back into the orange shells, sprinkle with the chopped herbs, top with the remaining prawns, and replace the lid. Serve the oranges slightly chilled.

EDITOR'S NOTE: cut a shallow slice off the bottom of the oranges if they do not stand level.

Pork fillet in an orange and green pepper sauce

Petty France, Dunkirk
chef/proprietors: Stephen and Jane Samuel

1¼ lb pork fillet
seasoned flour
4 oranges (approx) plus 1 for
    garnish
2 grapefruit (approx)
2 green peppers
2 oz butter
1 large clove garlic
1 tablesp brown sugar
1 teasp powdered rosemary
1 tablesp cornflour
salt, pepper

Trim any fat off the fillets and slice them on the slant into ½-inch thick oval pieces – about 16 in all. Toss these in seasoned flour. Squeeze enough oranges (leaving one for the garnish) and grapefruit to make ¾ pint of juice. Deseed and dice the green peppers.

Melt the butter in a large sauté pan, add the clove of garlic cut in two, and let it simmer for a few minutes without burning. Remove the garlic and put in the pork fillets. Let them cook gently for about 7 or 8 minutes on each side. Transfer them to a heated dish and keep them warm. Add the sugar, rosemary, and diced green peppers to the pan juices and simmer for 5 minutes, before adding the fruit juices. Simmer the mixture for 10 minutes or so until the peppers are tender. Thicken the sauce with the cornflour dissolved in a little cold water. Check the seasoning. Put the fillets back into the sauce for 5 minutes over a low heat. Slice the remaining orange, sprinkle with brown sugar and grill quickly until the sugar glazes.

Arrange the fillets, overlapping each other, down the centre of a serving dish, pour the sauce over them and decorate with the glazed orange slices.

Orange and green pepper salad

Cherwell Boathouse, Oxford
proprietor: Mrs A. Verdun

2 medium-sized green
    peppers
3 oranges
1 small clove garlic
4 tablesp oil
salt, sugar

Wash the green peppers and cut them into fairly thin rings. Peel two of the oranges, removing all the pith, and slice them in rounds. Arrange the peppers and oranges decoratively in a flat dish.

Make a dressing with the chopped clove of garlic, the oil and two tablespoonsful of orange juice. Season to taste with a little salt and sugar and just before serving pour the dressing over the salad.

EDITOR'S NOTE: use olive oil if you like the flavour, peanut or corn oil otherwise.

Chicken with lemon and mushrooms

Bowlish House Hotel, Shepton Mallet
chef/proprietor: Elaina Gardiner

1 4-lb chicken (or 4 joints)
salt, pepper
1 oz butter
2 tablesp oil
2 carrots
2 shallots
1 clove garlic
6 coriander seeds
2 tablesp chopped parsley
¼ teasp powdered saffron (or
    ½ teasp threads)

for the sauce
2 egg yolks
¼ pint double cream
½ lemon
1 oz butter
2 tablesp flour
2 teasp sugar
¼ lb button mushrooms

lemon slices, parsley

Cut the chicken into serving pieces and season with salt and pepper. Heat the butter and oil in a large heavy pan, and in it sauté the coarsely chopped carrots and shallots, stirring constantly until the shallots have softened. Place the chicken pieces on top and sprinkle over them the finely chopped garlic, the coriander seeds, the parsley and the saffron. Add enough boiling water to half-cover the chicken (about ¾ pint), bring it back to the boil, and simmer, covered, till the chicken is tender. Keep the chicken warm while you make the sauce.

Reduce the stock by about half, over a high heat. Combine the egg yolks, the cream, the lemon zest in fine matchsticks (or removed with a zester) and the lemon juice in a bowl. Melt the butter in a double boiler or heavy saucepan, stir in the flour and cook without browning. Add the strained stock. Caramelise the sugar with a little water, add a little more water to make a smooth syrup and add it also to the sauce. Simmer until the sauce is thick and smooth.

Add the mushrooms and the egg and cream mixture and whisk gently until it has thickened. Do not let the mixture boil, as it will curdle.

Pour the sauce over the chicken and garnish the dish with lemon slices and parsley.

Escalopes de veau orange et rhum

Au Bon Accueil, London
chef: Ronald Pearce

2 oranges
4 escalopes of veal
2 tablesp flour
1 oz butter
salt, pepper
2 fl oz rum
1 fl oz double cream
1 orange

Shred the peel of the two oranges finely, and blanch them for a few minutes in boiling water. Rinse in cold water.

Beat the escalopes out flat under polythene or waxed paper, using a rolling pin or meat bat. Pass them through the flour and fry them in the butter till golden brown and lightly cooked. Season. Add the juice of the two oranges, the blanched and shredded peel, and the rum. Let the sauce reduce a little until thick, and stir in the cream.

Serve the escalopes in the sauce, with a garnish of slices of fresh orange.

Roast duckling with mint and lemon sauce

Cleeveway House, Bishop's Cleeve
chef/proprietor: J. G. Marfell

a 5-lb duckling, dressed weight
salt, pepper
1 handful mint
6 oz butter
3 oz caster sugar
1 lemon

for the sauce
1 lemon
1 handful mint
1–2 tablesp sugar
¼ pint water
salt, pepper

1 lemon, watercress

Wipe the duckling inside and out, and sprinkle it with salt and pepper. Chop a handful of mint and mix it with the butter, sugar, and the grated rind and juice of a lemon. Spread the paste over the duckling, breast side up. Place it in a baking dish in a moderate oven (375°F, mark 5) and cook until brown on top (about 45 minutes). Turn the duck over on to its breast and put a cupful of water in the baking dish to prevent the mint burning. Continue roasting until the duck is cooked (about another 45 minutes). Remove the duck and keep it warm.

Drain any fat off the liquor left in the baking tin, add the juice of a lemon, the remaining chopped mint, a spoonful or two of sugar to taste, and ¼ pint of water. Let this reduce over heat until it is thick, and check the seasoning.

Carve the duck and serve it with the sauce, garnished with lemon slices and watercress.

EDITOR'S NOTE: prick the skin over the breast and thighs if the duckling is a fatty one.

Spiced oranges

Spread Eagle Restaurant, Greenwich
chef: Hannah Wright

At the Spread Eagle, these orange slices are served with roast duck. They are also good with pork, ham or game.

4 large, seedless oranges
½ pint wine vinegar
½ lb sugar
3 cloves
small piece of nutmeg
6 allspice berries
small piece of root ginger

Cut the unpeeled oranges into ¼-inch slices. Discard the end slices. In a saucepan cover them with cold water, bring to the boil, and simmer them gently, covered, for 40 minutes.

Make a syrup with the wine vinegar, sugar and spices. Allow it to boil for about 5 minutes. Using a fish slice, put the orange slices gently in the syrup. Add ½ pint of their cooking liquid, and

simmer, covered, for half an hour. Allow to cool in the syrup.

Serve the oranges with a little of the syrup.

CHEF'S NOTE: although the oranges can be used straight away, they improve by being stored in a wide-mouthed jar in the fridge for a couple of months, in their syrup with the spices.

Oranges monégasque

L'Aubergade, London
chef/proprietor: Maurice Manciet

5 seedless oranges (e.g. navel)
3 tablesp sugar
1½ tablesp Grand Marnier

Carefully remove the zest of one of the oranges. Cut these strips into thin juliennes – matchstick lengths. Put them into a saucepan with enough water to cover them and bring them to the boil. Strain off the water and cool them under running water. Put the juliennes back into the pan with just enough water to cover them and add the sugar. Cook them gently until the liquid starts to thicken and they begin to look shiny. Lift them out of the syrup with a perforated spoon and leave them to cool. Continue simmering the syrup and when it starts to caramelise, add the juice of the peeled orange and 4 fluid ounces of cold water. Allow the caramel to dissolve and then remove the pan from the heat and leave it to cool.

Peel the other four oranges very carefully, removing every trace of pith. Cut them into thin rings and arrange them decoratively in a shallow dish. When the syrup has cooled add the Grand Marnier and pour it over the oranges. Decorate them with the juliennes and chill overnight in the refrigerator.

Orange Boodles fool

Old Crown Inn, Messing
chef/proprietor: Elizabeth Law

4 dry sponge cakes
2 oranges
1 lemon
1 dessertsp caster sugar
½ pint double cream

Slice the sponge cakes in half horizontally and arrange them in one layer in the bottom of a glass bowl or soufflé dish.

Grate the rind of the oranges and half the lemon. Squeeze the juice of all the fruit, strain it and add the grated rind. Stir in the sugar until it has dissolved.

Whip the cream until it forms soft peaks and fold the fruit juice gently into it. Pour this mixture over the sponges and chill the fool in the refrigerator for several hours before serving.

CHEF'S NOTE: the cream has to be whipped fairly stiffly, as for a mousse or soufflé, so that it will hold the juice when it is folded in. If it is overwhipped, however, it will have a grainy consistency when it is mixed with the juice.

Mrs Beeton's baked lemon pudding

Tetthers, London
proprietor: Liz Tetther

6 oz shortcrust pastry (DPB,
    page 173)
2 lemons
¼ lb caster sugar
3 fl oz double cream
6 egg yolks
2 oz ground almonds
¼ lb unsalted butter

Line an 8½-inch flan ring with pastry.

Beat the grated rind of one lemon and the juice of both, with the sugar, cream, egg yolks, ground almonds and melted butter. Pour the mixture into the pastry case. Decorate it if you wish with lattice strips or whorls made from the pastry trimmings.

Bake the pudding in a warm oven (325°F, mark 3) until it has risen and is nicely browned – 40–50 minutes.

Serve cold.

EDITOR'S NOTES: you can bake the pastry case blind for 10 minutes in a hot oven (425°F, mark 7) before putting in the filling. (Line it with foil to keep it flat and prevent its becoming too brown.)

It is almost impossible to do tidy lattice-weaving in a flan ring because the filling is rather liquid. If you use a tin with a rim, the lattice will have something to hang on to.

The pudding is good hot or warm too, with cream.

Lemon Cotswold

Tudor Rose, East Horsley
chef: Mrs W. M. Chapman

3 oz butter
6 oz digestive biscuits
1 lemon jelly
6 fl oz water
2 lemons
6 oz Philadelphia cheese
½ lb caster sugar
½ large tin evaporated milk
    (chilled)

Put the butter to melt while crushing the digestive biscuits. Mix them together and line a loose-bottomed 7-inch cake tin with the mixture, bringing the lining well up the sides of the tin.

Dissolve the jelly in the hot water and squeeze the lemons. Cream together the cheese and sugar until they are light and beat in the jelly and lemon juice. Whisk

A simple sweet, rather like a cheesecake.

the chilled evaporated milk as stiff as possible and fold it into the cheese mixture. Fill the biscuit lining with it and put to chill in the refrigerator.

EDITOR'S NOTE: the biscuits can be crushed very easily between sheets of polythene or greaseproof paper, or in a paper bag.

MUSHROOMS

'Mushrooms are to be met with in pastures, woods, and marshes, but are very capricious and uncertain in their places of growth, multitudes being obtained in one season where few or none were to be found in the preceding.'
Mrs Beeton's Household Management

History

Yeast, penicillin and dry rot may, at first sight, seem to have little to do with mushrooms, but they are all fungi, some beneficial, others anything but. Mushrooms, of course, are the most appealing as something to eat, although they were also used as effective hallucinogens in Dionysian festivals and early Mexican rituals.

The Romans, instructed by Apicius, cooked truffles and ceps. Agrippina, wife of Claudius Cæsar, is said to have poisoned her husband with a dish of mushrooms, although he may simply have shared the misfortune of many other fungus-lovers since, in eating a lethal variety. The ever-practical French are careful to teach themselves to distinguish edible from poisonous wild fungi, and in the autumn staid chemists' windows are enlivened by bas-relief plastic charts indicating which are dangerous and which safe. There is no infallible test, and no substitute for knowledge. Collins *Guide to Mushrooms and Toadstools* is useful as an aid to identification.

It is only within the last 300 years that mushrooms have been cultivated. The French discovered how to do this by planting the spore of wild ones in manure, and by the beginning of the 19th century they were growing them underground in quarries near Paris. (Button mushrooms are still known as *champignons de Paris*.)

Nutrition

Mushrooms are renowned for flavour rather than nourishment, but they do provide a little protein, and most of the B vitamins, including folic acid, the blood-builder. If you have gout, some dieticians suggest you avoid them. Some people find them indigestible, and even more so if eaten along with steak or other animal protein. Try them, instead, with carbohydrates, as in crêpes surprise (page 156).

They are virtually free of calories and carbohydrate grams in their natural state – but taste so good with butter. . . .

Field mushrooms

If you are lucky enough to find them in late summer and autumn, freshly gathered field mushrooms have a far better flavour than cultivated ones. Unfortunately, horses and mushrooms have dwindled together.

Cultivated mushrooms

Over 35,000 tons are marketed every year. This sounds like a lucrative trade, but it is nevertheless best confined to commercial growers. In the August 1973 issue of *Which?* the home kits tested produced nothing but difficulties.

Buying	Mushrooms are graded by size and age. Choose the one which best suits a particular recipe:

BUTTONS are very young, with the membrane under the cap unbroken. They have less flavour than mature mushrooms but their neat shape makes them useful in cooking and in salads.

CUPS are open, with the membrane broken or breaking and the cap curved in a 'cup' shape. They are useful in stews, and flavourful grilled or fried.

OPENS or FLATS have a flat top and dark gills. They are full of flavour and good for grilling, stuffing, ketchups and soups.

STALKS are sometimes sold alone, relatively cheaply, and can be used in soups, purees and duxelles (DPB, page 168; crêpes surprise, page 156).

As mushrooms ripen, the gills darken from pinky beige to brownish black. While their flavour increases with age, their life expectancy shortens drastically, and thus opens are usually cheaper than small buttons or cups, which tend to hold their price because of their longer shop life.

Fresh mushrooms should be firm, dry, unbruised and unwrinkled. Bruising and dampness encourage decomposition. The cut ends of the stalks darken with age.

Tinned mushrooms have little true mushroom flavour and often a slimy rubbery texture. Dried ones, especially Chinese, have a strong flavour and are useful in stews or other made-up dishes.

Storing

No mushrooms keep very long. Unrefrigerated, they will last several days in a cool, dark, airy place, if they are spread out in a single layer. In the refrigerator, they will keep for up to a week if stored, unwashed, in a covered container, which will prevent their drying out. Mushrooms can also be dried or frozen.

Preparation

Mushrooms need not be peeled if they are in good condition. Wipe them with a damp cloth and cut off the crusty base of the stem. If you must wash them, rinse them quickly in a colander under running water and dry them carefully. They should never be soaked in water.

Buttons or small cups for a sauce or salad can be sliced vertically or cut in quarters to show off their pretty shape. A stainless knife will prevent their discolouring. Small buttons can be used whole in a creamy sauce (for example, chicken with mushrooms and lemon, page 147). Darker-gilled ones are likely to discolour a pale sauce or soup unless they are finely minced, wrung out thoroughly in a cloth, and cooked till dry in butter or oil before they are added to the mixture.

Cooking

DUXELLES is a marvellous invention of La Varenne in the 17th century, named in honour of the Marquis d'Uxelles (at least according to one story). The combination of minced mushrooms, finely chopped shallots and a little butter appears in bœuf Wellington, filet au château (page 191) crêpes surprise (page 156) and similar dishes where a savoury stuffing is called for. It freezes admirably, or can be kept in the refrigerator for some weeks under a layer of clarified butter.

Mushrooms have a great affinity with cream, eggs, garlic, parsley and wine, as the following recipes testify. And they make a fine savoury, served simply grilled on toast. The mushroom and cucumber salad shows how appetising they can be, served raw.

If by happy chance you have a glut of mushrooms, first eat your fill, then make duxelles, and finally consult Mrs Beeton for a strongly flavoured mushroom ketchup, 'one of the most useful store sauces to the experienced cook'.

Mushroom soup

Ballymaloe House, Shanagarry
chef/proprietor: Myrtle Allen

1 onion
2 oz butter
½ lb mushrooms
1½ oz flour
salt, pepper
¾ pint chicken stock (DPB,
    page 171)
¾ pint milk

for garnishing
cream or parsley

Chop the onion finely and cook it in the melted butter until it is soft. Add the finely chopped mushrooms and cook for a further 3–4 minutes. Stir in the flour, salt and pepper, and allow to cook for a few minutes, stirring constantly, before adding the stock and milk. Stir the soup until it comes to the boil and thickens. Allow it to simmer for 5–10 minutes longer, before serving garnished with a swirl of cream or some chopped parsley, or both.

Salzburg mushrooms

The Priory, Bath
chef/proprietor: Thea Dupays

½ pint thick pancake
    batter (DPB, page 172)
1 tablesp grated Parmesan
salt, pepper
8 button mushrooms
2 oz dried breadcrumbs
oil for deep frying

for the sauce
¼–½ pint mayonnaise (page 200)
1 dessertsp capers

Make the pancake batter slightly thicker than for pancakes by reducing the amount of milk, and allow it to stand for 1–2 hours. Add the grated cheese and some salt and pepper. Heat the oil to 325°F.

Remove the stalks, dip the mushrooms in the batter and roll them in the breadcrumbs so that they are completely coated in crumbs. When the oil is hot, drop them in and fry them for about 5 minutes, turning them over after a couple of minutes, until they are a lovely golden brown.

Serve the mushroom caps while they are hot, accompanied by the mayonnaise into which a dessertspoonful of crushed capers has been stirred.

Crêpes surprise

Le Caveau, Edinburgh
chef: Bernard Georgin

for the pancakes
3 eggs
¼ lb flour
pinch of salt
½ pint hot milk
2 tablesp oil

for the duxelles
½ lb mushrooms
1 medium-sized onion
2 shallots
parsley
½ oz butter
salt, pepper, nutmeg

for the béchamel
¾ oz butter
¾ oz flour
8 fl oz milk
4 fl oz cream
salt, pepper

for the topping
red Cheddar

Beat the eggs well, stir in the sifted flour and salt, pour on the oil and the hot milk and beat the batter thoroughly. Leave it to stand for 1–2 hours. Make 8–10 thin pancakes, putting them in a folded tea towel as they are made.

For the duxelles, chop the mushrooms finely and wring them out in a cloth to dry them as much as possible. Fry them in the butter with the finely chopped onion, shallots and parsley until all the liquid has evaporated and the mixture is cooked. Season it. Make the béchamel (DPB, page 174).

Fill each pancake with 2–3 tablespoonsful of the duxelles mixture, roll it neatly and place in a gratin dish. Cover the pancakes with the béchamel, sprinkle some grated cheese on top, and put under a very hot grill until the cheese is melted and brown.

EDITOR'S NOTE: this dish can either be prepared completely ahead, except for the final glazing (reheat gently in the oven before sprinkling on the cheese) or the pancakes and the duxelles can be made ahead so that the final assembly is not too lengthy.

Pousse d'automne

Pool Court Restaurant, Pool-in-Wharfedale
chef: David Armstrong

3 oz shallots or mild onions
5 oz butter
4 large cloves garlic
½ lb button mushrooms
½ pint dry white wine
oregano, basil
½ oz beurre manié (DPB, page
    169)
salt, pepper
4 thick slices white bread,
    crustless
1 lemon

In a large frying pan sauté the finely chopped shallots in 3 oz of the butter until transparent. Add the crushed garlic, and the finely chopped mushroom stalks, and cook them until tender. Increase the heat a little and add the mushroom caps, frying them quickly to keep them crisp. Pour the wine over, and at once, with a perforated spoon, lift out the mushrooms and shallots on to a heated plate and keep hot.

Add a pinch of oregano and one of basil to the liquor and reduce it by a third. Stir in two walnut-sized pieces of beurre manié to thicken the sauce and season it well. Put back the mushrooms to reheat for a minute or so while frying the slices of bread in the rest of the butter. Pile the mushrooms and sauce on top of the croûtes and serve immediately with a wedge of lemon.

CHEF'S NOTE: field mushrooms, cut up coarsely, give the finest result of all.

Mushrooms arménienne

Cleeveway House, Bishop's Cleeve
chef/proprietor: J. G. Marfell

1 lb button mushrooms
5–6 oz streaky bacon
2 fl oz olive oil
pepper
8 fl oz red wine
2 large cloves of garlic

for garnishing
parsley
red peppers
celery
walnuts

Wipe the mushrooms. Rind and trim the bacon and cut it into small squares.

Heat the olive oil quickly in a deep baking dish until it begins to smoke. Add the mushrooms, stirring with a wooden spoon. When they are just brown, add the bacon and pepper, all the time keeping the heat high. Pour in the wine and add the crushed garlic. Cook until the liquid is reduced by half, stirring occasionally. By this time the mushrooms should be cooked.

Transfer the mushrooms to a serving dish when cool, and sprinkle with chopped parsley. Serve with sliced red peppers and celery, and walnut halves.

CHEF'S NOTE: you need a well-ventilated kitchen for this dish, since the smoke and steam are as powerful as the aroma.

EDITOR'S NOTE: if the bacon is salty, you should need no additional salt. Taste before serving.

Rissolés à la bergère (sweetbread rissoles)

Houstoun House, Uphall
chef/proprietor: Keith Knight

An aristocratic and distant French relative of the British rissole, always pastry of some sort, with a forcemeat filling (chicken, fish or game), either deep-fried or baked.

½ lb lambs' sweetbreads
¼ lb onions
2 oz mushrooms
2 oz butter
1 oz flour
½ pint milk
salt, pepper
½ lb puff pastry (page 199)
egg wash
oil for deep-frying

Soak the sweetbreads in several changes of water for 2 hours, and for a further hour in cold water with a teaspoonful of vinegar for each pint. Pull off as much of the membrane as possible without tearing the sweetbreads. Trim them by cutting the lobes from the connecting tube. Put the sweetbreads in a saucepan and cover them by 2 inches with cold water. Add salt (1 teaspoonful per quart) and cook them, uncovered, just below simmering point for about 10 minutes. Leave them to cool in the water, then dry them on absorbent paper. Cut them into half-inch dice.

Chop the onions and mushrooms finely. Melt one ounce of the butter in a saucepan and sauté first the onion, then the mushrooms. Finally add the sweetbreads.

Make a roux (DPB, page 169) with the remaining ounce of butter and the flour. Stir in the milk (or half white stock, half cream), allow the sauce to thicken and cook it for several minutes over very low heat. Stir in the sweetbread mixture, and season to taste.

Roll the puff pastry out thinly and cut it into eight 5-inch rounds with a crimped cutter. Put a small heap of the mixture in the centre of half the rounds, egg wash the edges, and seal on the remaining rounds as lids. Egg wash the tops, and deep-fry the rissoles at 375°F, for about 3 minutes, turning them at least once. Drain them on absorbent paper and serve them very hot.

Any remaining filling can be thinned with a little milk and served as a sauce.

EDITOR'S NOTE: the rissoles are so crisp and delicate that we preferred not to serve them with the sauce. Any left-over filling is good served reheated on toast as a light snack.

Deep-fried mushrooms with cucumber sauce

George and Dragon, Fordwich
chefs: Alison Page, Jacky Dadds,
Elizabeth Crittenden

for the sauce
½ cucumber
½ medium-sized onion
1 sprig watercress
½ pint mayonnaise (page 200)

8 medium-sized field
  mushrooms
2 oz well-seasoned flour
2 eggs
2 oz dried breadcrumbs
oil for deep-frying
lettuce, lemon

Prepare the sauce first, since the mushrooms should be cooked at the last minute. Peel and deseed the cucumber, then cut it into dice. Chop the onion and the watercress finely. Stir these into the mayonnaise.

Put the oil to heat to 325°F. Trim the stalks of the mushrooms level with the caps and dip them into the seasoned flour, then coat them with beaten egg and finally the breadcrumbs. When the oil is hot enough, drop in the mushrooms and fry them for about a minute on each side, turning them until they become golden. Lift them out to drain on absorbent paper and serve them while they are hot on a bed of lettuce with slices of lemon. Hand the sauce round separately.

Mushroom and cucumber salad

Henderson's Salad Table, Edinburgh
chef/proprietor: Janet Henderson

½ lb mushrooms
1 cucumber
½ oz parsley

for the dressing
6 fl oz corn oil
3 fl oz wine or cider vinegar
½ teasp salt
¼ teasp pepper
½ clove garlic, crushed
1 teasp mustard powder
1 teasp soft brown sugar

Slice the mushrooms, chop the unskinned cucumber into small pieces, and chop the parsley finely.

Put the dressing ingredients in a bottle and shake them together vigorously. Pour the dressing over the salad and mix gently.

EDITOR'S NOTE: if you have too much dressing, the extra will keep for a few days if stored in a dark place.

Mushrooms with lemon and coriander

La Chandelle, Marlow
chef/proprietor: Tom Hearne

1 lb small button mushrooms
4 tablesp olive oil
2 or 3 bay leaves
salt, pepper
1 heaped teasp crushed
   coriander seeds
juice of 1 lemon

Wipe the mushrooms with a damp cloth. Heat the olive oil in a large, heavy-bottomed frying pan. When it is really hot, put in the crushed coriander and fry it for half a minute before adding the mushrooms and bay leaves. Stir and allow them to brown over a high heat for a minute or two. Then add some salt and pepper, reduce the heat and leave the mushrooms to cook for another 2 or 3 minutes. They must not be overcooked. Add the lemon juice, check the seasoning and serve cold.

EDITOR'S NOTE: coriander seeds should be pounded in a *deep* mortar to prevent their flying about the kitchen. Failing that, put them in a piece of cloth or polythene bag and crush them with a hammer or rolling pin.

Tranche de jambon morvandelle

8 2-oz slices cooked gammon
½ lb button mushrooms
2 oz butter

for the sauce
1 small onion
1 clove garlic
1 oz butter
2 fl oz wine vinegar
4 fl oz dry white wine
1 tablesp tomato puree
6 tablesp sauce espagnole
   (page 200)
salt, a few black peppercorns
¼ pint double cream
1 oz grated cheese

Randalls Restaurant Français, Brixham
chef: John Randall

Trim any fat off the slices of ham and arrange them in an ovenproof serving dish. Quarter the mushrooms and sauté them in butter. Sprinkle them on top of the ham.

Prepare the piquant sauce by softening the finely chopped onion and garlic in an ounce of butter. When they are transparent, add the wine vinegar and reduce it to a tablespoonful. Add the wine, tomato puree, sauce espagnole and

Morvan is a district in Burgundy noted for its ham and its mushrooms.

some seasoning. Cook until the sauce has reduced by about a third. Warm the cream and stir it into the sauce. If it is not thick enough, continue the cooking until it has reduced to the right consistency, then strain it over the ham and mushrooms. Sprinkle the cheese on the top and bake in a moderate oven (350°F, mark 4) for 12–15 minutes. If the top has not glazed sufficiently at the end, brown it quickly under a hot grill.

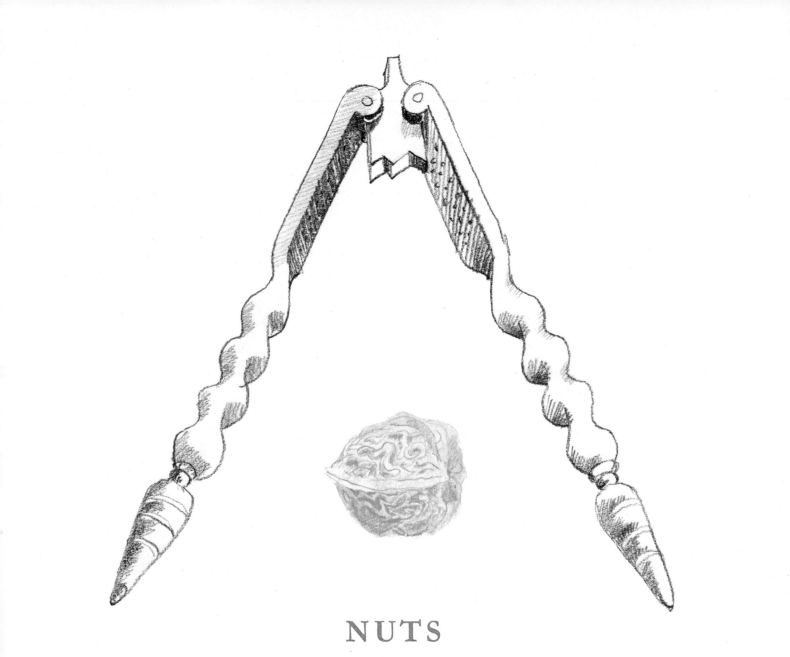

NUTS

'He that will eat the kernel must crack the nut.'
LATIN PROVERB

The earliest Celts ate wild woodland fruit and nuts, and while the Ancient Britons were smearing themselves with woad, other civilisations were using unguents made from nut oils. Mrs Beeton tells us that the Romans believed six almonds would guard them against drunkenness – perhaps this is the origin of contemporary cocktail nibbles. On the other hand, the medieval theory was that nuts were a digestive and 'closed the stomach' after a meal. We obviously subscribe to this theory too, since nuts are offered as dessert.

Nutrition

Nuts are a good source of protein: almonds, peanuts and cashews have approximately 20% of their weight as protein. Their high oil content (up to 55% by weight) provides necessary fat in the diet. They score high on calories: 170 per ounce for almonds, 182 for brazils, 50 for chestnuts, 177 for desiccated coconut, 170 for peanuts and 155 for walnuts. While most nuts have one or two carbohydrate grams per ounce, chestnuts have ten.

Buying

Nuts are at their best early in the season before the kernels shrivel. The peak periods are October and November for walnuts, November for chestnuts, and September for homegrown nuts like hazelnuts, cobs and filberts (so named because they ripen near St Philibert's Day, August 22). Almonds are available all the year round.

In general nuts with clean bright shells are likely to have sound kernels, stained or cracked ones are not. The heavier the nut is in proportion to its size, the meatier the kernel. Shelled nuts are trickier, since their high oil content makes them go stale very quickly. Try to buy them from a grocer with cool shelves and a rapid turnover of stock. Chopped, flaked and ground nuts go rancid even more quickly than whole ones. They should be pale rather than yellowish in colour.

Storing

Most nuts in shell will keep for several months in a cool, dark, dry place. Chestnuts should be stored in loosely-covered containers or ventilated plastic bags, to keep them moist. Nut kernels can be deep-frozen in a tightly-closed container for up to two years. They will also keep in the refrigerator, similarly packed, for about six months.

Almonds

Sweet almonds come in two varieties. The long tapered Jordan ones (from Mediterranean countries) are considered the finer, and eaten for dessert. Valencia almonds, short and chubby, are generally used for cooking. You can buy them whole, shelled, blanched, flaked, shredded, nibbed or ground, paying, of course, for the various processes. Or you can blanch your own and grind them in a coffee-grinder.

BLANCHING Drop the shelled nuts into boiling water and leave them for one minute. Drain them, plunge them into cold water, and drain them again. Squeeze each nut between thumb and forefinger, and it will pop out of its skin. Dry the nuts carefully.

SALTING For half a pound of nuts (nicest with Jordan) you need a small knob of butter to grease a shallow baking tin. Put in the blanched almonds, and cook them in a slow oven (300°F, mark 2) until they are pale brown, in about 20–30 minutes. Toss them in two tablespoonsful of sea salt on greaseproof paper, and wrap them up and leave them for an hour or two before serving. They are at their best within six hours or so, and are less good the next day, or so they tell us . . .

Old recipes called for one bitter almond to every few dozen sweet ones, and you may now find a few drops of almond essence recommended to accentuate the almond flavour in a dish (for example, in bavaroise aux amandes, page 169 and bobotie, page 138).

Chestnuts

English chestnuts are too small to make the effort of peeling them worthwhile, and it is the Spanish variety which you find in the shops, imported from Italy, Portugal and France, as well as Spain. The nuts should be plump and glossy in appearance.

The chestnut is more like a floury vegetable than a nut, and the sieved cooked kernel can be used in cakes, stuffings and purees. Whole kernels are used in savoury dishes (chicken pie Ste Nicole, p. 166) and, of course, to make marrons glacés. The high cost of marrons may inspire you to do your own. Our attempt convinced us that a glacé-er earns his money.

SHELLING is not a difficult job, but a tedious one. Make a cut on one side, or all round, each chestnut. Either boil them in water for about ten minutes or bake them in a moderate oven for 15 minutes. Remove them a few at a time, and with a sharp pointed knife take off the hard outer shell and the clinging inner skin. If you are lucky, the inner skins may rub off with a cloth. The rest should be kept warm while you are working. Tinned chestnuts are truer to the original than are many other tinned products, and come either whole or in pieces in syrup (lovely with ice cream), and as a puree, both sweetened and unsweetened. Dried ones seem more successful in savoury dishes than sweet, and should be simmered gently in stock for 15–30 minutes, depending on their age.

PUREE A fresh puree is delicious, and easy to make once the initial shelling is done. Simmer a pound of shelled chestnuts gently in enough stock and water or milk and water to cover them, until they are tender (about an hour should do) and most of the liquid has evaporated. Puree them in the liquidiser or sieve them. Reheat the puree in a double-boiler with an ounce of butter, and salt and pepper. Try a puree of chestnuts and potatoes with game (DPB, page 101). Chestnut flour makes interesting cakes and sauces.

Walnuts

English walnut trees do not produce enough to satisfy our demands, and we import walnuts from California and China as well as Europe. They are probably the most widely used nut in British kitchens, in stuffings, salads and cakes, and as decoration, where their brain-like convolutions provide welcome contrast to the endemic glacé cherry.

WALNUT OIL This ranks for us just a little below truffles as one of France's most precious foodstuffs. The price is just a little below truffles too, but the flavour is so intense that a little goes a long way. (Unfortunately it goes rancid more quickly than other oils.) Our favourite salad is a mixture of leaf lettuce and chicory, dressed with an oily vinaigrette (one spoonful of vinegar to four or five of oil) made with half walnut oil, half peanut oil. We find that garlic alters the walnut flavour unpleasantly, and omit it from all our walnut-oil recipes. It is lovely with tomato salad, leeks vinaigrette or a mixed rice salad containing salted peanuts, plumped raisins and diced celery.

Guinea fowl baked with walnuts and cider

Rivermede Country House Hotel,
St Michaels-on-Wyre
chef: Elizabeth Fielding

2 guinea fowl, 1½–2 lb dressed
   weight
¼ lb butter
3 oz shelled walnuts
2 cooking apples
1 oz cornflour
¾ pint dry cider
¼ pint double cream
salt, pepper

Remove the wings from each guinea fowl and cut along either side of the backbone and breastbone, dividing each bird into two halves. Trim off the legs at the knee joint, if this has not already been done.

Melt the butter in a large, heavy casserole and put in the pieces of fowl to seal on both sides. (If necessary, seal two halves first and put to one side.) While they are cooking, finely chop the walnuts and the peeled and cored apples. Put a few of the nuts aside. Add the rest, and the apples, to the casserole and continue to cook gently for 5 minutes.

Lift out the pieces of guinea fowl and, off the heat, sprinkle the cornflour into the pan juices. Mix it in and gradually blend in the cider and the cream. Return the pan to the heat and bring the sauce to the boil, stirring until it has thickened; simmer it gently for a few minutes. Put back the pieces of bird, cover the casserole and put it into a warm oven (325°F, mark 3) to cook for about an hour. If after half an hour it is simmering too fast, reduce the heat, since the sauce may separate.

Serve the guinea fowl smothered in its sauce and sprinkled with a few chopped nuts. Pommes parisienne (DPB, page 163) go well with it.

Terrine of chicken and walnuts (16)

Chanterelle, London
chef: Peter du Toit

for the stock
3–4 lb chopped veal bones and/or 2 large split pig's feet
1 lb Spanish onions
½ lb carrots
1 bouquet garni

for the terrine
1 roasting chicken, about 4 lb dressed weight
1 lb unsmoked streaky bacon, in the piece
bay leaves
¾ lb minced veal
3 oz shelled walnuts
1¼ teasp salt
15 peppercorns
1 small clove of garlic
1 tablesp brandy or 2 tablesp sweet sherry

In a large saucepan, cover the ingredients for the stock (the vegetables coarsely chopped) to a depth of 2 inches with cold water. Bring to the boil slowly and simmer gently for 3–4 hours. Strain and return the stock to the saucepan.

Put the chicken in to the stock, which should come to just above the legs and thighs. Bring the stock to the boil, cover the saucepan and reduce the heat so that the stock barely simmers. Poach the chicken for 1½ hours.

Meantime, in a separate pan, gently boil the bacon with a few bay leaves for 1½ hours.

Remove the chicken and bacon and allow them to cool a little. Strip off the flesh, discarding all rind, skin and bones. Chop the chicken and bacon together to give a medium-rough texture. Add the raw veal, the walnuts broken into large pieces, the salt, the crushed peppercorns, the chopped garlic, and the brandy or sherry.

Reduce by half the stock in which the chicken was poached, and add about ¼ pint to the mixture.

Grease one large or two smaller terrines with butter, sprinkle them liberally with flour, and shake out the excess. Put in the mixture to within half an inch of the top, cover carefully with foil, and the lids. Place the terrines in a bain-marie (BFB, page 168) with the hot water reaching one-third the way up their sides, and cook in a warm oven (325°F, mark 3) for 1½–2 hours.

The terrine is cooked when the mixture begins to shrink from the sides of the container and a skewer pushed into the middle comes out clean and hot.

Remove the terrines from the oven, drain off some of the liquid, and place weights on top of the foil. Leave in a cold place for at least 24 hours to mature.

CHEF'S NOTE: if the stock is properly reduced, its jellying action helps the texture of the terrine.

EDITOR'S NOTE: if you wish to serve the terrine from its dish rather than in slices, decorate the top with half walnuts, parsley, watercress, or bay leaves, since its colour is pale.

Chicken pie Ste Nicole (6)

Inigo Jones, London
chef: Santosh Bakshi

In Austrian cooking, Ste Nicole is a term applied to a dish containing cranberries.

1 lb puff pastry (page 199)
2 chickens
18–24 chestnuts
seasoned flour
2 tablesp cooking oil
1 medium-sized onion
1 oz butter
¼ pint white wine
½ pint chicken velouté
¼ pint double cream
salt, pepper
4 tablesp sweetened cooked
    cranberries, fresh or tinned
1 egg yolk

Make the puff pastry and put it to rest in a cool place. Skin and bone the chickens, putting the legs, thighs and breasts – which go into the pie – to one side. Make some stock for the velouté with the carcases and wings by simmering them with the usual vegetables, herbs and seasonings. Reduce this stock until it is very strong. Slit the chestnuts, cook them in water or stock until they are tender, then peel them.

Cut the legs and breasts of the chickens in half, dip them in seasoned flour and fry them in hot oil until they are slightly browned. In a large casserole, sauté the chopped onion in butter until it is transparent, put in the browned chicken, the white wine and the velouté sauce, made with the reduced chicken stock. Cover and simmer for 10 minutes or so. Add the cream, season with salt and pepper and continue to cook for a further 10 minutes before adding the chestnuts. After another 5 minutes remove the casserole from the heat, turn the contents into a large pie-dish and leave to cool a little. Sprinkle the cranberries on top.

Roll out the pastry on a floured surface to ¼-inch thickness and into a shape similar to but larger than the top of your pie dish. Cut off a ¾-inch strip from round the edge and lay this round the damped rim of the dish. Brush it with water and put the pastry lid in position on top. Press the edges firmly together. Trim away any surplus pastry, then flute the edges with the back of a knife. Make a slit in the top to allow the steam to escape and roll out any trimmings to make decorative leaves for the top. Brush the pastry with beaten egg and leave it to stand for about 30 minutes. Bake the pie in a hot oven (450°F, mark 8) for 10 minutes. Reduce the heat to 375°F, mark 5, and cook for 15 minutes until the pastry is golden brown.

EDITOR'S NOTES: if you are using fresh cranberries (obtainable, vacuum-packed from many grocers) cook them as follows: 1 lb cranberries, 14 oz sugar, 4 fl oz water. Simmer gently until the cranberries are translucent and start to pop. Let them cool in the syrup.

Cranberries may be frozen, just as they come, in the vacuum pack.

Chicken velouté is béchamel (DPB, page 174) made with reduced chicken stock instead of milk.

Chicken noix

Crown Hotel, Lyndhurst
chef/proprietress: Mrs F. H. Kramer

This recipe is very useful because it uses the chicken legs, leaving the suprêmes for more delicate dishes.

4 fresh chicken legs
1 medium-sized onion
6 oz celery
2 oz walnuts
2 oz butter
½ pint white wine
½ pint demi-glace (DPB, page 172)
salt, pepper
a little chopped parsley

Skin the pieces of chicken and carefully remove the thigh bones. Dice the onion and slice the celery finely. Chop the walnuts roughly.

Melt the butter in a heavy-bottomed saucepan and brown the chicken, onions and celery in it. Drain off any excess fat and pour in the wine. Allow it to simmer for a minute or two before adding the demi-glace. Bring the sauce to the boil and continue cooking, uncovered, for about 25 minutes, turning the chicken in the sauce occasionally and allowing it to reduce slightly. Add the chopped walnuts, check the seasoning and serve the chicken sprinkled with a little chopped parsley.

White cabbage salad

Toastmaster's Inn, Burham
chefs: Christopher Dimech and Gregory Ward

This salad partners the Saalbacher à la crème recipe (page 192), accompanied by small, new, boiled potatoes, scrubbed but not peeled.

for the dressing
2 large cloves garlic
salt
2 teasp dry English mustard
1 teasp caster sugar
pepper
2 tablesp white wine vinegar
6 tablesp oil

½ medium-sized white cabbage
1 oz chopped walnuts
2 oz currants
a little chopped parsley

Crush the cloves of garlic with a little salt. Add all the other ingredients for the dressing and mix them well together.

Cut out any thick stalk from the cabbage and slice the rest thinly into shreds. Toss it in the dressing and sprinkle the chopped walnuts, currants and parsley over the top.

Rhubarb and almond tartlets

Ballymaloe House, Shanagarry
chef: Mrs M. Allen

2–4 sticks of plump red
    rhubarb, according to size

for the syrup
6 oz sugar
8 fl oz water

3 oz butter
3 oz sugar
3 oz ground almonds
½ pint whipped cream

Cut the rhubarb into 16 one-inch lengths. Bring the sugar and water for the syrup gently to the boil and poach the pieces of rhubarb in it until they are just tender, then drain and cool them.

Beat the butter, sugar and almonds together to a cream and put a heaped teaspoonful of this mixture into 16 small buttered patty tins. Bake them in a moderately hot oven (375°F, mark 5) for about 10 minutes or until they are nut-brown. Allow them to cool a little but not set before removing them onto a wire rack. Just before serving, place a chunk of rhubarb in each tart and top with whipped cream.

EDITOR'S NOTE: these crisp little cases could also be filled with other fruit, such as fresh raspberries or peaches.

Frozen almond creams (8)

Highbullen Country House Hotel,
Chittlehamholt
chef/proprietor: Pamela Neil

¼ lb flaked almonds
½ pint double cream
2 egg whites
3 oz caster sugar
a pinch of salt
2–3 tablesp sherry, Marsala or
    brandy

Turn the refrigerator to its coldest setting.

Toast the almonds until they are golden brown and leave them to cool.

Whip the cream lightly. Beat the egg whites until they start to foam, then add the sugar and salt and continue beating until the mixture is stiff and glossy. Fold in the cream and the toasted almonds, keeping some for decoration. Stir in two or three tablespoonsful of sherry, Marsala or brandy, checking the flavour, which will be less strong when chilled. Spoon the cream into eight individual cocotte dishes and sprinkle the tops with a few almond flakes.

Freeze in the ice-making compartment of the refrigerator or the deep freeze for 2–3 hours. Serve straight from the freezer.

Bavarois aux amandes (8)

Swan House Hotel, Wilmcote
chef: Miss J. Burton

1 pint milk
¼ teasp almond essence
3 eggs
3 oz sugar
½ oz gelatine
3 tablesp water
6 almond macaroons
2½ fl oz crème de cacao
½ pint double cream

for decoration
whipped cream
¼ lb split almonds

Heat the milk to blood temperature and add the almond essence. Separate the yolks from the whites of the eggs, add the sugar to the yolks and beat them till creamy. Soften the gelatine with the water. Pour the milk on to the yolks, whisking rapidly all the time. Strain the mixture into a double boiler, and cook the custard very gently, stirring continuously, until it coats the back of a wooden spoon. Do not allow it to boil. Stir in the softened gelatine and leave the custard to set.

Soak the macaroons in the crème de cacao, and toast the split almonds. Whip the cream and fold it into the set custard. Whip the egg whites stiffly and fold them in gently. Half fill a mould or glass dish with the custard, put in the macaroons, and fill the dish with the remaining custard. Leave in the refrigerator for at least two hours. If you are using a mould, turn the bavarois out onto a serving dish. Decorate it with cream and sprinkle it liberally with the almonds.

EDITOR'S NOTE: this sweet is best made the day it will be eaten.

Büntertorte (Gâteau des Grisons) (4-6)

Old Manor House, Knaresborough
chef/proprietor: E. W. Schwallen

6 oz pâte sucrée (DPB, page 173)

for the filling
½ lb sugar
4 tablesp water
½ lb walnut halves
¼ pint double cream

for the topping
3 oz dark dessert chocolate
   (e.g. chocolat Menier)

Line an 8-inch flan ring with the pastry and bake it blind at 400°F, mark 6.

Put the sugar in a very heavy pan, moisten it with the water, and allow it to boil till a dark mahogany colour. Immediately add the walnuts, bring the mixture back to the boil, stirring all the time. Stir in the cream off the heat, since it will splutter a little. Bring the mixture back to the boil once again, then allow it to cool and thicken.

When it is cold, fill the flan case with the mixture and pour a thin layer of melted chocolate over the top, smoothing it as far as possible with a spatula.

CHEF'S NOTE: since the filling keeps 'indefinitely', you might as well make large quantities at a time, and have an instant dessert ready.

EDITOR'S NOTE: if the filling looks untidy, decorate it with piped whipped cream.

SMOKED FISH

Smoking your own fish has now become a pastime for some, but originally smoking was a vital way to preserve both fish and meat. In warmer countries further south salting became the standard method, whereas smoking seems to have been – and still is – the speciality of Northern Europe.

In medieval times fish had to be ready for the frequent fast days decreed by the Church, and the fish was first salted and then smoked. Both salting and smoking are done very much more delicately now, although the principle is unchanged. As a result, some smoked fish goes off almost as quickly as fresh.

Smoking

There is a preliminary soaking in salt or brine to accentuate the flavour of the fish and to firm the flesh by dehydrating it somewhat. The fish is then hung in a kiln in a stream of smoke from smouldering hardwood chips and sawdust (generally beech or oak). The chemicals from the wood smoke give the fish a distinctive smoky flavour and also, of course, act as a mild preservative. Traditional smoking produces the genuine glossy golden coating which is now often fabricated commercially. In cold-smoking the kiln temperature is kept at or below 86°F and the fish remains uncooked. In hot-smoking the fish are cooked during the smoking process.

Nutrition

Fish is an excellent source of first-class protein, providing about the same amount, weight for weight, as meat. It also provides calcium and various minerals; oily fish (herring, mackerel) are a good source of vitamins A, B and D. Dieters love fish because it is relatively low on calories – about 40 an ounce – and scores no carbohydrate grams. White fish is less calorific than oily fish.

Buying

Correctly smoked fish feels firm and springy without a trace of flabbiness. Dryness is a sign of poor quality. Smoked fish deteriorates if kept in a warm place for any length of time – worth remembering next time you see kippers sweltering in the fishmonger's sunlit window.

Cold-smoked fish

HADDOCK Large ones are filleted before smoking, smaller ones (finnan haddock) are split open but smoked on the bone. The latter are regarded as the finest, especially those which come from Aberdeenshire where the village of Findon claims to have given its name to the breed. The best are undyed and pale in colour, unlike the bright yellow or orange of the artificially coloured. They are at their best from September to February.

Golden cutlets are very small haddock, first filleted, then smoked.

HERRING If gutted, split, and lightly brined before smoking, the result is a kipper. Most are artificially coloured to a reddish-brown, but the finer, undyed ones are walnut-hued or yellow-brown. The best come from the Isle of Man (where dyeing is forbidden by law), Loch Fyne and Northumberland. Available all the year round, they are at their best from August to April.

Bloaters and red herrings are processed ungutted, the bloaters dry-salted and very lightly smoked to preserve their bright silvery skin, the red herrings heavily salted and slowly smoked so that they will keep well. Both originated in East Anglia, but while bloaters are not hard to obtain, red herrings are almost all exported.

COD The smoked fillet is similar to haddock fillet, though with less flavour. It is golden yellow, and at its best from October to May. Cod's roe is, naturally, at its best in spring. It is heavily dry-salted to firm it and should be dark red and easily sliced.

Hot-smoked fish

These are ready to eat and always expensive.

HADDOCK Small ones, usually from Arbroath, and smoked whole, become smokies. They are especially good in early spring, but highly prized at any time. The skin should have an oily sheen.

HERRING Gutted, beheaded, brined and slowly smoked whole, herring become buckling. The skin is golden and silvery, the flesh pale gold with a flavour similar to smoked trout, although they are less expensive than trout. The skin should have an oily sheen, and the flesh should be soft in texture.

MACKEREL Less well known and cheaper than most, but with a delicate flavour and fine texture.

EEL Lightly brined and sold either filleted or on the bone. The flesh should be firm and buttery rather than tough, the flavour smoky and not too salt. Two to three ounces, preferably sliced lengthwise rather than across the bone, make an adequate helping for one.

TROUT Lightly smoked on the bone but gutted, trout has become the easiest hot-smoked fish to find, probably because rainbow and other trout are now reared in hatcheries in Britain so that we do not depend entirely on imported ones. The skin should have an oily sheen, the flesh be moist. Allow one 4-ounce trout per person for a light supper or as an hors d'œuvre when the main course is rather insubstantial; half a trout per person is ample before a heavy main dish.

SALMON Probably the most popularly prized of all smoked fish. Salmon is usually dry-salted and mildly smoked over oak chips. Scottish or Tamar smoked salmon, regarded as the finest, are a darker red than other varieties. Young salmon or grilse is pinkish red. Norwegian and Canadian salmon (both Atlantic and Pacific) are saltier, drier and usually less expensive. All should have an oily sheen. Allow about two ounces per head as an hors d'œuvre. Trimmings can often be bought cheaply for cooked dishes or sandwiches.

Storing

The two aims in storing smoked fish are to prevent its drying out and to prevent its communicating its smell to other food in the larder or refrigerator. Luckily the solution to both problems is the same: wrap the fish carefully in greaseproof paper and store it in a covered container. Unless it is to be eaten on the day of purchase, it should be stored in the fridge where it will stay in good condition for at least 4 days, except for herring which should be eaten within three days. Smoked salmon loses its flavour as well as drying out if kept too long. (It can be lightly brushed with oil if it looks dry.) Frozen smoked fish should also be carefully wrapped before storage.

Smoked fish in recipes

Delicate smoked fish is perhaps at its best with brown bread and butter and a wedge of lemon, but if you are lucky enough to become bored with the taste and want something new, you will find that trout and eel make an interesting mousse-like pâté (page 177), that haddock and kippers combine well with eggs and cheese (page 176), and cream.

To poach haddock, cover it with milk or milk and water to prevent the flesh going dry (and save the smoky, fishy stock – if it is not too salt – for a chowder, perhaps with chopped onion, parsley, cubed potato, kernel or creamed corn, and some left-over flaked fish).

Kippers are always controversial: some swear that they must be grilled or fried, others that they are at their best plunged in a jug of boiling water and left to stand, covered, for 5 minutes. The latter method certainly cuts down on the smell, as does baking the fish in foil in a moderate oven for about 15 minutes.

Kipper fillets are obtainable in packets, even deep-frozen, and while they are not for the purist, they are very convenient for a quick pâté (DPB, page 152).

Bloaters can be soaked for a couple of minutes in hot water before being split, filleted, trimmed and grilled. Or they can be split, floured and fried.

Pans, plates, grills and cutlery should be rinsed in *cold* water as soon as possible after use to help remove the clinging smell.

It is very difficult to find good, undyed smoked fish if you live outside a large city – and sometimes difficult even within one. The following addresses have all been recommended by people whose judgment we trust, though obviously we cannot guarantee supplies or quality. We should be glad to have comments on these or others which you know about.

Ernest Cox Ltd
The Smokehouse
PO Box 19, 44a Cleethorpe Road
Grimsby DN3 13LE
tel: Grimsby 55488

5–7 lb boxes (consumer packs) of mackerel, buckling, sprat, or cold-smoked haddock fillet. Delivered by British Rail.

L. Robson & Sons Ltd
Fishcurers, Craster, Alnwick,
Northumberland
tel: Alnwick 76223

Kippers, from two pairs of the smallest size to 10–12 pairs of the largest. Sent by post. (Replaced if they arrive unfit for consumption.) Smoked salmon by the side.

Ritchie Brothers
37 Watergate, Rothesay, Bute

Loch Fyne kippers by post.

Curtish, Fishmonger
Douglas, Isle of Man

Kippers by post.

Old Farmhouse smokies (6)

*Old Farmhouse Restaurant, Armitage
chef/proprietors: Richard and Ishbel Speight*

2 8-oz Arbroath smokies
4 tomatoes
½ oz flour
½ oz butter
4 tablesp single cream
1 oz butter

Cover the fish with boiling water, and leave them to stand for 5 minutes or so to soften them. Drain the fish, keeping the water, and fillet them, putting the bones and skin back into the water. Break up the flesh into flakes. Skin, deseed and chop the tomatoes.

Bring the water and bones back to the boil and reduce the liquid until a strong stock is obtained – but stop before it gets too salty. Make a roux (DPB, page 169) with the butter and flour and blend in half a pint of the fish stock. Add the cream, the chopped tomatoes and the flaked fish and reheat gently.

Fill four large cocotte dishes with this mixture, dot them with butter and brown them under the grill.

Taramosalata (6-8)

*Highbullen Country House Hotel,
Chittlehamholt
chef/proprietor: Pamela Neil*

*A Greek/Cypriot dish, originally made from
the roe of grey mullet.*

½ lb smoked cod's roe
juice of ½ lemon
½–¾ pint salad oil
a little boiling water
1 tablesp chopped parsley
1 clove garlic

Soak the cod's roe for at least an hour, preferably two. Rinse and drain it, and peel off the skin. Put the roe into a mixing bowl and mash it to a pulp with a fork. With an electric beater (table or hand-held) start whisking the roe at top speed, pouring in the lemon juice slowly. Then start adding the oil drop by drop, still whisking, as when making mayonnaise. Keep adding it until the mixture is really solid and dry: it should be forming lumps and working its way up the sides of the bowl. When it reaches this stage it is safe to start beating in a little boiling water – about 2 fluid ounces – just sufficient to

turn the mixture into a soft mousse. If the water is added before it has become very solid, the mixture will separate.

Stir in some chopped parsley and crushed garlic and serve the taramosalata with hot pitta bread (page 91) or toast.

CHEF'S NOTE: as with mayonnaise, it is advisable to have the oil and the cod's roe at a similar temperature. Should the mixture separate it can be rescued by beating it into an egg yolk as you do to save a curdled mayonnaise.

Smoked haddock mousse (4-6)

*Pink's, Fairford
chefs: Alison Gregory and Jane Hill*

½ lb smoked haddock
milk, water
bouquet garni
½ pint aspic
1 teasp gelatine
¼ pint mayonnaise (page 200)
¼ pint double cream
salt, pepper
slices of lemon or cucumber

Poach the haddock in a little milk and water with a bouquet garni. Remove all its bones and skin and break it into flakes.

Warm the aspic slightly and dissolve the gelatine in it. Put aside half of it to set in the refrigerator as garnish. Add the rest to the fish and blend them together in the

liquidiser until smooth. Fold in the mayonnaise and the lightly whipped cream. Check the seasoning.

Pour into individual cocotte dishes – 4 large or 6 small ones – and decorate with lemon or cucumber and a little chopped aspic.

Moscow smoked salmon

Old Crown Inn, Messing
chef/proprietor: Elizabeth Law

for the filling

2 oz jar black caviar or
  lumpfish roe
4 oz cream cheese
1–2 tablesp double cream
salt, pepper
1 teasp lemon juice
a pinch cayenne pepper

½ lb smoked salmon
1 lemon

Mix the caviar or lumpfish roe with the cream cheese and enough cream to give a smooth texture. Season it with salt and pepper – not too much salt – lemon juice and a pinch of cayenne. Cut and trim the smoked salmon into eight slices, then put some of the caviar mixture on each one and roll it up neatly.

Garnish the rolls with wedges of lemon and serve them with slices of buttered brown bread.

Smoked haddock and cheese bouchées

Crispins, London
chef: James Stewart

½ lb puff pastry (page 199)
  or 4 fairly large vol-au-vent
  cases
1 egg plus 1 yolk
1 lb smoked haddock on the
  bone
½ pint milk
½ oz butter
½ oz flour
2 oz grated Cheddar cheese
pepper, cayenne, nutmeg
2 tablesp double cream
chopped parsley

Roll out the pastry to ¼-inch thickness and stamp out an equal number of rounds with a 3-inch and a 1½-inch fluted cutter. Arrange them on a damp baking tray and brush with beaten egg. Mark the centres of the larger rounds gently with the 1½-inch cutter and put the tray in the refrigerator to chill for 15 minutes. Heat the oven to 450°F, mark 8, and bake the rounds for 10–15 minutes when they should have risen spectacularly and turned a golden brown. Transfer to a wire rack and scrape out any soft pastry from the centres of the larger cases. Keep the smaller ones for 'hats'. Leave them to cool and reheat when required in a moderate oven (350°F, mark 4) for 15 minutes.

Poach the haddock in the milk. Drain and flake the fish, removing all skin and bones. Make a roux with the butter and flour and, using the milk the fish was cooked in, prepare a white sauce. Season with pepper, cayenne and nutmeg and blend in the grated cheese, then the flaked fish. Just before serving add an egg yolk beaten with the cream. Heat through gently, then fill the hot pastry cases to overflowing, set a 'hat' at a jaunty angle on each and sprinkle with chopped parsley.

Trout and eel pâté (6-8)

Pool Court Restaurant, Pool-in-Wharfedale
chef: David Armstrong

This smoked fish pâté has a creamy mousse-like texture.

for the béchamel
½ oz butter
½ oz flour
6 fl oz milk
seasonings
3 eggs
2 oz butter

2 smoked trout (3–4 oz each)
¼ lb smoked eel
fresh chives
3 fl oz double cream
salt, pepper

Make the béchamel using the butter, flour, milk and seasonings. Allow it to lose a little heat and whisk in the egg yolks and butter. Skin and flake the trout with a fork (checking carefully for small bones) and chop the eel finely. When the sauce is quite cool, fold in the fish and some chopped chives.

Stiffly beat the double cream and then the egg whites and fold first one, then the other into the mixture. Season it to taste. Refrigerate the pâté till about 30 minutes before serving it.

CHEF'S NOTE: at Pool Court the pâté is served on a bed of watercress, shredded lettuce and finely sliced green peppers, topped with butter-fried almonds and lemon zest, with hot brown toast.

Quiche with Irish smoked salmon (4-6)

Snaffles, Dublin
chef/proprietor: Rosie Tinne

6 oz shortcrust pastry (DPB, page 173)
4 eggs
¼ pint double cream
¼ pint milk
2 tablesp chicken stock
salt, pepper
a pinch of freshly grated nutmeg
¼ lb Irish smoked salmon
½ oz butter (approx)

Bake a 9-inch pastry case blind (DPB, page 173) and allow it to cool.

Whisk together the eggs, cream, milk and chicken stock. Season the mixture well, and pour it into the pastry case. Cover the top with small slices of smoked salmon and dot the surface with butter.

Bake on a baking sheet in the centre of a moderate oven (350°F, mark 4) for 30–40 minutes until it is set and beginning to brown.

WATER ICES

'The ice of her Ladyship's manners,
The ice of his Lordship's champagne.'
WINTHROP MACKWORTH PRAED, *Good-night to the Season*

Sorbets, sherbets and granitas are varieties of water ice. Although each is basically a sugar syrup mixed with fruit juice or some other flavouring, they differ somewhat in the proportions of their ingredients and in their preparation.

Origins

Almost ten centuries ago ice was used in China and Japan to chill fruit and tea, and later, in the Middle East, cold fruit drinks were chilled by being left in a draught with their container swathed in a wet cloth. From such humble beginnings comes the sorbet. (*Shariba* is the Arabic verb *to drink*.) Italy is credited with the next appearance of the water ice – the *sorbetto* of Renaissance times – and from there it travelled to France and, much later, to England and the United States where, confusingly, the name sherbet has come to mean a water ice with milk or cream added.

By the 1870s ices were so fashionable in Paris that a book called the *Glacier National* was published to help their creator, the *glacier-limonadier*. It contained detailed instructions for making ices in *sorbetières*, metal tubs surrounded by water, ice and salt, in which the ice was stirred by hand. It also provided recipes for every imaginable fruit ice, and others using violets, amaryllis, jasmine, orange flowers, elderflowers, tea, wine and kirsch. According to the density of their sugar syrups they were classified as ices ($21°$), sorbets ($17°$) and granitas ($14°$). And in case your etiquette was shaky, it also issued instructions on serving ices at a *soirée dansante* or *bal* – during the second interval, with fruit syrups during the first, and hot chocolate or soup saved for a reviver during the third.

Sorbets, usually those made with wine or liqueur, were also served between courses during formal banquets as a palate cleanser and aid to digestion. This custom has virtually disappeared, but happily a few restaurants in *The Good Food Guide* still perpetuate it, and London's Capital Hotel's sorbet à la Fine Champagne, an extravaganza in itself, fits the role perfectly.

Types

An ice with a relatively low sugar content and little air beaten into it will form fairly small ice particles or grains, rather like soft snow. The coffee granita (page 182) is this type and forms beautifully dark glistening crystals. A sweeter ice, part frozen before the incorporation of air or whipped egg white, becomes a sorbet. Its consistency is smoother and lighter, an effect often accentuated by the addition of alcohol towards the end of the freezing process, which lowers the freezing point and thus produces a softer texture. The most important point to remember is that the quicker the freezing the less likely your water ice is to form large crystals.

Modern electric ice-making machines still adhere to the principles of the old *sorbetières*: the fruit syrup hardens against the sides of the metal container, and is scraped off by the paddle which replaces hand-stirring. The simplest are used in a freezer or the ice-making compartment of the refrigerator. Mechanical stirring not only ensures that the ice freezes more evenly, but also incorporates air into the mixture, which prevents large crystals forming.

Sorbetières and ice-making machines are on the market, but you can make good ices with a freezer or an efficient ice-making compartment in your refrigerator. Domestic freezers and three-star fridges maintain a temperature of around 0°F (−18°C) and are thus ideal. Two-star fridges with compartments at 10°F (−12°C), and one-star at 21°F (−6°C), need to be pre-set on their coldest setting for at least 30 minutes before the liquid is put in to freeze.

Chilling both the liquid and its container beforehand helps rapid freezing. A metal container conducts cold better than plastic.

Beating air or whisked egg whites into the mixture lightens its texture and virtually doubles its bulk, so choose appropriate containers and do not fill them too full. The egg whites also act as a stabiliser so that the ice will not separate out.

Water ices are easy to make and require a minimum of equipment. An electric beater makes the whisking easier: remember to use a large bowl, since the partly frozen mixture tends to fly about. You will also need ice-making trays or polythene containers. A sugar hydrometer, to be found in good kitchen equipment suppliers', is useful for measuring sugar density.

The following recipes are mainly for sorbets. Some – the raspberry, the grapefruit and mint, and the elderflower – have additional egg white. Those without it – the gooseberry, the blackberry, and the orange and grapefruit – will not hold their shape for very long, and it is a good idea to chill the glasses in which they are to be served. This is particularly true of the brandy sorbet which freezes with difficulty because of its high alcohol content, and melts quickly.

All the water ices will liquefy quickly at room temperature, but will be too cold to serve straight away if they have been frozen in a three-star fridge or freezer. They should be left for an hour or so in the main compartment of the fridge before serving, or, better still, six-hours in the ice-making compartment at 21°F (−6°C), where they will keep for two or three days. Ices made at this temperature (i.e. a one-star refrigerator) will take a long time to freeze and may not have quite so smooth a texture as those made more quickly at lower temperatures.

Stemmed glasses or dishes are probably best for serving water ices. If you have made the ice from fresh fruit, save a little for garnishing. Crisp, not-too-sweet biscuits go well with ices, and provide a contrast in taste, temperature and texture.

Sorbet à la Fine Champagne (6)

Capital Hotel Restaurant, London
chef: Richard Shepherd

Virtually frozen white wine and brandy – delicious, fragrant and refreshing. As this sorbet contains a high proportion of alcohol, it freezes at a lower temperature than a fruit sorbet.

9 oz sugar
6 fl oz water
about ½ bottle good Chablis
2–3 fl oz Fine Champagne
   cognac
juice of 1–2 lemons, according
   to size

Prepare the sugar syrup by dissolving the sugar in the water and bringing it slowly to boiling point. Leave it to cool.

When the syrup is cold, stir in the Chablis and the cognac. Add some strained lemon juice, carefully checking the flavour. There should be a good balance between the dry Chablis and the slight harshness of the brandy which the lemon juice should blend together and accentuate without overpowering either. Pour the mixture into either an ice-cream machine, or a metal or plastic container or bowl and put it into the deep freezer or the freezing compartment of the refrigerator. When it starts to solidify round the edges (after about 2 hours in the refrigerator or less by other methods) turn the edges into the middle and continue stirring the mixture every so often as it sets in order to form a smooth consistency – the more stirring the better.

The sorbet will never become really hard but should have the consistency of firm snow. Serve it in chilled goblets to prevent its melting too quickly.

Coffee granita (10)

Walnut Tree Inn, Llandewi Skirrid
chef/proprietor: Franco Taruschio

6 tablesp instant coffee
1¼ pints water
5 oz sugar
6 ice-cubes
whipped cream (optional)

Measure the coffee into a saucepan, blend in ¾ pint of water and add about 5 ounces of sugar. Bring the liquid to the boil, stirring continuously, then reduce the heat and leave it to simmer for 5 minutes. Away from the heat, pour in another ½ pint of cold water and drop in six ice-cubes. Stir until the ice has melted, then pour the liquid into a metal or plastic container and freeze in a deep-freezer or in the ice-making compartment of the refrigerator, turned to its coldest setting.

After two hours or more and when the ice has frozen round the edges but is still softish in the centre, turn it out into a bowl and whisk with an electric beater at medium speed until the ice is smooth. Replace it in the freezer and continue the freezing until it is almost solid.

Serve the ice in chilled glass goblets with a little fresh, whipped cream.

Elderflower sorbet (6)

Pinks, Fairford
chefs: Victoria Lawrence and Jane Hill

½ lb lump sugar
½ pint water
1 handful elderflowers, rather
   unopened
2–3 lemons
1 egg white

Dissolve the lump sugar in the water, bring it gently to the boil and boil it for 10 minutes. Remove the pan from the heat, put in the elderflowers and leave until the syrup is quite cold. Pre-set the refrigerator if necessary.

Strain the syrup, then add the juice of 2 or 3 lemons, taking care to check the flavour of the syrup so that it is not overpowered by the lemons.

Freeze the mixture until it sets firm, then chop it up into cubes. Beat the egg white until it is very stiff, then add the chopped mixture, beating hard all the while. When it is well blended, return it to the freezer.

Gooseberry sorbet (6)

Bistro One, Penzance
chef/proprietor: Roger Harris

¾ lb gooseberries
1 lemon
9 oz granulated sugar
1 pint water
2 egg whites

Wash the gooseberries but do not top and tail them. Remove the zest of the lemon in strips with a peeler and squeeze the juice. Put the gooseberries, lemon juice, rind, sugar and water into a pan and bring them slowly to the boil. Simmer for 15 minutes, remove the pieces of lemon zest and rub the cooked fruit and syrup through a sieve (into the container it is to be frozen in). Leave it to cool before putting it to freeze.

After an hour or more when the edges are beginning to solidify, whip the egg whites until they are very stiff and beat them into the puree, making sure that any frozen edges of the ice are beaten in well. Return the container to the freezer. Beat the mixture another couple of times before it is firm, say, every half hour or so.

Grapefruit and mint water ice (6)

Provans, London
chef/proprietor: Fergus Provan

¼ lb caster sugar
½ pint water
1 lemon
a handful fresh mint leaves
2 grapefruit
2–3 drops green food colouring
1 small egg white

Make a syrup with the sugar and water and the zest of the lemon; bring it to the boil and simmer it for 5 minutes. Add the mint and simmer the syrup for two further minutes, then leave it to cool completely before removing the mint leaves. Preset the refrigerator to its coldest setting if necessary.

Squeeze the lemon and grapefruit and strain the juice into the cooled syrup. Freeze if possible in a *sorbetière* (ice-cream making machine). Failing that, put it into a container in the freezer or in the ice-making compartment of the refrigerator, stirring as often as possible until it is firm. Whip the egg white and fold it into the ice, then return it to the freezer for a further two hours before serving it.

Sorbet de framboises (6)

Le Talbooth Restaurant, Dedham
chef: Derek Driver

½ lb caster sugar
½ pint water
½ lb fresh raspberries (or
    frozen, unsweetened)
1 egg white
juice of 1 lemon
1 fl oz Framboise liqueur

Make a syrup by dissolving the sugar in the water and simmering it for 3 minutes. Leave it to cool. Turn the refrigerator to its coldest setting.

Liquidise the raspberries. Rub the puree through a sieve and mix in the sugar syrup. Pour the syrup into a container and put it to freeze, either in the deep freezer or in the ice-making compartment of the refrigerator. When it is firm but not too solid, turn it into a bowl and beat it with an electric whisk. Whisk the egg white separately then fold it into the ice, together with the lemon juice and liqueur. Whisk again until the mixture is smooth. Return the ice to the freezer or refrigerator for a further 2 hours before turning the fridge back to its normal setting.

Serve with a wafer biscuit and decorate with fresh raspberries.

Sorbet à l'orange et pamplemousse (10)

Old House, Wickham
chef: Mr C. White

for the sugar syrup
7 oz caster sugar
17 fl oz cold water

3 large oranges
1 large grapefruit
¼ pint semi-sweet white wine
3 tablesp red wine
1 tablesp kirsch

To make the sugar syrup, stir the sugar into the cold water in a pan until it dissolves, then gently bring it to the boil. Leave to cool. (It may be tested with a syrup meter which should read 15°.)

Grate the rinds of one of the oranges and half of the grapefruit, taking care to use only the thin outer peel. Then peel all the fruit completely, removing the pith and any seeds. Rub the flesh and the grated rinds through a sieve or food mill into a bowl. Add the white and red wine and the kirsch. Stir well and leave it to stand for 1 hour. Combine the liquid with the cooled sugar syrup and freeze it in a *sorbetière* if available (otherwise, use a metal or plastic container) in the freezing compartment of the refrigerator, turned to its coldest setting. When it is firm, serve in chilled goblets with sponge fingers or plain biscuits.

Blackberry sorbet (6)

Walnut Tree Inn, Llandewi Skirrid
chef/proprietor: Franco Taruschio

¼ lb sugar
¼ pint water
1 lb blackberries
2 tablesp rosewater

Make a syrup by simmering together the sugar and water for 5 minutes, then leave it to cool. Turn the refrigerator to its coldest setting.

Wash the blackberries and rub them through a sieve into a metal or plastic container which will fit into the freezing compartment of the refrigerator. Add the syrup and the rosewater, cover and put to freeze.

After an hour or so, scrape the freezing ice from the sides of the container into the middle. When all the ice is firm but *not* solid (in 1½–2 hours), turn it into a bowl and whisk it smooth with an electric beater. Return it to its container in the freezing compartment for another 2 hours before turning back the setting to its normal reading. Serve in sorbet glasses or dishes, with langues de chat or almond-flavoured biscuits.

EDITOR'S NOTES: when sieving the blackberries, it helps if the fruit can be slightly pureed in a liquidiser with a little of the syrup. The rest of the syrup can then be poured through the sieve with the puree and this also makes the job easier.

Rosewater can be obtained from most chemists.

Raspberries sorbetière

Carrier's, London
proprietor: Robert Carrier

¾–1 lb fresh raspberries
¼ pint double cream
1–2 teasp icing sugar
4 scoops raspberry sorbet
    (page 184)
a few toasted slivered almonds

Wash the raspberries, removing any that are too soft or discoloured, and drain them.

Whip the cream, adding a little icing sugar to taste. Just before serving, put one scoopful or large spoonful of raspberry sorbet into four large balloon glasses or individual glass dishes. Top these with the fresh raspberries, reserving a perfect berry for each glass. Pipe a swirl of whipped cream on top and decorate with a raspberry and a few slivered almonds.

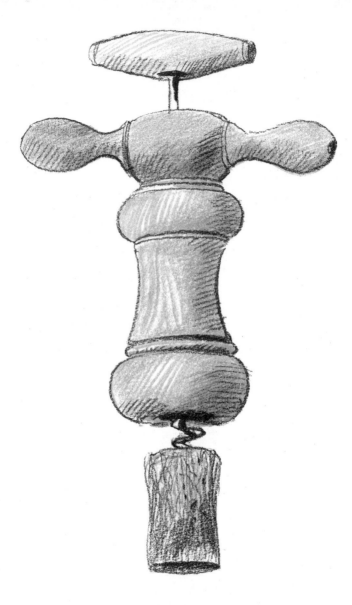

WINES AND SPIRITS

'A man cannot make him laugh; but that's no marvel; he drinks no wine.'
SHAKESPEARE, *King Henry IV*, part 2

'There's some are fou o' love divine,
There's some are fou o' brandy.'
ROBERT BURNS, *The Holy Divine*

It seems no time since a glass of wine added to a casserole was a bohemian gesture of great extravagance. Now that not just the meat but even the onions may cost more than the wine, it is worth considering wines and spirits as you do the other basic materials for cooking. In other words, do they make a dish taste good, or better? Do they bring out the best in the other ingredients? Do they improve texture and appearance as well as flavour? A happy yes to all those questions, with the sole caveat that no wine or spirit can be all things to all dishes, and that you must choose appropriately. But then that is true of the meat and onions too.

WINE

Type

Wine cooked slowly in a casserole enhances the dish immeasurably, adding richness and subtlety to both aroma and flavour. But this is true only if the wine you use tastes good in the first place. A poor bottle of near-vinegar will leave the essence of near-vinegar behind it when the alcohol evaporates. Wine for cooking need not be *premier cru* but it should be drinkable and appropriate.

With reds, this probably means that if you are making bœuf bourguignonne, you will use a modest burgundy, or a glass or so of the wine you plan to drink with the dish. Entrecôte bordelaise deserves a Bordeaux wine, or at least one with claret characteristics – perhaps a Spanish Rioja or a Rumanian Cabernet. For humbler dishes and ordinary family meals, you may like to do as we do, and cook with a Moroccan or French regional wine.

Acceptable white wines seem harder to come by at a modest cost, but your supermarket may help, since their range is constantly being extended. Avoid the *very* dry and the *very* sweet, unless the recipe specifically calls for them. We have cooked contentedly with Mâcon Blanc, Gaillac, Entre-Deux-Mers, and many of the lesser white burgundies.
If you are cooking a dish from any wine-producing country, use the national wine if you can come by it reasonably. You can then be sure that you are doing what the French, Italians, Spaniards, Greeks and Moroccans would do.

Colour

There are no inflexible rules about which colour of wine to use with any given meat or fish. Most frequently red is used with meat, especially in hearty beef or lamb dishes, but veal, pork and chicken recipes often suggest white wine. Fish is usually cooked in white, but the fish stew called a matelote (DPB, page 158) and Basque chiorro (page 59) use red. Game is almost always cooked in red wine, but the pigeon casserole with celery and walnuts (DPB, page 49) shows what white wine can do for an often ungrateful little bird.

Sweets using wine are generally restricted to simple fruits – pears baked in red wine, a fresh peeled peach sliced into a glass of white wine. Syllabubs were traditionally made with white wine, but rosé makes a pretty and delicious one (page 196). It is seldom otherwise used in cooking, since it lacks adequate body and flavour.

Quantity

Some dishes call for a spoonful or two of wine to complement a delicate sauce; others require a bottle. Both quantities are effective in their different ways. Don't be tempted to think that if one glass works wonders, two will be even better.

Left-over wine

If a bottle of wine is unfinished at a meal, transfer the wine to a smaller bottle and cork it securely. With air thus excluded, it will keep for a week or so and will be drinkable for the first few days, fit for cooking for a few more. Opened white wines should be stored in the fridge. Small quantities of left-over wine can be used to top up your vinegar bottle.

Marinating

As well as adding flavour to meat, wine has the effect of making it more tender, breaking down the fibres as does any acid. One way of achieving this is to marinate dry meat, cheaper cuts, or game in wine, oil, herbs, onions and garlic. The common proportions are three parts wine to one part oil. A recipe might recommend anything from 12 hours to four days' marinating. The strained marinade is generally used as the cooking medium and the basis for the sauce, as in pigeon ramier (page 194) and venison casserole (page 195). Fish is usually marinated in white wine and oil, and for about an hour only.

Cooking

Wine is used in cooking in one of two ways, in both of which the wine itself is actually cooked and the alcohol driven off. In slow cooking, as in casseroles and daubes, tough cuts of meat are cooked at a low temperature for several hours in wine, or a mixture of wine and stock or water, with vegetables, herbs, spices, and so on. On the other hand, a recipe may suggest sauté-ing tender pieces of meat, such as escalopes of veal, in butter or oil, removing the meat, and deglazing the pan with wine. This means scraping up all the residue in the pan and combining it with the wine. Then the wine is reduced over high heat to a syrupy glaze which forms a little sauce requiring no further thickening. Sometimes cream is added, as in steak à la moutarde and tournedos Médicis (DPB, page 60).

FORTIFIED WINES

Port, sherry, Madeira and Marsala are most often used in the fast-cooking method described above, perhaps seen at its best in Italian dishes such as veal Marsala. Sherry does fine things for trifle, even if used very generously. The same is not true of consommé, where too much sherry can mask the original taste almost completely. Remember that sherry and Madeira come very dry and very sweet, with many gradations between. Choose appropriately. Even the cheapest ruby port enriches the dish it is used in. Our port and prune fool (page 39) tastes splendidly vintage. Port and cream are combined to advantage in duckling Marshal Robert (page 192) and filet au château (page 191). Dry vermouth makes an interesting alternative to sherry or white wine in some recipes, but comes into its own in coq au vermouth (page 193).

SPIRITS

BRANDY is the spirit most commonly used in cooking, either to provide a 'lift' at the end of the cooking process, as an ingredient in pâtés and other meat dishes, or to flame dishes during the cooking process. The high cost of brandy will help reinforce our plea not to overdo any of these. Restaurants are particularly guilty of pouring a hefty shot of cheap brandy into an otherwise tolerable lobster bisque, thus making the soup unpalatable. And their lamp-cooking pyrotechnics often demonstrate how *not* to get the best out of flambé. Keep it all decently in the kitchen, and safely under control on your stove. If a recipe suggests pouring lighted brandy over sautéed chicken or meat, heat the brandy in a small pan or ladle, set fire to it, and pour it over the meat while it is still flaming. Shake the pan around so that it burns as long as possible. In doing so it will remove any excess fat from the dish, crisp the skin of the chicken, and concentrate the flavours wonderfully. (See chicken Mère Michel, page 190.)

GIN, with its juniper flavour, is particularly suited to dishes containing juniper berries.

CALVADOS, often rough and forceful, but speaking firmly of apples, goes particularly well in the cooking of its home region, Normandy. It is often combined with apples and cream (crêpes normande, page 13). While there is no close substitute for calvados, kirsch and whisky are probably the best alternatives.

RUM has a remarkable affinity with chocolate and orange, as demonstrated in veau au rhum et orange (page 147) and Amaretti Schokoladentorte (page 34). Unless a recipe specifies otherwise, use dark Jamaican rum.

The white spirits, or *eaux de vie*, such as kirsch, framboise and mirabelle, are subtler than fruit-flavoured liqueurs because they are unsweetened and carry just a memory of the fruit from which they were distilled. For that reason, they are perfect for delicate dishes such as fruit compotes and salads, or in fresh-fruit sorbets (see sorbet de framboises, page 184), or the simple but effective kirsch and pineapple.

MACERATION is the term applied to the process of soaking fresh fruit in a little spirit or liqueur. Dried or glacé fruits are sometimes macerated before being used in a cake or trifle.

LIQUEURS

Sweet, fruity, herby or spicy, liqueurs are perhaps at their best in puddings: apricot brandy with dried or fresh apricots in tarts or fool; orange flavoured liqueurs (Grand Marnier, Cointreau, Curaçao) in crêpes Suzette, chocolate mousses and creams (see chocolate Cuisinier, page 32); cherry brandy with fresh or bottled cherries; Crème de Cacao and Tia Maria or Kahlua in chocolate or coffee dishes. Liqueurs make the best instant sauces for ice cream, if you need a sweet in a hurry.

If you have never used liqueurs in savoury dishes, you might like to experiment with an orange liqueur in the sauce for duck, crème de menthe with lamb, and anisette with fish.

Chicken Mère Michel

Highbullen Country House Hotel,
Chittlehamholt
chef: Pamela Neil

This dish originates from the little restaurant La Mère Michel in Paris.

1 roasting chicken
salt, pepper
2 oz butter
1 bunch fresh tarragon *or*
   2 teasp dried tarragon
1 tablesp brandy
5 fl oz double cream
2 tablesp Madeira

Season the inside of the chicken with salt and freshly ground black pepper and stuff it with the butter and tarragon. Rub a little butter all over the bird and put it in a roasting tin into a hot oven (400°F, mark 6) for 20 minutes until it begins to brown. Remove it to the top of the stove, pour the brandy over the chicken and set fire to it. Turn the bird onto its side and continue to roast it for a further 20 minutes, basting frequently. Then turn it over onto its other side for a final 20 minutes. When it is cooked – its juices should run clear when the skin is pricked – cut the chicken into serving portions and keep it hot while making the sauce.

Drain off any excess fat from the roasting tin but leave the pan juices and into these whisk the cream. Reheat gently and simmer until the sauce has reduced a little, then stir in the Madeira and continue reducing until it is thick and creamy. Pour the sauce over the chicken to serve.

CHEF'S NOTE: the sauce may be reinforced, if necessary, with some reduced stock.

Marinated mackerel

Carlo's Place, London
chef: J. Delahaye

2 medium-sized mackerel
salt
9 fl oz dry white wine
9 fl oz wine vinegar (approx)
1 sliced onion
1 sliced lemon
4 bay leaves
4 chillies (optional)
12 peppercorns
1 tablesp salad oil

A refreshing starter, which can also be served as a lunch dish with a salad.

Fillet the mackerel (or have the fishmonger do it). Place the four fillets in a single layer in a shallow baking dish, skin side up. Sprinkle them with salt to taste. Add enough wine and vinegar just to cover the fillets. Add the sliced onion and lemon, the seasonings and the oil.

Cover the dish tightly with foil and bake it in a moderate oven (350°F, mark 4) for about 25 minutes. Remove the fish from the oven, and leave it to cool, still covered.

Serve the fillets with the lemon and onion rings on top, and some of the marinade spooned over.

Filet au château

French Partridge, Horton
chef: D. C. Partridge

4 thick fillet steaks
salt, pepper

for the duxelles
½ lb mushrooms
butter
4 shallots or 1 small onion
salt, pepper

4 thick rounds of white bread
oil and clarified butter
2 cloves garlic

¼ pint port
¼ pint double cream

Trim the steaks and tie them into tournedos with string. Season them with salt and pepper.

Make the duxelles (DPB, page 168).

Fry the bread rounds (roughly the size of the steaks) in a mixture of oil and clarified butter. Rub each side of the croûtes with a cut clove of garlic. Keep them warm.

Heat a little oil in a frying pan, fry the tournedos to the desired degree, remove them from the pan and keep warm.

Deglaze the pan with the port, scraping up any residue with a wooden spoon. Stir in the duxelles, and finally the cream. Check the seasoning.

To serve, remove the string, place a steak on each croûte, pour a little of the sauce over each, and serve any remaining sauce separately.

EDITOR'S NOTE: even with cheap ruby port this dish tastes very good, and 'expensive'.

Saalbacher à la crème

Toastmaster's Inn, Burham
chefs: Christopher Dimech and Gregory Ward

4 veal escalopes
2 oz butter
2 tablesp oil
1 tablesp paprika
1 tablesp capers
2 tablesp dry sherry
salt, pepper
4 fl oz double cream
chopped parsley

Beat out the escalopes. Fry them lightly in the butter and oil for about 4 minutes on each side. Remove and keep hot.

Mix the paprika and capers with enough of the vinegar in which they were bottled to form a thin paste – about 2 teaspoonsful. Blend this into the pan juices, with the sherry and seasoning, and simmer gently for 10 minutes. Add the cream and stir until the sauce thickens, then pour it over the escalopes. Sprinkle with chopped parsley and serve the dish as quickly as possible.

Duckling Marshal Robert

Swan House Hotel, Wilmcote
chef: Miss J. Burton

1 large duckling (or 2 small ones)
salt, pepper
2 tablesp honey
¼ lb duck or chicken livers
2 oz pâté maison
¼ lb mushrooms
2 oz butter
2 tablesp French mustard
4 fl oz ruby port
¼ pint double cream
a little chopped parsley

Before roasting prick the skin of the duckling over the breast and legs to let out the fat as it cooks. Sprinkle inside and out with salt and pepper, and roast by the quick or slow method, whichever you prefer (see DPB, page 162), using the honey for basting.

Towards the end of the roasting time, chop the livers and pâté roughly, and slice the mushrooms. Sauté them together in the butter, and when they are ready, stir in the mustard. Portion the duckling into four and keep it hot. Pour off the fat from the roasting tin and stir the sediment into the sauté mixture. Pour in the port and after a minute or two, lift out the livers, pâté and mushrooms with a perforated spoon. Divide them into four helpings on a serving dish and put a piece of duck on top of each.

Pour the cream into the port and let them bubble gently together until the sauce amalgamates and reduces a little. Season it, pour a little over each portion and serve the rest separately. Garnish the duckling with a little chopped parsley.

EDITOR'S NOTE: try this recipe with wild duck for a change.

Coq au porto

La Chandelle, Marlow
chef/proprietor: Tom Hearne

1 large roasting chicken

for the marinade
½ bottle ruby port
1 lb onions
2 cloves garlic
2 bay leaves
salt, pepper

1 oz butter
1 lb button mushrooms
6 fl oz double cream
2 egg yolks

Joint the chicken into 8 pieces and leave them overnight in the marinade. Make stock with the giblets and carcase (DPB, page 171).

Heat the butter in a heavy pan. Take the chicken pieces out of the marinade, dry them, and brown them in the butter. Remove the chicken to a large heavy pan. Strain the marinade and fry the onions in the first pan (adding more butter if necessary). Stir the marinade into the onions, and scrape up any residue from the bottom of the pan. Heat the marinade and pour it over the chicken. Add the whole mushrooms and enough stock barely to cover the chicken. Bring to the boil and simmer, covered, until tender, about an hour.

Remove the chicken pieces and keep them warm. Skim off any excess grease from the sauce, check the seasoning, and just before serving stir in the cream and egg yolks, beaten together. Do not allow the sauce to boil again. Pour it over the chicken, and serve the dish with rice.

EDITOR'S NOTE: if you have added more than ½ pint of stock, you should reduce it considerably before adding the egg and cream liaison.

Coq au vermouth

Simple Simon, London
chef: Simon Delgado

1 chicken, 3½-lb dressed
    weight
a few vegetables and herbs for
    making stock
3 tablesp olive oil
½ lb button mushrooms
1 bunch fresh tarragon
salt, pepper
¼ bottle dry vermouth
1 small onion
2 slices bacon
½ pint double cream

Divide the chicken into four – two breasts and two legs – discarding the backbone and breast bone, and skin them. Make stock with the bones and trimmings.

Heat the olive oil in a frying pan and seal the pieces of chicken on all sides. Transfer them to a flameproof casserole with the whole mushrooms and the tarragon, add salt and pepper and pour in the vermouth. Slice the onion very finely and fry it with the chopped bacon until they are both soft, then add them to the chicken. Pour over about ¼ pint of the prepared stock, cover and cook in a moderate oven (350°F, mark 4) for 45–60 minutes until the chicken is tender.

Discard the bunch of tarragon and transfer the chicken to a warm place while you reduce the stock in the casserole by fast boiling. When it has reduced by three-quarters, put back the chicken and add the cream. Allow the sauce to simmer gently until it thickens, and check its seasoning.

Pigeon ramier

Normandie Restaurant, Birtle
chef/proprietor: Y. R. L. Champeau

*A comforting winter dish of pigeon named
after the wild pigeon of the Midi.*

4 wood pigeons
1 bottle red wine
a pinch or sprig of thyme
bay leaf
1 clove garlic
salt, pepper
2 oz flour
4 tablesp olive oil
2 tablesp brandy
¼ lb boiled ham
¼ lb smoked bacon or ham
1 large onion
½ lb button mushrooms

Wipe the pigeons with a damp cloth. Marinate them in the wine for 24 hours with the thyme, bay leaf and chopped garlic, turning them in the marinade from time to time.

Remove the pigeons from the wine, putting it to one side, and dry them carefully. Roll them in seasoned flour. Heat the olive oil and fry the birds briskly in it until they are completely sealed and lightly browned. Put them into a casserole and flame with the brandy. When the flames have died down, pour over the reserved marinade.

Dice the ham and bacon, chop the onion and cut the mushrooms in half. Fry them together, using the same frying pan in which the pigeons were browned, until they start to brown, then put them into the casserole with the birds. Cover with a tight-fitting lid and simmer slowly either on the stove or in a slow oven (275°F, mark 1) for 1½ hours, or until the pigeons are tender.

Serve with plain boiled potatoes, and a red burgundy or Rhône wine.

CHEF'S NOTE: this dish may be cooked the day before, put in the refrigerator overnight and reheated just before serving.

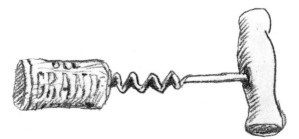

Venison casserole

Le Caveau, Edinburgh
chef/proprietor: François Aliane

This simple dish is very dependent on the 'height' of the venison for its flavour.

2 lb venison
¾ pint red wine
2 bay leaves
2 onions
2 carrots
bouquet garni
4 tablesp flour
2 oz butter
¼ pint red wine
1 oz cornflour
1 oz red fruit jelly
　(redcurrant, rowan, etc.)
salt, pepper

Cut the trimmed venison in 1½–2 inch cubes and marinate it for at least 24 hours in ¾ pint of red wine containing the bay leaves, the coarsely chopped onions and carrots, and the bouquet garni.

Remove the meat, dry it on paper towels, roll it in flour and sauté it in the butter until it is well browned. Transfer it to a heavy saucepan. Use the strained marinade to deglaze the frying pan, scraping up all the bits. Pour it over the venison and simmer gently until the meat is tender. (If you use leg or other tender cut, it should take about an hour; stewing cuts will take correspondingly longer.)

Blend the remaining red wine, the cornflour and the melted jelly together and add the mixture to the saucepan. Bring the liquid back to the boil and check the seasoning before serving.

EDITOR'S NOTES: venison is often dry or coarse, and cheaper cuts need very slow simmering.

Barley and red cabbage go well with this dish, as with other game.

Sauce bordelaise

Randalls Restaurant Français, Brixham
chef/proprietor: John Randall

In the restaurant, this sauce is served with grilled entrecôte, fillet or rump steak.

½ pint sauce espagnole
　(page 200)
1 small onion
1 unpeeled clove garlic
6 peppercorns
½ pint red wine
1 teasp tomato puree
1 teasp brandy
salt, pepper

Prepare the sauce espagnole. While it is reducing, chop the onion and put it in a saucepan with the garlic, peppercorns and red wine to simmer until the wine is reduced by half. Add it to the finished espagnole together with the tomato purée and brandy and continue to simmer the sauce for a further 15 minutes. Strain and check the seasoning.

EDITOR'S NOTE: if, at the end, the flavour of the sauce needs a little pointing, add a dash of red wine vinegar.

Courgettes in red wine and almond sauce

Bistroquet, Southport
chef: Enrique Garcia-Darias

for the sauce
1½ oz almonds
3 tomatoes
1 dessertsp olive oil
½ oz butter
1 small onion
1 clove garlic
¼ pint veal or chicken stock
¼ pint red wine
1 teasp sugar
salt, pepper

6–8 courgettes
seasoned flour
6 tablesp cooking oil

Roast the almonds until they are brown, then pound them in a mortar or a liquidiser. Peel, deseed and chop the tomatoes. Heat the oil and butter in a large thick saucepan and fry the finely chopped onion and garlic until they are golden. Add the chopped tomatoes and cook until any liquid has evaporated and the mixture is fairly thick. Stir in the stock, wine, pounded almonds and sugar, and continue simmering until the sauce has reduced by one third. Season.

Cut the courgettes into ¼-inch slices and toss them in seasoned flour. Heat the cooking oil and fry them lightly on both sides. Drain the slices on absorbent paper before adding them to the sauce. Cover and simmer gently until the courgettes are just tender, but not soft.

EDITOR'S NOTE: the sauce can be prepared in advance and reheated, if this is more convenient.

Rosé syllabub

White Moss House, Grasmere
chef/proprietor: Jean Butterworth

1 lemon
4 tablesp rosé wine
3 oz caster sugar
½ pint double cream
pink colouring

for garnishing
crystallised rose petals
tuiles

Stir together and leave overnight the juice and finely grated rind of the lemon, the wine and the sugar. Fold in the cream and enough colouring to tint a very pale pink. Whisk the mixture until it falls in soft folds. Put it in individual glasses, scatter with crystallised rose petals and serve with tuiles, or other crisp, sweet biscuits. If you wish to chill the syllabub – and it can be made several hours ahead – scatter the rose petals just before serving.

CHEF'S NOTE: if you use a hand whisk there is less danger of overwhipping the syllabub.

Crêpes Mercédès

The Close, Tetbury
proprietors: Mr and Mrs John Hastings

½ pint pancake batter (DPB, page 172)

for the filling
2 egg yolks
2 oz sugar
½ oz flour
¼ pint milk
2 fl oz double cream
1½ tablesp curaçao

for glazing
1 tablesp curaçao
a little icing sugar

Make the pancake batter and allow it to stand for about 2 hours. Also prepare the filling in advance, as it has to be chilled.

Put the egg yolks, sugar and flour into a double boiler and cream them together with a wooden spoon until they are quite smooth. Boil the milk and stir it into the creamed mixture. Have the water in the double boiler just simmering and heat the mixture, stirring it continuously, until it thickens enough to coat the back of the spoon. Pour this custard into a bowl and allow it to cool, then fold in the stiffly whipped cream and the curaçao. Put it to chill in the refrigerator for an hour or more.

Just before serving, make eight small pancakes, keeping the first ones hot while preparing the others. Place a little of the chilled cream in the centre of each of the hot pancakes, roll them up and arrange them side by side in a gratin dish. Sprinkle a tablespoonful of curaçao and a little sifted icing sugar on top and flash the crêpes quickly under a very hot grill to glaze the top. Serve them immediately – they should provide a contrast of hot exterior and cold filling.

EDITOR'S NOTE: the pancakes can be prepared ahead and kept hot so that they have only to be filled and glazed at the last minute.

Irish coffee meringue

Ballymaloe House, Shanagarry
chef/proprietor: Mrs M. Allen

2 egg whites
2 oz caster sugar
2 oz icing sugar
1 tablesp instant coffee
½ pint double cream
1 tablesp Irish whiskey

Whisk the egg whites until they are stiff. Add the caster sugar and continue beating until they are very stiff. Sift the icing sugar, mix the coffee into it, then fold this gently into the egg whites.

Cut two 7-inch rounds of silicone paper, oiled greaseproof or foil and spread the mixture over each. Bake them in the oven at its lowest setting for up to 4 hours, until the meringue is quite dry on the outside but slightly soft inside.

Half an hour before serving, whip the cream until it is quite stiff and stir in the whiskey. Spread this on top of one meringue and press the other on top to form a sandwich. Chill for a short time.

EDITOR'S NOTE: it would taste nearly as delicious made with Scotch.

Rum cake (8-10)

Bowlish House, Shepton Mallet
chef/proprietor: Elaina Gardiner

The lightest of fatless sponges, marbled with coffee and rum.

5 eggs
½ lb caster sugar
grated rind of ½ lemon
¼ lb flour
a pinch salt
8 fl oz sweetened very strong
   black coffee
4 tablesp dark rum (approx)
½ pint double cream

Preheat the oven to 350°F, mark 4.

Oil and flour a tube cake tin (or a Kugelhopf mould), about 9 inches in diameter and 4 inches deep. Separate the eggs and beat 2 ounces of the sugar into the yolks with the grated lemon rind until the mixture is light and thick. Beat the egg whites until they start to stiffen, add the remaining sugar and continue beating them until they are quite stiff. With a metal spoon, lightly fold into the yolks first the whites and then the sifted flour and salt. Turn this mixture into the cake tin and bake it in the centre of the oven for about 50 minutes. When it is cooked –

test it either by pressing the top lightly to see if it gives slightly and then rises again, or check whether a skewer or needle comes out of it cleanly – leave the cake to cool for a few minutes before turning it out on to a rack.

When the cake is cold invert it again and gently pour the warm or cold coffee over it, making it fairly moist, but leaving patches unsoaked so that when the cake is cut there is a marbled effect. Sprinkle the rum all over, being as generous with it as you feel inclined. Turn the cake right side up and serve it in slices with thick cream.

Basic recipes

Puff pastry

$\frac{1}{2}$ lb strong flour
$\frac{1}{2}$ teasp salt
$\frac{1}{2}$ lb unsalted butter
a squeeze of lemon

The coolest possible conditions, utensils and ingredients are essential when preparing this kind of pastry which contains a high proportion of fat; on the other hand, it is baked in a really hot oven so that the air trapped between the layers will quickly expand and puff up the pastry.

Sift the flour and salt and rub in about $\frac{1}{2}$ oz of the butter. Make it into a fairly soft dough with about 4 fl oz of ice cold water and a squeeze of lemon (the lemon strengthens the dough but too much liquid toughens it), and knead it well on a floured surface until it is smooth. Rest it for 15 minutes in the refrigerator.

Roll out the dough into an oblong roughly 12 inches by 4. Flatten the remaining piece of butter – it should be slightly softened – into a rectangle about half the size, and place this on one half of the dough, or cut the butter in thin slices and place them evenly over half the surface of the dough. Fold the other half over and press the edges together with a rolling pin or with the side of your hand. Turn the fold to one side and roll out the pastry again in short quick movements into an oblong the size of the original one. Keep the pastry regular in shape with square corners and do not roll the pin over the edges or stretch the

dough. Fold it into three and seal the edges to trap the air inside. Wrap the pastry in greaseproof paper and put it to rest in a really cool place or the refrigerator for 20 minutes.

Repeat this turning, rolling and folding operation five more times, always starting with the fold to the same side and chilling the pastry between each rolling.

To make bouchée cases see page 176.

To cover a pie: see page 166.

First rollings are used for vol au vents, bouchées and patties, second rollings or trimmings for sausage rolls or fleurons – small shapes (usually crescents) used as garnishes for meat and fish dishes. These second rollings do not rise as high as the first ones. If vol au vents or mille-feuille consistently overbalance while they are baking, it would be worth checking your oven shelves with a spirit level.

Puff pastry can be made in quantity and frozen – it freezes very well. Prepare it up to but not including the last rolling. Bought puff pastry is an acceptable alternative but should be rolled out to a thickness of $\frac{1}{8}$ inch as it rises very well.

Mayonnaise

2 egg yolks
½ teasp salt
pepper
½ pint olive oil
lemon juice or wine vinegar

The eggs and the oil should be at room temperature. Beat the yolks with a wooden spoon until they are thick before adding the salt and a little pepper.

Start dripping in the oil, a little at a time, beating continuously. When the mayonnaise has thickened a little, the oil can be added rather more quickly, but it is essential to start drop by drop. When half the oil has been beaten in and the mayonnaise has become very thick, whisk in some lemon juice or vinegar to thin it a little. Continue beating in the rest of the oil. Taste and add more lemon juice or seasoning if required.

If the oil is added too quickly at the beginning, or if the eggs or oil are too cold, the mayonnaise may curdle during the operation. To rescue it, start in another bowl with another egg yolk and add to it the curdled mayonnaise, teaspoonful by teaspoonful, beating continuously as before.

If the mayonnaise is to be kept for some time, or if you need to thin it for coating, whisk in 2 tablespoonful of boiling water at the end.

Sauce espagnole or brown sauce

1 oz butter
1 oz flour
1 pint beef stock (DPB, page 170)
1 slice unsmoked bacon
1 medium-sized onion
1 carrot
1 stick celery
1 or 2 mushrooms
2 or 3 tomatoes or 1 tablesp puree
a few peppercorns
a bouquet garni
salt, pepper

A grande sauce de base which is the basis of a demi-glace (see DPB, page 172), and, amongst others, sauce madère, sauce périgueux and sauce bordelaise (page 195).

Make a brown roux (DPB, page 169) with the butter and flour and blend into it ¾ pint of the stock. Bring this to the boil, stirring it continuously, and put it to simmer gently. Chop up the bacon and vegetables and fry them until they are brown. Add them to the sauce with the chopped tomatoes, the peppercorns and the bouquet garni and continue to simmer it, partially covered, for at least 2 hours so that it reduces. From time to time skim off the fat which rises by adding a little of the remaining ¼ pint of cold stock, bringing the sauce back to the boil and skimming off the top. When the sauce is reduced by at least a half, rub it through a sieve into a clean pan and add some seasoning.

Sauce hollandaise

3 large egg yolks
1½ tablesp cold water
a pinch of salt
6 oz Normandy butter
lemon juice

An elegantly creamy sauce, served with asparagus, artichokes, broccoli, salmon, sole, chicken, eggs (as in œufs bénédictine) and crêpes (délices d'Argenteuil, page 45). This method is what Pomiane describes as cooking beside a bain-marie rather than in it.

Boil a quart of water in a large saucepan. Turn off the heat. In a small enamelled pan whisk the egg yolks and cold water with a wire whisk. Add the salt. Cut the butter into 16 pieces. Lower the small pan into the hot water and continue to whisk until the eggs start to thicken. Remove the pan, add the first piece of butter and, off the heat, beat until it melts. Add the second piece and continue to beat. As soon as a piece of butter fails to melt, put the pan back in the hot water until the butter melts, remove it, and continue in this way until all the butter has been incorporated. Add about half a teaspoonful of lemon juice and check the seasoning. Return the pan to the hot water, still beating, until the sauce thickens slightly and is warmer than lukewarm. Serve it at once, or keep it warm over hot water.

EDITOR'S NOTE: this makes a rather bland, buttery sauce suited to salmon or other delicacies. For a more rugged flavour, reduce 3 tablespoonsful of white wine or white wine vinegar by half, by boiling, and use that, cooled, instead of the cold water.

Fish stock

1–1½ lb fish, fish bones and/or
    trimmings
1 onion
6 parsley stems
½ lemon
⅛ teasp salt
8 white peppercorns
1 pint water or
    ½ pint water
    ½ pint dry white wine

This can be used as the basis of a fish velouté sauce. Use less fish for a lighter stock to use for poaching fish or making a fish soup.

Wash the fish and trimmings thoroughly in cold water. Break them into pieces and put them with the sliced onion, the parsley stems, the juice and rind of the half-lemon, the salt, pepper and water, or wine and water, in a large saucepan.

Bring slowly to the boil, skim, reduce the heat, and simmer the stock slowly, partly covered, for 30 minutes. Strain it, and either use it at once or refrigerate it.

This stock has a delicate flavour. For a heartier stock add a bouquet garni or thyme, diced carrot or turnip, celery or mushroom trimmings.

Equivalent temperatures and measures

Gas	Fahrenheit	Centigrade	
$\frac{1}{2}$	250°	121°	very slow
1	275°	135°	very slow
2	300°	149°	slow
3	325°	163°	warm
4	350°	177°	moderate
5	375°	190°	moderately hot
6	400°	205°	moderately hot
7	425°	218°	hot
8	450°	232°	very hot
9	475°	246°	very hot

Measures

Solids
1 kilogramme (1000 grammes) = 2 lb 3 oz (approx)
100 grammes = 3½ oz (approx)
1 lb = 450 grammes (approx)
1 oz = 28 grammes (approx)

Liquids
1 pint = 20 fl oz = 4/7 litre (approx)
1 cup (BSM) = 10 fl oz = ½ pint
1 gill = 5 fl oz = ¼ pint
1 litre = 35 fl oz (approx) = 1¾ pints (approx)

Handy measures
1 tablesp = ½ fl oz (approx)
1 standard bottle of wine = 26 fl oz (approx) = 6 glasses
1 liqueur glass = 1 tablesp

Index by restaurant

General Index